No. 1

THE

DAILY

JOURNAL,

FOR

1860

PUBLISHED ANNUALLY, BY

FRANCIS & LOUTREL,

MANUFACTURING STATIONERS,

45 MAIDEN LANE,

NEW YORK.

MANUFACTURERS OF
Account Books, Manifold Writers,
Croton Inks, &c. &c.

Augusta's Journal
Volume IV

Augusta Seeks Her Fortune
In Gold Mines of two New Territories:
Colorado; Montana
1860 - 1870

Ralph & Marjorie Crump

authorHOUSE®

AuthorHouse™
1663 Liberty Drive
Bloomington, IN 47403
www.authorhouse.com
Phone: 1-800-839-8640

First published by AuthorHouse 7/19/2010

ISBN: 978-1-4520-1777-8 (hc)
ISBN: 978-1-4520-1778-5 (sc)
ISBN: 978-1-4520-1779-2 (e)

Library of Congress Control Number: 2008902972

Printed in the United States of America
Bloomington, Indiana

This book is printed on acid-free paper.

DEDICATION

These four volumes
are dedicated
to all the girls
who have descended from Augusta's line
that her legacy to you of endurance,
to prevail over
unusual personal
disappointments and tragedy
will be an inspiration to you
to prevail over your own difficulties

CONTENTS

ILLUSTRATIONS

ACKNOWLEDGEMENTS
Volume IV

Donnali Fifield of San Francisco who has edited for Forbes Publications and recently translated "March of the Penguins" and other books from French to English, painstakingly edited all 69 chapters (and more) ...(a task of one and a half years)

My brother, James L. Lund, Esq., inherited Augusta's three original journals from our mother, Hazel. Sometime in the 1980s he passed them on to me.

Dr. Ramon Powers, Executive Director of the Kansas State Historical Society in Topeka in the early 1990s invited us to use their library and gave us access to twelve volumes of the transactions of the Kansas State Historical Society, where several references of the territorial period verified or corresponded to many of Augusta's journal entries, in volumes I through III. Augusta has provided some of the best accounts of the first few years of Eldorado and its founding by her father and a few like-minded abolitionists in the summer of 1857.

Mrs. Kim Stagliano, a professional editor and author, edited this volume for punctuations, typos, etc.

The Kansas State Historical Society, Topeka, KS, graciously gave us permission to use the two pictures of John Brown and one of Sara Robinson.

Ms. Lin Frederickson, Head of Reference, Kansas State Historical Society, Topeka, Kansas generously provided the best military and other source material on Captain John Graton, Adda's husband, which helped flesh out his military career. She also discovered wartime letters exchanged between Adda and Captain Graton...some were very difficult to read. Her excellent archival "finds" on Quantrill's raids on Lawrence helped with chapters 58 and 59.

Research by our daughter, Constance S. Crump Najar, a Colorado resident, reinforced Augusta's entries on the geography of the early mining camps and the role of the Green Russell party in early Colorado mining. Her research on the western explorer, Jim Bridger, and the many trails he established used by pioneers, particularly after 1849, helped us expand Augusta's acquaintance with the western movement and Bridger's safer route from Colorado to Montana, that Augusta and George's party used to get there. Her searches fleshed out many references to Augusta's relatives past and contemporary.

Of these four volumes, in not one does Augusta fail to include some significant contribution of James Lane to the early History of Kansas. She was in good company. Many of his contemporaries wrote entire biographies on the man. A close friend, John Speer's 1896 book, William Connelly's 1899, Wilder's *Annals of Kansas 1875*; Governor Robinson's 1892, and his wife Sara, who attributed Lane's shortcomings to his "phrenological defaults." Stephen Oates explores Jim Lane's association with John Brown in his *Biography of John Brown*. One of the most thoroughly researched and easiest to read is Robert Collins 2007 work on Lane. We have gratefully used them all.

VOLUME IV
Historical Prologue

During that terminal summer of 1860 – a summer of historical droughts – the girls abandoned hopes for Eldorado, sold their claims, the sawmill and returned to Lawrence with enough money to buy the little house, they'd looked at earlier on Rhode Island Street, (later numbered #627) and two cows.

Through 1860 and up to the March 1861 inauguration of President Lincoln the organized fighting in Kansas by the two opposing militia had decreased, though random raiding, killing and property rights denial continued, mostly from Missourians coming over for a day or two of mayhem, while free stators gradually became the majority. The vote for the state constitution, which was at the core of Popular Sovereignty, was in the end, that Kansas would be admitted with no slavery and signed by, of all people, President Buchanan! Most of this was due to the organizing genius of Jim Lane.

The question is, for seven years, just what were the two sides fighting about? Early Southern immigrants to the territory expected that slavery would be their right and starting in 1854, did dominate in population and their preference for slavery. That proslavery majority quickly established a like-minded territorial administration including the courts. It took two years for the North to wake up. The alarm clocks were the radical speeches in the Northeast by John Brown and his violent, ruthless, well-publicized retaliatory actions in the territory, where he and his extended family lived. More effective were the speeches in the same area by Jim Lane (ex congressman, ex officer in the Mexican War) and his Free Soil state committeemen.

Their organizing and financial efforts finally produced wagon trains of indignant abolitionist immigrants with varying degree of zeal. Their move to the territory terminally destabilized the unstable political equilibrium.

When more abolitionists and free soil advocates arrived, to join those already there, they met resistance by forms of opposed Southerners and threats from the pro slavers already there, their Missouri neighbors plus the "establishment", which included the U. S. Army and the local courts. Pro slavery oppression was met with sporadic fighting, which soon escalated to where organized militia on both sides were fighting small but pitched battles. Cannons were involved, but in the summertime fighting of 1856 the northern immigrants, better trained, better organized (by Jim Lane), much better armed and more of them, finally prevailed in the field, which, was quickly followed by their prevailing at the ballot box.

Every U. S. school kid learns a little about "Bleeding Kansas." But this is what the bleeding was all about. That the matter of slavery or freedom could only be solved by bloody battle, as John Brown had predicted, so it was in Kansas and so it would soon be for the all the thirty-four states, north and south, except the central issue had changed to the question of whether the South had the right to secede.

In November of that year, Adda, who had returned to Lawrence in July, married John Graton, the ambitious gunsmith the same day that Abraham Lincoln was elected President.

In the early days of the Civil War Adda's husband, Graton enlisted for six months and was commissioned captain by Governor Robinson.

Four months later Augusta writes, "Except for a formal declaration of war, I can't see that our life out here is any different now than it was before Fort Sumpter. Two years before the first destruction of Lawrence 'til now we've had our own seven-year civil war with raiding parties coming from as far away as Georgia and Florida, not to mention the continual forays of the Missouri

Hooligans to which, of course, we responded in-kind. When John Brown was alive, the pro slavery folks shuddered at his response. Now since Sumpter I guess the difference is the level of excitement and public involvement. Since the first of the year the papers have been full of war anticipation. Hardly a week goes by without news of one (Southern) State or another threatening or announcing secession."

Just as Adda moved out to accommodate her sister's marriage in Eldorado, Augusta moves out of their house in Lawrence to accommodate Adda, except the difference this time is Augusta owns half the house. She soon came to feel like she's been dispossessed and evicted without compensation. Augusta and Graton seem to bear a mutual and on-going animosity. In one entry Augusta writes, "I took an instant dislike to the man and he to me. I kept waiting to see some behavior, not towards me but my sister, which would redeem him in my estimation. It never happened. His infidelity and rude behavior towards Adda always outweighed his sincere abolitionism and his patriotism."

From hundreds of slaves flocking to freedom in Lawrence Adda's husband and others volunteer to recruit and train an all black regiment, Although Governor Robinson commissions these officers, in the field, and in the early months of the war the Militia seems to be commanded by General Lane. Later with skepticism and Army reluctance they are "mustered" in to the Union Army, because everybody knows that you can't make a soldier out of an ex slave. This involvement of Graton was to put Adda's life in danger when Quantrill rides into Lawrence in the summer of 1863 to wreak havoc in general and to right some specific wrongs. On his revenge list is the wife of Captain Graton, the organizer of the Black Regiment. Quantrill's gang locates Adda and, as usual, she outwits her foe in an episode that swings from disaster to humorous triumph. Adda writes to her sister that she and a companion allow a state legislator's brother, who was also on Quantrlll's list, to hide behind and under their hooped skirts while the women are being questioned. While they are setting fire to her house, Adda convinces Quantrill's men they have the "wrong woman" and wrong house. All three go shaken but unharmed. She assures her sister she still carries her little Colt-4 shot pistol… just in case. All the while Adda copes with a humiliation that her husband has been "carrying on" with one of her girl friends and with reluctance stemming from her bitter disappointment with her husband, she discusses it with her sister.

Through the balance of '61 and '62 Augusta describes the early phases of the Civil War in the West, noting with sorrow and alarm the departure for the war many of her friends and her father's old associates. Dave Upham, returning empty-handed from the gold fields, volunteers with Sam Tappan for the Union Army. Due to his experience in Jim Lane's militia, Upham is "made" corporal. Colonel Deitzler and Captain Frank Swift, who joined Kansas 1st and 2nd Regiments, return from early Missouri battles, both wounded but alive. She notes a whole procession of generals that Lincoln appoints to defend Kansas and Missouri, which have both been quickly declared by Lincoln to be Union States. The second of Lincoln's appointments (for Kansas and Missouri) General Nathaniel Lyons, a West Pointer, was quickly killed (July) and replaced by the famous explorer, John Fremont, the Whig politician who Preston Plumb was certain would beat Buchanan in '56 for the White House. In three months General Fremont had been replaced. Augusta refers to Southern Forces as "Secessionists". As the war expands, Mr. Gates is killed; Mrs. Gates remarries.

Lexington, (Missouri) is taken by Secessionists on September 22, 1861. 2,000 Union troops were trapped and captured. Many are killed and buried in shallow mass graves.

Graton and his Negro Regiment are ordered to defend Wyandotte (Kansas City).

Mr. Rackliffe, her Eldorado neighbor, taking Sam Stewart's place in District 17 is elected to the Territorial Legislature. He gets Augusta a better job as chief cook in a Topeka boarding house catering to Legislators. Augusta is both flattered and mystified by proposals of marriage from Mr. John Slack, a casual acquaintance from Emporia. Twice she declines but acknowledges that he is a substantial, widowed farmer and a considerate gentleman.

In the summer of '63, she leaves for the Rocky Mountains with Elizabeth and Tom Cordis, the Eldorado blacksmith, to accept a better paying job cooking for a mining outfit in Kansas Territory, south of Denver's current site. After the death of her husband, Mary Rackliffe and little Ermie soon join the trio. In October '63, Augusta commences volume II of her journals and on April 18, 1864, five years after Chase has died, she married George Washington Blackman in newly named Denver.

On their honeymoon trip they can't resist the call of "Gold Strike" in Virginia City, Montana Territory. They arrive just as the Vigilantes are establishing law and order in Alder Gulch after discovering that it was the Sheriff Plummer himself who had been master-minding the robbery of wagons leaving Virginia City with smeltered gold. Over several weeks that cold winter the Vigilantes sought out and hung the whole Plummer gang, two dozen of them.

George stakes a claim on the mountain behind the mining camp and to defend it stays on it through the bitter winter, while Augusta has their first baby without him and later runs a boarding house for miners.

Alder Gulch was to produce one of the largest placer mining strikes ever, though to this day they've never discovered the mother lode, the source of all the nuggets and gold dust mined from the down-stream gravel.

Back in Lawrence, Adda gives birth to a daughter, Alice (later, Alice Graton Kincaid). Adda writes that her husband, John, has been taken prisoner and put in a Southern prison camp where he takes sick. After her "close call" during Quantrill's raid in August of 1863, fearing for her own life and the baby's, Adda leaves the state until the war is over. In 1872 John Graton dies from diseases contracted during the war. Adda never remarries.

Years later, Alice, Adda's only child, edits "Memories of Addie Stewart Graton" from her mother's journals.* Adda lived ninety-one years.

She died in 1932, having out-lived Augusta by eighteen years and is buried in Lawrence, Kansas.

After years of bitter struggle, Augusta and George grow modestly prosperous owning and operating small Montana mines. From their union three of four children survive. One of them is Adelaide, the Gold Miner's daughter, who grows up in Silver Star and later moves to Bozeman, Marjorie's grandmother, the first inheritor of these journals.

Augusta Stewart Chase Blackman continues her journal and finally sees some of her writing in print. The May 10, 1901 issue of the Walnut Valley Times prints her recollections of early Eldorado, filling two pages.

She dies of natural causes on may 31, 1914 and is buries on a windswept hill above the mining town of Silver Star, Montana looking east over the beautiful Valley of the Jefferson River.

Ralph E. and Marjorie L. Crump
Trumbull, Connecticut

---

* Watkins Community Museum of History, which is on loan to the Kansas State University Genealogical Section, where it exists today as a minor item in their vast archives.

INTRODUCTION TO VOLUME IV

This volume brings to a close our four volumes on the chronicled life of Augusta during a very turbulent and pivotal period in the History of the United States: the opening-up of the West, the question of whether slavery would prevail nationally with political attempts to legitimize it in the new territories, starting with Kansas; a serious depression brought on by over expansion of our then growth industry, the railroads; the explosive discoveries of gold in most of the Western Territories; one of the worst wars in our history to settle once and for all whether we were to be "one nation indivisible" with slavery or not.

Augusta's original three bound journals, which I inherited, with some 2,000 entries, beginning before she was seventeen, records not only her personal and occasionally tragic involvement in all of these events, but the influence these events had on her life at the time.

Her journal entries from 1857 to 1860 present a record of the founding (by her father and a few other abolitionists) the town of Eldorado, Kansas that is better and more authentic than any professional early history of the city we've seen. She described in detail these two or three-dozen mostly young pioneers that were willing to go far beyond the Frontier to establish a voting district free of proslavery domination.

She was not, nor was her father, a "Mover or a Shaker" of the period, though Sam may have become one through his territorial legislative activities, had he not been cut short by his senseless murder. She was simply a comparatively well-educated youngster, endowed with an engaging interest in the culture of her time, concerned with whether she would find a suitable husband, whether she could continue to run the family sawmill. Once she reached maturity, she recognized the importance of her economic well being, even if it meant working in one frontier boarding house or another, which in every case she became the chief cook and would ultimately try to own it. Over all those years Augusta and Adda remained loyal and communicating friends.

July 1860

When Adda and I got back to Eldorado from Lawrence on the 8th we found it as hot and dry as the prairie we had just crossed to get home. Our well was almost dry. The water I did crank up was unfit to drink. When I turned to the spring over by the river, to my utter amazement that old reliable source of sweet water flowing down out of the sandstone cliff was not only dry but its absence was disorienting. I thought maybe I'd gone to the wrong place, so I looked elsewhere, back and forth along the yellow-brown laminated stone face, I discovered I was right the first time. There was absolutely no water trickling down anywhere out from the ledges. The Walnut River below was low, muddy and moving sluggishly.

I went home empty-handed, hoping that some of our neighbors' wells were not dry.

That summer my carrots were runts, as were other root vegetable I'd put in that spring and to make matters worse, the grasshoppers had eaten the tops off all the carrots, turnips and radishes. During the two weeks or so that Adda and I were back we took stock of our situation. Adda really preferred to live and work in Lawrence. Since it looks like the corn crop we put in this spring will hardly make silage, never mind grain; if I did stay on, I don't know how I would make it through the winter. I suppose if I got an order for lumber, I could find help to fire up the boiler and saw the wood, but it would probably be a credit sale and I'm no different than others. I need a minimum of cash to get along. But I guess a credit sale is better than no sale. Mr. Watt's sale was mostly credit and he pays me little by little.

I was a widow. Although I'm sure that I could manage the sawmill, if there was enough regular business to keep full-time employees, like we did in Michigan but there isn't and that's a shame. And if I did stay, I'd need help with plowing, planting and harvesting.

We had both looked at an available house in Lawrence, which we would like to buy in the unlikely event that we could find a buyer for our three claims and the sawmill out here. But if we do, that's the house we'd like to buy and fix up. It was new, never occupied and not completely finished inside.

Adda has made it clear she has no interest in staying out here. She wants to live where there is plenty of work for her and that's Lawrence. Real life is always more complicated. Adda's major reason for returning to Lawrence is to test the promise of romance with an ambitious, young, handsome gunsmith, who boards at the Whitney House where she works. He has flattered her into believing that he has a serious interest. Adding to Adda's desire to return to Lawrence is a friend and coworker, Jule Johnson; who has also gained the eye of the gunsmith and Adda has always been competitive.

It only took us three or four days to make up our minds that if for the time being we want to remain together, we've got to look for a buyer of our claims and hopefully find someone interested in the sawmill, which, with the boiler, is really an outstanding piece of well-crafted and well-tested machinery. Thanks to Father's experience and planning and thanks to the old Scotch millwright, Mr. Eastwood, from the day it started, when we had the orders, we've sawed wood with it, and never spent a nickel on repairs.

As for the Sorghum mill a year ago this spring Mr. Eastwood and his family came through Eldorado to wait for a westbound Iowa outfit, all headed for the new and promising goldfields of the Rocky Mountains. Gold that others found, escaped Chase who had returned empty-handed in August two years ago. The

Eastwoods had come west early intending to take with them 10,000 board feet of sawed lumber and he knew that task would take several days, even if we had the logs on hand, which we did. It soon became obvious and a bit humorous that he also had his eye on our sorghum mill. He had always thought that the sorghum mill with an auxiliary still using excess heat from the big boiler should also make alcohol and he said so, often. During the two weeks that it took to saw-up his order, he would point out that the sorghum mill was idle, noting that even when it was working, it was not up to its "full usefulness".

It soon became clear to me that it was his intent to "take the idle sorghum mill off my hands." In the end, with Adda's blessing, since she was here and helped saw-up their order, I traded the sorghum mill for the one share of stock he owned in the sawmill. He had teased us about our abstinence and reminded us that he would make better use of the fermented cane-mash than our cows had by "teasing" some rum out of it, where in his "humble" opinion, the rum would serve a more useful purpose than the cane-mash, because the value of his product would please his customers more than the slightly fermented mash could please my cows. "There's always more profit in pleasing humans than pleasing animals," he added philosophically.

In the end he prevailed. He got the mill but we got much needed cash for the lumber and the one share of stock he owned in the sawmill. We agreed on $25 per 1,000 board feet and netted $200 after paying Jerry and Mr. Rice for their help. Adda and I split the $200 cash, 50/50. Lord knows we both could use it.

Luck was certainly with us that July. We had a short but successful negotiation with a Mr. Little, who needed more space and a better supply of water than he had up in Chelsea. Mr. Little's expanding business was selling calves to others from his breed stock. Buyers in turn fattened them on the prairie, and with grain and silage from their own acreage. It turns out that some of Mr. Little's customers were right here in Eldorado. He raises his own cattle feed, both grain (corn) and silage, to avoid being dependent on others. In that way he said, "I walk my crops to market". He liked the location of our three claims on the Walnut River particularly because of a meandering crick that starts from the river above a natural rock ledge dam that carries small amounts of running water across each of our three 160 acre claims. Until we heard from him that the crick was an asset we'd viewed it as a nuisance because we had to plow around it. He explained the advantage for cattle of running water and little muddy ponds, over well water, which is what he was currently relying on. Adding value to their claims was the dry summer. The girls suspected that his wells were as dry as theirs.

The sisters used Judge Lambden, a lawyer and a political friend of their Father's to write the buy-sell agreements for the land-transfer. The lawyer cleverly arranged it as an estate sale where the girls were the beneficiaries. There was some legal/territorial question as to whether females (unmarried or not, particularly those not yet 21 years of age) could be owners of territorial land initially owned by the Government. Judge Lambden also helped with the sale of the sawmill.

During the third week of July they packed up their reliable Studebaker and began the return trip to Lawrence and bought the two-storey house on Rhode Island Street that they had "looked at" earlier.

They found Lawrence that summer as dry as Eldorado. The Kaw River was so low, oxen wading it were pulling ferries from one shore to the other.

Augusta's entries for the balance of the summer and well into early winter deal mainly with daily events, friends coming and going and Adda's on-going romance with the gunsmith, who had been courting her, previously but not exclusively, while she was working at the Whitney House. He hadn't exactly turned a blind eye to Adda's competitor, Jule Johnson.

On the same day in March that Lincoln is inaugurated Adda and the gunsmith marry. Although he chose Adda over Jule, he fails to treat her with the courtesy and respect that Augusta thinks is due her sister. But the trouble doesn't stop there. There remains some deep-seated animosity between John Graton and Augusta.

Although their house at #627 Rhode Island Street is a beehive of social activities, her journal entries makes clear that she is very lonely, unfulfilled and often melancholy over the realization that their plans have failed terribly to work out the way they began in Eldorado and the way she planned them to work out. Augusta, the young widow, makes entry after entry dealing with the loss of her father and all he stood for, that their business ventures had failed to materialize, and because of all this, the change in their social status. But mostly she wrote about her loneliness and of her longing for her husband's lost love and companionship. She "Hopes it is Heaven Chase calls home and that one day I may join him." This hope (she says) "is the greatest consolation I have." And the poignant entry continues in this melancholy mood for several paragraphs. Manifestations of her depression continues on in other entries for the next four years. Finally in 1864 In a Colorado mining camp she meets, falls in love with George Blackman and marries the gold miner in Denver.

Returning to Lawrence that summer of 1960 the girls visit their old friends at the Cincinnati House and the Whitney House where they are offered their old jobs, neither sister decides to work for a while, which suggests that they want to enjoy getting along for a while using surplus proceeds from the land and sawmill sale, not consumed by their new house, its repairs and the usual furnishings. The neighborhood appears to be suburban enough that they buy and keep two cows, like some of their neighbors.

After Adda's marriage, her husband moved in with the girls, an arrangement that immediately causes family friction. On one occasion, Adda's husband suggested that for privacy they buy an extra "cook" stove, put a bunk in the kitchen for Augusta, and divide the house into two separate living quarters. Augusta writes that she is absolutely opposed to this silly suggestion. She had always wanted a proper parlor, an anti room from the outside to it, a dining room adjacent to a kitchen…that and two upstairs bedrooms was what their house had. Augusta is convinced that Graton wants her out of the house (never mind that she owns half of it).

Jim Lane stays in the headlines by protecting President Lincoln and the Capitol prior to and after the inauguration with a regiment of Kansas Militia hastily called to Washington by President Buchanan. Following Lincoln's inauguration, Civil War is declared…within weeks the war draws close to Eastern Kansas.

Commissioned a Lt. General by the President, Lane returns having been asked by Lincoln to recruit for the Union in Kansas. "General" Lane expands his assignment, by taking two Regiments of Jayhawks or "Red Legs" into Southwest Missouri. He raids, plunders the countryside and liberates slaves, escorting them back to Kansas and enlisting the able bodied for military service. These acts offend the moderates and Lane's political foes, the same people who for more than a generation thought the question of slavery could be settled by compromise. Now that war has been declared, they think it should be conducted with "moderation." Even Lincoln believes that with moderate behavior of the Union troops in the field he can keep the Border States, like Maryland, Kentucky and Missouri on "his side." Governor Robinson is of the same mind. General Lane disagrees with both.

Adda's husband goes up to Fort Leavenworth and volunteers to train a (territorial)Militia Company of ex slaves. Their regiment is ultimately mustered into the U. S. Army. To the surprise of many early doubters they fight with as much enthusiasm and courage as white soldiers. When Captain Graton is on leave he threatens Adda with violence and is unfaithful to her. In desperation to defend herself physically and to save their marriage she threatens to expose his tawdry marital behavior to his superiors through their personal contacts with Governor Robinson, who had commissioned Graton or General Jim Lane, who Graton's superiors report to..

Looking to improve her prospects, Augusta accepts a job as chief cook in a Colorado mining camp, where she meets an old-time miner from Georgia, learns the rudiments of primitive placer mining and modestly prospers.

It's in Colorado that Augusta begins to confront her five-year, self-imposed mourning and wonders how long she should live with this melancholy and what real benefit, if any, was she deriving from this secret solitude. No doubt this introspection was initiated by the first male that she's met since Chase's death with whom she seems to have an affinity, if she will allow herself to accept it.

Finally after five years of mourning for her first love, she remarries (in Denver.) The newly weds honeymoon on a six week trek to a new gold strike in the Idaho territory, part of which soon becomes the Montana Territory.

They spend several years in the Virginia City area. Augusta buys and runs a rather large boarding house while her husband George continues to search for the Mother Lode in the mountains behind Virginia City, he and all others fail to find it.

They ultimately settle nearby in Silver Star, still in mining, where they raise three children and achieve a modicum of commercial success and domestic happiness.

The ever-loyal sister, Adda, continues their correspondence. Before statehood Augusta and George are acknowledged as Montana Pioneers.

At Eldorado's 50th anniversary she is asked by the town's newspaper to write an early history of the founding of the town. Using her journal entries, she writes a full page in the *Walnut Valley Times*, May 10th, 1910.

She survives her husband by twenty-two years and finally succumbs in May 1914. They both are buried in Silver Star Cemetery, Montana.

53.

RETURN TO LAWRENCE
1860

Returning to Lawrence that July we found the area as dry as Eldorado. The river was so low, oxen wading the Kaw River were pulling ferries from the New Hampshire Street slip to the other side.

We arrived on Thursday, about noon, in late July leaving the horses and wagon at the end of Connecticut Street, close to the river, upstream two blocks from the ferry landing, where there were still patches of green grass for the horses and walked over to Mrs. Fiske's place. She was back from Emporia with her health restored looking so much better than she did when we offered her a ride out there earlier this summer. She's a widow, but she looks ten years younger than she did last June when she was "under the weather". She has resumed running her boarding house, though it seems rather small to me, if she intends to "make it pay".

She was most hospitable and immediately suggested that we help her run her business. We told her about our selling out in Eldorado, but she already knew. Can you beat that? She had already heard about it. In fact, she said both Mr. Stone over at the Whitney House and she had discussed it, hoping we'd both be available to one or the other of us. I thought there must be a shortage of female help.

I asked Mrs. Fiske if she was full.

"Yes, but I can always make room for you two. My own bed is too big for just me. You can just crawl in with me. Every other bed in the house has two men in it, but I have an upstairs room with two dormer windows. I can dress it up and put a bed up there for you two.

I looked at Adda. It was obvious that Mrs. Fiske's offer was better than nothing.

Adda response was "I'd like to walk down to the Whitney House and see if we can board and room there for a week or so until we figure out where to live."

I said, "Adda, I can't go there. Have you forgotten how that man treated us? How many weeks we all went without pay until our friend from Plymouth, Mr. Montague, took Mr. Stone to the woodshed on our behalf? He'll never forgive me for that embarrassment.

"Well, I need a bath. I've been sweaty and dusty for a week and I don't want to live in the wagon when I know I can rent a bed and buy some hot water in a half dozen places in this town. I can put up with Mr. Stone."

"What happens if he doesn't have a room?"

"We'll try the Cincinnati House. With Aggie Rourke the food is better there anyway. There are three or four places in town... How about the Killam's place? If the whole town is full, the three of us in Mrs. Fiske's bed beats another night in that dusty wagon and Mrs. Fiske has a bathtub."

Mrs. Fiske piped up, "Just say the word and I'll buy a bed and we'll fix-up that upstairs room for you."

It was obvious that Adda wasn't going to spend another week in the wagon, knowing she had better alternatives...all within walking distance.

"I have an idea. I'll go down to the Whitney House. I'll ask Mr. Stone if he's got space. I'll be able to tell in a second if we are welcome. Yes or no, I'll come back and tell you."

"Well, if you are so determined, I'll go with you."

"Fine, but let me do the talkin'.'"

About five o'clock we walked over to the Whitney House. I was apprehensive. To my surprise Mr. Stone could not have been nicer. We had learned from Mrs. Fiske that Mr. Stone had his family out here from Detroit for the summer. When Adda asked if he had a room for two more boarders for a week or so, much to our surprise Mr. Stone invited us to be his guests for supper and said he had a spare room if we wanted to stay at the Whitney House.

Adda asked, "Can I get some hot water for a bath before supper?"

"Certainly."

He seems to have changed, especially towards me. He knew my name, used it and behaved as though all that difficulty over our back wages and Mr. Montague's visit never happened. The Stone family, which includes Mrs. Laura Stone and their three "children", all eat at their own table. Mr. Stone invited us to join them. I counted seventeen boarders. Some of them, like Mr. George Burt and Mr. Esterbrook have been boarding here for several years. Many board here but live elsewhere. That's customary. At supper we walked around and said hello to several of the "old timers".

Then I saw why Adda was so insistent about a room and a hot bath before supper. Who was at table number three, shaking hands with my just bathed sister, none other than John Graton., the handsome gunsmith.

So, I thought, that's what all this has been about. Although we both sat at Mr. Stone's table, Mr. Graton came over mid meal to bid a good evening to Mrs. Stone but it was really to make another hello to Adda…who was beaming.

Well, who am I to deny my little sister some romantic attention from an eligible bachelor, although he appears to be several years older.

The quality of the main course made it obvious that Aggie Rourke was not running his kitchen anymore, but he had arranged a special dessert…a rum-flavored bread pudding. I wondered what has come over the man. He actually allowed the cook to use eggs and cream and a generous amount of rum-soaked raisins in making a delicious bread pudding, which is more than he ever allowed us to use when we were working for him. Adda says it's all because his Misses is with him. I suspected that Mrs. Stone had made the dessert.

During dessert Mr. Graton graced our table again. This time his excuse was to compliment Mr. Stone on the quality of the bread pudding, saying he hadn't had a pudding like that since a banquet at the Parker House in Boston several years ago. Mr. Graton boards mainly at the Whitney House and rooms with the Reed family.

Before we left at 9 o'clock, Mr. Stone asked if we would both come back to work. Adda said she'd think about it, but would need a day off each week and said she'd expect to get paid regularly each week…on Friday. He said, calling her Miss Stewart, that she could not only count on it but she could expect to make more this year than last. He walked us to the front door and in making his good night he held my sister's hand in both of his, like she was a daughter.

At the front door I explained to him that we had left the horses and our wagon down by the river. Had it been a brighter night, we probably could have seen them from the front porch. I asked him to hold the room…that tomorrow we'll board the horses at the livery and find a safe place to leave the wagon, but that we'll take all three meals tomorrow with him and a room for the two of us.

After the long prairie twilight it began to get dark and we were concerned about our two horses and the wagon with all our "stuff" unattended. The nice old dining room that Adda and I knew so well, the prepared hot supper and unusual hospitality with the Stones would soon be quite a tempting contrast to spending the night as we had the recent five in the wagon. We walked in the dark back down 7th Street toward the river until we could hear the horses by our humble mobile accommodations.

As we "turned in", we could faintly hear, down river, some activities from one of the docked riverboats. I asked Adda if she had her little revolver...in case of prowlers.

"You betcha".

Before we went to sleep, I asked Adda if she wants to go back to work.

She said, "Not for a while, but if I do I'll go back to the Whitney House. Did you notice Jule Johnson was waiting tables tonight? Do you remember her?"

"Certainly, I remember the whole family...fine abolitionists. I think Mr. Johnson, Jule's father, was in one of Jim Lane's militia. Why do you ask?"

Well, I think she also has her eye on Mr. Graton." It was quiet that night and very warm.

Just a note: August 8, 1860. Today is my 21st birthday. Young in years...old in heart"...I seem to have known so much misery and disappointment for someone so young...and I'm a widow. Among all my friends I don't know of a single girl widowed so young. Why me?

A letter from Sam Chase, my husband's father, finally caught up with me. He complains that he had written several letters (all unanswered). I must find a way to explain that some mail simply doesn't get out here to the territory and I guess I should tell him that I no longer live in Eldorado.

During a week inspecting available houses and visiting old friends, we made a call at the Riggs bank. Now that abolitionists are in the majority, I noticed the bank has hired a few people with northern accents. When we asked to speak to one of the managers who was familiar with the Diggle fraud of last year, he informed us that Mr. Diggle had never gone to trial. "Oh? Why?" asked Adda.

"Several weeks ago he died of complication from back injuries." My little sister gave me an under-the-table poke on my thigh but said in almost mock-somber tones, "Oh, what a shame." But immediately she was grinning ear to ear.

We still owed the bank some eighty dollars including interest. We said we wanted to deposit two checks: one from Mr. Martin and the other from Mr. Little, using those deposits, we opened an account, telling the banker that he could expect that we would be drawing on it to buy a house here in Lawrence and that the bank, in time, could expect checks drawn to us from two gentlemen from Eldorado. We explained to them the sale of the sawmill and land.

Three days later on the 14th of August we met the seller of the house in the 600 block on Rhode Island Street at the Riggs Bank and after a little good-natured haggling bought it. The two-storey house is within sight of the cottonwoods along the river and not far from the docks. Our block is bounded by two streets, later named Warren and Henry. It will be nice to see the riverboats come and go. It turns out that the bank was carrying a loan on that new but vacant house. Leaving the bank Adda said we ought to try and invite Mr. and Mrs. Gates over. I laughed and said "Well, Adda, let's get some furniture, some rugs and plaster all those bare spots first.

Even though the house needs some inside lathe and plastering, and the stairwell casing has never been adequately anchored in-place, Adda and I decided to move right in. Adda, thinking of her beau, I'm sure, said, "Let's board at the Whitney House 'til we're ready to cook here, eh?"

We did have one bed, the one we brought up with us, but with two upstairs bedrooms, we'll need another bed. We were impressed that the builder had installed one of those new, short-handled cast iron pumps, right on our back porch, which with a pump or two brought up "good quality" drinking water. I expected that we'd have the usual crank-up well close by, some place in the yard. But to have it on a covered back porch is quite a luxury. The pumping action moves a vertical rod up and down, which must lift up the water that's already in a pipe. Being near the river, I suspect that the water table is not very far below us. We're only twenty to twenty-five feet above the river.

We wondered how or when that well was dug, since it was just outside the kitchen door. It was customary for the well to be some distance from the house to accommodate farm animals as well.

A family from Indian Creek, who claims the Indians stole their child, recently has decided to return to Ohio. They had two cows and we obliged them by the purchase of both. "It's an ill wind that doesn't blow somebody some good." We'll need to build a cow shed before winter sets in and I'll get some heavy planking for a walkway to the outhouse.

There's plenty of space in our backyard for a garden, though I'll need some help to get that ground turned over. I suppose it's too late for my cantaloupe seeds but I'll certainly get carrots, turnips and potatoes in.

We returned to some optimistic news and town excitement. We heard that ground was broken by the Missouri-Pacific railroad in Kansas City near the river, (old Wyandotte) with plans to go southwest through Emporia, Council Grove and on out to Fort Riley. Of course, we were anxious to see if it would go through Eldorado.

Mr. Stein from Eldorado is here with the bad news that Mrs. Carey, our old neighbor out there, has died. She was sick only two days. There is something wrong with that valley. I remember how quickly last year our two faithful oxen were taken...with a totally unknown disease.

Well, the plasterers said today they are finished.

This is the worst piece of plastering I have ever seen. They must have used sticks trying to get a smooth surface. Little hard lumps and grooves are all over the place. How can I ever paint it? I made the mistake of not being here for two days to supervise these two incompetents. Mrs. Leiby was sick and she sent a note recalling my nursing days during the small pox episode at the Gates here in town and would I come care for her? I was only gone two days and counted four empty whiskey bottles tossed in our backyard when I got home. I certainly won't use these two blockheads to finish the stairwell. We need a good carpenter to address the one-inch gap between the stair casement and the walls on both sides. The staircase wobbles insecurely whenever we go up and down the poorly anchored stair well. I immediately thought how quickly Chase would handle this problem.

Adda, with or without me, takes all her meals at the Whitney House, has gone riding again today with "you know whom", so I can't count on her to help me deal with these two scoundrels.

Yesterday we were delightedly surprised by the delivery of a half a keg of sweet, ripe peaches and some absolutely white, fine-grain sugar. They must be from Missouri or Iowa, but what a pleasure. I asked Adda who in the world would send us such a generous amount? Adda thinks it's Mr. Graton. He's invited her to go riding again today. I've given some thought to asking him to help me deal with these pestering plasterers. I haven't paid them yet, though I certainly paid for the plaster and lathes. They come by every day looking for their money. As the plaster dries, it turns yellow and emits an awful odor. I've asked them twice what in the world they dissolved that plaster with to give off such a smell. They just grin at each other. Now, I'll have to paint over their plaster job, but it will be fun to choose the paint color.

While Adda and I were enjoying the ripe, juicy pealed peaches sprinkled with some of that complimentary sugar, that didn't need it; I asked Adda what she knew about Mr. Graton.

"He was born in Leicester, Massachusetts, which he says you pronounce as Lester. 'Lester' is a few miles northeast of Springfield, where the Gates had their hotel. His mother's maiden name is Lucy Adams. He takes particular pride that she's from the Boston Adams family.

"Like us, he went to private schools…then to Shelburne Falls Academy, which combined three years of high school and two years of college with drafting, mathematics, physics. He calls it "Mechanics Arts."

He was accepted as an engineering and design apprenticeship in an armory located in Providence, Rhode Island, where he learned to design gun parts, make them, assemble them, and test-fire them. He had classes of gunpowder chemistry and knows how to make it. This armory often made special guns for both the Navy and the Army, so he traveled throughout New England demonstrating their gun models to get arsenals to manufacture them. He claims he knows every major gun manufacturer in New England and New York State.

"How long was he in the Armory??"

" At least two years including the summers."

"He said he occasionally attended anti-slavery lectures and rallies around Boston, which is close to Providence, both rabidly anti-slavery. In 1857, a year after us, he joined a group and came out here. They were able to put their wagons and teams on the boats in St. Louis and came across Missouri on the riverboats, unthreatened. He's very patriotic. He writes to his folks in Leicester regularly and has a sister here in town named Julia. She's a little older than Mr. Graton and I get the feeling that she's been married before but I've never asked. In fact, what little I know about Julia, I've learned from her brother.

There's also a brother-in-law here in town, Mr. Haskey, but I haven't met him."

"How old is Mr. Graton?"

"I don't know."

"Well, do you now when he was born?"

At first Adda pretended she didn't know or had forgotten.

" Is he as old as Frank Robinson?"

"Oh, yes, now I recall. He was born in 1836.

"Adda, he's three years older than me and four years older than you."

"Has he been married before?"

"Not that I know of."

"Is that all you know?"

Our discussion over the delicious peaches was interrupted by a knock on the door by the swain, himself. When Adda answered the door, I overheard him say, rather gruffly, "Why aren't you ready? Just look at you. What have you been doing?"

Giggling, like a schoolgirl, Adda said, "Eating peaches with my sister."

"I told you when I would be here."

As Adda ran upstairs to change, she shouted for him to take a seat in the parlor. We had been in the kitchen. I thought I would put Mr. Graton at ease by saying hello and give my excited sister time to change.

I found him pacing back and forth in front of the bay window. I said something to the effect that we had met briefly in July while Adda and I were having supper with the Stones at the Whitney House. Although he's not a tall man, nor heavy, he stands very erect. Father would say, "He carries himself well." He seemed to have trouble looking me in the eye.

"Adda and I were enjoying some of the nicest peaches I've ever tasted… from a mystery donor…they will be enjoyed for some time, because of our benefactor's generosity. May I assume you were the donor?"

"You may assume anything you please."

Ignoring his haughtiness, I asked if I could offer him a sweetened peach.

"No. I never eat between meals. What's keeping your sister? What smells in here?"

"This is a new house. It required some inside plastering."

He turned his back on me, looked out the window and began pacing again like the train he was waiting for from Detroit might be late. Finally Adda appeared and rushed by me in the anteroom in a rustle of skirts…wearing long grey riding gloves swinging a (silly) little purple parasol. Some time ago she had shown me a sketch in the fashion section of Graham's Magazine of a similar going-for-an afternoon- ride costume.

Adda grabbed Mr. Graton's sleeve and hustled him down the front steps. As she swept by me I caught the unmistakable delicate fragrance of the cologne that Howland had given her two years ago, when he learned that Glennis Bemis had left for the Gold Fields. Obviously the perfume and a new dress was intended for Glennis, and my little sister was sure making good use of it today.

I followed them out to the front porch in my apron. I wanted to see what his "rig" looked like. I was not disappointed. It's certainly apparent that he's a good judge of horseflesh and wants everybody to know he has a new two-wheel shay with a collapsible cover...on this bright, sunny occasion it was fashionably down. As they rode off, Adda was coyly twirling her little parasol.

Jerry Jordan is in town and has dropped by but is very formal. I suppose it's because I have refused his proposals...twice. I hope he hasn't quit work at the Chelsea flourmill, but I didn't ask whatever came of his budding romance last summer with Glennis. Of course, I was also curious about Glennis myself.

SUNDAY, SEPTEMBER

I have been thinking about joining a church, so this morning I got properly dressed and attended the 9am services at Reverend Brant's church, the one Adda favors among those she's attended. It was a nice service. I particularly enjoyed the familiar hymns. He had used a passage from Mathew, comparing our quest for a state without slavery, to a pearl with a great price on it. Mathew speaks (he said) of a merchant who so wanted a fine pearl that when he finally located one, he sold all he had to buy it. His message was that many of us have sold all we had to come out here to seek this "Pearl of freedom"...and so on and so on.

There was a notice on the church's bulletin board about a lecture that evening. It was to deal with the consequences of a harsh religious culture that existed in Puritan New England during Colonial times as described in Hawthorne's novel, "*The Scarlet Letter*". I had read a book report in Leslie's Magazine not long after we moved to Eldorado, maybe two years ago with a comment about it from of all people, Edgar Allen Poe, but I never got around to ordering the book. I went to the lecture anyway and found it stimulating.

Reverend Brant, this morning's preacher, introduced the speaker, reminding us that he had used a parable from the book of Mathew in this morning's sermon alluding to a pearl of great value. He said he suspected that the evening's speaker would explain why, when this poor Dutch immigrant (to Boston), Hester Prynne, believing that after an absence of two years her husband was dead, took up with a local pastor, Dimmsdale, and bore him a child they named Pearl. And how Hester, when in the dock accused of adultery noticed that in the very courtroom stood her long-lost husband. In a very convoluted, but best selling story, Hawthorne tells how both she and the pastor had paid, like Mathew's merchant, a great price for their Pearl.

Obviously Reverend Brant is a well-read gentleman. He certainly had a nice turn out for his morning service as well as this evening's cultural event, which his church had sponsored. The speaker was from a Chicago speaker's agency and except for summer is a professor at some older New England college, Bowdoin.

As sorry as I am that we abandoned our "best laid plans" out west, life in Lawrence does have these cultural recompenses.

An old beau of Adda's, Mr. Hubbard, has sent a small package for her from the Rocky Mountain gold fields. The package contained a piece of quartz rock that has a thin visible vein of gold in it. I asked Adda what else the letter contained, but she declined my curiosity. Adda and I walked up to the post office to get a second letter from her gold-mining friend.

When she showed Graton the quartz containing gold, he sniffed and said he'd bet there wasn't seven dollars worth of gold in the rock and invited Adda for another afternoon ride. They didn't get back until after 10 O'clock this evening.

Sunday night he spent the night at our house. I asked Adda if she thought it was proper for one of her beaus to spend the entire night...even if he did sleep in the parlor. She said, "Well, you were our chaperone, so you know we behaved ourselves." I reminded her that this is a small town…full of gossips. But you know Adda… blithe spirit that she is…I might as well talk to the wall.

Adda and I hosted a supper party here for Sarah Goss even though we are running low on "resources", Our guests were Mr. George Burt (a successful businessman here in town, Dr. Lewis (Sarah's beau), Mr. Graton, Mr. Randall and Mr. Critchett, who has just returned from the gold fields, with what he brags is a sizeable "poke". He's become very friendly with Mrs. Fiske and has been boarding with her.

They all stayed so late after the meal and parlor games, we said if we could find suitable accommodations for them, they could stay the night. It was so windy. Mr. Critchett asked me why our staircase wobbled. When I explained the situation, by inviting him to walk up and down them, he said that if I located some one-inch thick pine, he could fix it. Two days later he showed up with the wood and in no time the stairs were as solid as they should have been. Although he says that I'll need some molding to make the staircase conform to the two walls. He's a little less than Father's age and very congenial.

At the party I tried to show the appearance of having a good time and I think everyone thought that I was enjoying myself, but this supper comes exactly one year after my darling husband's death but I saw no need to say so.

Mrs. Spicer sent a note asking if Adda and I can come over and help her "put up" peaches. She said she had bushels of them and if they weren't put up, they'd spoil. So here we are and here I am writing about it, but Adda and I will get four quarts of canned peaches for our neighborly help

A day later another note: Sarah Goss is sick and I'm with her at the Goss's place on the edge of town. Doctor Lewis is here now. Adda and I have been here all night. This is very serious. For some reason Adda sent for Mr. Graton. I don't know what earthly purpose he can serve but he's here. Adda said his presence would give her comfort if Sarah dies. Well, Sarah *is* sick, but she is *not* going to die. You can mark my word on that.

To add to my frustration, while we were attending Sarah, as I suspected, Mr. Critchett (the recently wealthy middle-aged gold-miner, and fixer-of-stairs,) married Mrs. Fiske. It was quite a party, I'm told. Graton and Adda snuck away to attend but, for me, duty called. Sarah, my patient, was still gravely ill.

Three days after the Critchett/Fiske wedding the newlyweds got off on their honeymoon to visit relatives in New England, near Concord, New Hampshire. Mrs. Fiske simply closed her boarding house. Although I was taking care of Sarah, I got up very early and walked over to 7th and Massachusetts, the stage depot, to see them off. I gave serious thought to asking them if I could go along… at least as far as Concord. It would be so nice to spend time with Chase's people. I did send several letters and a likeness of Adda and me, taken by the new studio here in town.

But Dr. Lewis had prevailed in asking me to stay with Sarah, instead of going to New Hampshire with the Critchetts. She remains a very sick young lady. But it's my opinion that after two weeks she's much better now than when she first came down with it, if for no other reason than for the last few days what she eats, stays down and that's a very good sign.

George Burt, who called on us after supper, said he knew what was wrong with Sarah.

I said, in jest, "George, Sarah took sick two weeks ago. Where were you when we could have used your services?" "She's coming along just fine."

Nevertheless, as soon as Dr. Lewis left, George mesmerized Sarah (a treatment he learned he said from studying a magazine on healing.) His "treatment" he claims would bring her "out of it". I've never seen such "carrying on" by George or any other "healer". First, he made sure she was awake Then he made her stare at him or his watch, which he dangled as a pendulum before her eyes. He spoke in monotones, repeating sentences like, "I am getting better. I will be well" over and over. Sarah sweat profusely, then fell into a

14

deep sleep. About midnight George woke her up, slapped her face smartly and said, "You will be just fine" and he left.

She now thinks George is a genius, a faith healer. She seems to forget Doctor Lewis has seen her as a patient every day for two weeks and I've been here that long myself, cooking, doing her laundry, taking out the slop jars, etc. She was over most of it long before George and his mesmerizing tricks arrived on the scene. When Sarah explained to Dr. Lewis, George's miraculous cure, he just looked at me, shrugged his shoulders and in winking, worked at stifling a smile.

Hank Morse, who is still single and rather handsome, came by for supper last night. He said he was going back to Michigan. He said four years is enough. He came out here to do his Christian part, served with Jim Lane, voted for our new constitution without slavery. We have prevailed, he said, so he's going home. He knows we are from Michigan and invited me to go with him, but I have this house and other responsibilities, as intriguing as the offer is.

Adda and I had a nice quiet supper here tonight at our place with Dr. Lewis and we believe his "intended" Sarah, who has recovered, but is very pale and tires easily. Mr. Graton was also with us. After the meal the doctor had to make a house call. Sarah and I were in the kitchen cleaning up. Adda came out and asked if she could be excused from doing the dishes, etc. Looking at each other and smiling we said, "certainly". She proposed that the two of us stay in the kitchen for a while to give her and Mr. Graton some privacy in the parlor. Well, their need for privacy went on and on to where Sarah and I were thinking about bedding down in the kitchen. There is plenty of room and it's warm, but we could use some blankets but they are upstairs. I don't want to see Sarah go into a relapse by sleeping on a chilly floor.

Augusta's entries for the balance of the summer and well into early fall deal mainly with their daily events, friends coming and going and Adda's escalating romance with the gunsmith, who she'd been seeing long before her recent return to Eldorado. In fact, Augusta suspects he was the major reason she had no longer cared to stay in Eldorado. Although he appeared to be a successful businessman from Massachusetts with a bustling shop in an excellent location on New Hampshire Street, where he sells guns and repairs them, he fails to treat Adda with the courtesy and respect that Augusta thinks is due her sister. But the trouble doesn't stop there. There seems to be some deep-seated animosity between John Graton and Augusta, a cautious distrust, which has led to a mutual disliking. Her disapproval, though not enough to cause serious concern between the sisters, seems to increase Adda's interest in Graton, who, like her previous beau, is several years older, except this one seems better educated, is successful and more ambitious.

Throughout the fall of 1860 their house at #627 Rhode Island Street is a beehive of social activities. Nevertheless, her journal entries makes clear that she is personally, very lonely, unfulfilled and often melancholy over the realization that things have failed terribly to work out the way they began in Eldorado and the way she planned for them to work out. Augusta, the young widow, makes entry after entry dealing with the loss of her father and all he stood for, that their Eldorado business ventures had failed to materialize, and because of all this, the change in their social status. But mostly she wrote about her loneliness and of her longing for her husband's lost love and companionship. She "Hopes it is Heaven Chase calls home and that one day I may join him." This hope (she says) "is the greatest consolation I have." And the poignant entry continues in this melancholy mood for several paragraphs and its melancholy theme continues on in other entries for the remainder of that year.

For months, maybe years after Chase's death Augusta not only fails to get beyond mourning for her loss, but he is hardly in his grave and like the mythical Greek sculptor, she creates out of her taciturn, rude, often indifferent inconsiderate husband a prairie male Pygmalion. In her self-serving imagination he becomes the ideal sweetheart/husband that he never really was. In her self-contradictory recollections she forgets dozens of her pre and post wedding entries where Chase ignores her acts of kindness, where he could have been, but wasn't appreciative or grateful. She reinvents him into a paragon among men. She forgets his coldness and aloofness towards her as well as his occasional rudeness, when he could have been even minimally responsive to her acts of consideration and affection, but wasn't.

She forgets his dishonest behavior when she wrote of bringing him noon meals at the sawmill, hoping for a little companionship at most or the opportunity to please him at least, as he pretends to be too busy, but as soon as she with disappointment returns to the cabin, he eats it with relish.

Within months of his funeral she remains so depressed that during a church service a passage from St Paul makes her so anxious that she must leave the church mid-sermon…and does.

Finally, in widowhood, while remaining loyal to this recreated visage of Chase, little-by-little she gains her own identity. It's not until four years later, when she meets George W. Blackman in Colorado in the winter of '64 that she begins to realize who she is, that she can be somebody separate and distinct from her father and the self-created image of her ungrateful first husband that she never seems to abandon.

late fall 1860

The Sisters The Summer of 1860 Left to Right Adelaide Stewart Augusta Stewart Chase (copied from a small tintype Lawrence, Kansas Territory)

54.

LAWRENCE
ADDA MARRIES

Winter of 1860 to Spring 1861

Although the girls discuss employment when they visit their old friends at the Cincinnati House and the Whitney House where they are offered their old jobs, neither sister decides to work for a while, which suggests that they want to enjoy getting along for a while using surplus proceeds from the land and sawmill sale, not consumed by their new house, its repairs and the usual furnishings. The neighborhood appears to be suburban enough that they can keep their two cows, like some of their neighbors.

This morning Adda was all dressed-up in the latest Lawrence fashion of hooped skirts, looking very elegant, but when I inquired as to the occasion, she said she's about to have a few sessions with a new dentist in town and suggested that I come along. Lord knows I should, but I can't afford it just now.

She said, rather nonchalantly, that she wanted to get her teeth fixed before the wedding.

"Who's wedding?"

"Mine"

"Are you and Graton formally engaged?"

"Yes"

Pause, "Have you announced it?"

"Graton doesn't want to yet"

"What's he waiting for?"

I thought to myself, I think I know why.

"When's the big day?"

"November 6th"

"Adda, that's less than three weeks!"

"Yep"

I know that Graton "sees" Jule Johnson here in town but I don't think Adda knows. I certainly can't tell her. She will impute it to my prejudice against her man. It's my opinion that Graton simply wants time to explain "things" to Jule before a public announcement; well, he'd better get on with it.

Adda and her gunsmith marry the same day that Abraham Lincoln was elected President. Augusta's entry of Tuesday, November 6, 1860 notes that she "stood up" for her sister, a Mr. Johnson stood-up for Mr. J. R. Graton, and she names other members of the wedding party; that Reverend Brant, a friend of the bride groom, performed the ceremony here in our new house and that, later that evening several guests returned to give the newly-weds a noisy "Shivaree", that had been arranged by Mrs. Spicer. Augusta writes that this is a quaint, uncouth, and unnecessary singing of ribald songs and banging on pots and pans, a rather pagan custom brought out here by the eastern lower classes, mostly Southerners, which detracts, she writes, from the dignity and purity of our ancient Northern European and solemn marriage tradition. These social activities continue right up to the eve of the Civil War.

Thursday of this week Dr. Lewis and his "intended", Sarah Goss, dropped by to invite Adda and me to be their guests for a "gala" celebration this Saturday night to honor the election of President Lincoln. I accepted immediately. I really didn't need to explain to this couple that Adda, having wed two days ago was… unavailable.

I asked him where we planned to celebrate. He said he would try for a table at the Eldridge House and he left. I immediately started to plan what I would wear.

Later in the day he sent a note that the Eldridge House was full up, but he was able to get a reserved table at the Cincinnati House.

They called for me at 8 o'clock in a rather elegant two-horse shay with a driver. Dr. Lewis was quick to admit that it was a "livery." Sarah looked lovely.

Well, it was just a great supper with many spontaneous toasts from prominent citizens. Mrs. Gates could not have looked more elegant. She said she'd heard we'd bought a house not far from the Ferry slip. It was so nice to see her again. I hadn't seen her for several months.

Just as soon as I could, I excused myself and went out to the kitchen. I wanted to see Aggie Rourke. To handle the extra cooking load for the evening banquet, Aggie had two extra cooks and two helpers. They were all so busy that it wasn't the pleasant reunion that I looked forward to. I should have come over earlier in the fall.

The "popular" vote of Mr. Lincoln's election became official Wednesday, November 7th. The electoral college had yet to take its tally and announce its decision and wouldn't until mid February. Today, December 22nd, I read in the Leavenworth paper that South Carolina has taken the lead in "dissolving the Union, that these seven Southern states has declared themselves free of the rest of us. In time four more would join them in seceding.

An editorial in a St. Louis paper has summed up what the editor calls "the big picture" by questioning the idea that, if out of fifty year's of North-South tension over slavery, that war somehow will solve this problem and that the South can possibly prevail; they cannot, given the simple demographics.

According to the editorial, prior to secession, our population was about thirty-one million (10% of them recent immigrants); eight to nine million of them were in the South, that's not counting three and a half million slaves, Hence twenty-three million in the North. Of the Southerners only about 250,000 families or 5% are significant owners of slaves. And that aristocracy and its wealth will be called upon to pay for the war. But before a single shot is fired and the bullet paid for, they are already in hock to the North for $200 million.

Of course throughout the North most still believed that the moral argument carried such weight that "right" would prevail over bloodshed. However, there was a small militant minority led by John Brown, while he was still alive, financed by a handful of either well known or well to do, mostly in New England, who were convinced that ultimately only by violence and bloodshed would the slavery issue be laid to rest. They really hadn't considered secession as an option, even though it's been a perpetual option and threat: North and South.

The St Louis editor concluded by saying that if John Brown from the grave is proven to be correct, those fighting for the wealthy 5% slave owner will be the young white lower class male. The South has a miniscule middle class. In spite of their bravery and loyalty to the Southern cause, they will be no match for the industrial North with three times their population and its enormous engines of wealth, to have in ten years invested $400 million for 20,000 miles of railroad and another $60 million for canals allowing steamboats to carry the cargo railroads can't handle. Most of the American factories, 100,000 of them with one million workers, are north of the Mason-Dixon line. Most of the corn for their beloved grits and wheat for their bread, all raised in the North and transported to the South on railroads and boats owned or paid for by the North. The Southern military problem will be exacerbated by the fact that of the 1.2 million of combat age, most of the males going west in recent years, particularly for California in 1849 and the Rocky Mountains in '57 and '58 were young Southern white males, which would only add to the disadvantage that the South will suffer if their actions (secession) provokes war. They have one-fifth the number of factories of the north and one-tenth the number of skilled factory workers.

Lincoln has been elected but until March 4th. Mr. Buchanan is president and in this article he has tried to calm things in a very disturbed Congress and Senate.

Congressman Thomas Crittenden has proposed a compromise that to keep the seven states in the Union, Congress would agree never to abolish slavery and several politicians endorsed his idea... not the least of them Lincoln's old debating opponent Senator Douglas, plus Jefferson Davis, Secretary of War and several other... even the *New York Herald* embraced the idea.

Besides a compromise aimed at tolerance, William Lloyd Garrison whose abolitionist stuff I've been reading since we came to Kansas, has suddenly decided that if the South wants to secede, let them. It's not worth fighting over. The New York Tribune's Horace Greeley agrees. He says if the cotton states think they can make it on their own, let them try.

Both these attitudes surprise me, because Garrison and Greeley have continually opposed slavery. They've insisted that the slave be free. It seems to me that this secession business doesn't free the slave. It simply frees the South.

Nevertheless by the first week of February the South was organizing a provisional and independent government, and Jefferson Davis has resigned his cabinet post to be its president. Mississippi has seceded.

On New Year's night (1861) our two old friends, Dr. Lewis and Sarah Goss, were married. I recall it was to this Lawrence doctor that I turned, two years ago to discuss the details of my husband's short illness and death. He confirmed my suspicions that in Chase's case the use of morphine was questionable and the excess use of it was probably the cause of his death, not "ague" from bad water.

They were married by Reverend Perkins, the same preacher who married Chase and me in Eldorado when he was looking for a parish out west. I would like to say that it was pleasant renewing my acquaintance with Reverend Perkins, but seeing him again rekindled the painful episode I had in his church shortly after Chase's death, when the preacher used for his sermon a passage from Paul, taken from the Corinthians. I know now that his sermon on the uselessness of those who had lost love was not aimed at me personally but that Sunday, while I was still in mourning, mistaken or not, his words pierced my heart, reinforcing my own despair making me so acutely anxious that I had to leave the church mid-sermon. But I did go back and apologize for my behavior. And it was from his sermon notes, which he loaned me that I had been able to reconstruct in one entry that whole painful episode. Nevertheless, I've attended several of his Sunday sermons since I've been back and I've considered joining his congregation.

Immediately after Adda's marriage, her husband moved in with the girls, an arrangement that soon causes family squabbles. On one occasion, Adda's husband suggested that for privacy they buy an extra "cook" stove and divide the house into two separate living quarters, suggesting that Augusta have a bunk built in the kitchen where she can sleep. Augusta writes that her brother-in-law's ridiculous suggestion borders on lunacy and she is absolutely opposed to it. She had always wanted a proper parlor, an ante room to it, that acts as a cloak room during bad weather, a dining room adjacent to the kitchen…that and two upstairs bedrooms. And that is exactly what they had in this place, and she writes she sees no need to renovate the house even if it's for Adda's new husband. Both girls agree that there's no need to alter the house arrangement. Their kitchen was simply too small to be partitioned. Needless to say these quarrels put some pressure on Adda. Augusta understands that her sister needs to "side" with her husband but Augusta also knows that she owns half this house…and the deed clearly says that.

Within weeks of Adda's wedding Augusta writes that "Graton is determined that I shall not stay here. From the wedding on, he has wanted to evict me…not like a landlord evicting a tenant arrears in rent. He simply feels that by marrying my sister, some sort of property rights have transferred to him that preempts mine." Well, what am I to do? When Adda and I decided to buy a house, one of the conditions was that it would be so modest that there would be no mortgage or mortgage payments to contend with. In lean times we would always have a place, rent free, to stay (except for taxes)...and we've accomplished that. Now, simply because he has married my sister and moved in with her, with us, he can't simply ignore my needs. I need a roof over my head and I don't intend to forego my needs to satisfy his, maybe for my sister, but not him.

When I asked Adda if they had considered buying their own house, she said that although Graton's business is good, he always has loans to pay off. He borrows money at the bank to pay for his new inventory. During weeks of slow sales, he borrows money to make payments on the shop mortgage (which is in a very valuable commercial location). Adda says he does have a savings account at Riggs. He would like to own commercial property here in Lawrence and is saving for such a purchase.

I said, "Well, the 1860 census lists your husband's net worth at over $1,300, so it would seem to me that if he really wanted to own a house, just for the two of you, rather than usurp my ownership, he's certainly financially able to do so.

"How did you find that out?"

"Mrs. Killam and I were discussing my eroding domestic situation and she asked me if I had simply looked-up the Lawrence census information. I said I didn't know how. Four or five days later she gave me a little slip of paper with that information on it.

"Adda, he's perfectly able to draft a check to me for half what we paid for this house and get my name off the deed and his on it. With that money I could reestablish myself. Mrs. Fiske has offered me an arrangement. For $500 she will sell me half interest in her boarding house, which has a rather large attic with two dormer windows. I could make that into a very comfortable bedroom. In fact, that's where I stay when I'm not home. But I don't have the cash. If I'd had it, I could be running her now empty place, while they are in New England on their honeymoon.

I asked her if he was a gambler and she thinks not and he doesn't seem to depend on alcohol in excess. But I'm just rambling, because if he can find a way to evict me at no cost to himself, I'm sure he'll do it.

The sisters agree that when Graton is absent, they should try to be together, Adda seems to need her big sister's support. To further complicate matters, Graton's sister, Julia, who also lives in Lawrence occasionally takes room *and* board with them. Augusta notes that Julia is so much more agreeable than her brother.

January 13, 1861 Although it was a cold day, I had an errand to run up town and in the process bumped into two old neighbors from Eldorado, Phil Woodard and Mr. Carey. They were both coming out of the Riggs Bank. Mr. Carey said he was planning on returning to Indiana. He presumed correctly that I knew his wife had died, so neither of us brought up the painful subject. It was Mr. Carey that volunteered to go with Chase down into the Cherokee Nation where Father had been killed to retrieve the two horses, saddles and other personal effects. That was more than two years ago. He was most cordial and I invited him over, but he excused himself. Mr. Woodard and I went over to the Eldridge House and renewed our acquaintance over several cups of coffee. He said he'd left his claim in the lower Colorado Mountains when the snow got so deep they weren't sure they would get out and it had started to get very cold. Even though I was of the impression that he was doing well on his claim north of the Martins (Eldorado), I remember now he was one of the recruits when the Mountain-bound party came through in May of 1858 that also claimed Chase.

The last I knew of him he was in the mountains working his mine.

When I asked him how he fared out there, he said, "pretty well". It appears he had joined the Russell boys, and prospected with them in '58, stayed out there that winter and took a good claim on Clear Creek (near Central City), due west of Denver in the low mountains and worked the claim at least six months of 1858. "And as soon as we could get in last year, which was March or April I worked the same claim about seven months. I didn't leave until the snows got so heavy, we were afraid we couldn't get out...October, I'd guess. I couldn't make up my mind whether to stay out there again last winter, but several of us got a chance to sell our claims to an Eastern group called Consolidators. You know, Mrs. Chase, I made about as much selling our claim as I did mining it, so with no claim we came home."

"Was Mrs. Woodard with you all that time?"

"Yes, that is, she came out with a party later in the summer of '58."

"What did she do when you were mining?"

"Before the weather was safe for her to come up and stay with me in the tent, she stayed down below, out of the mountains in a little town called Aurora, working in the boarding house that we used both winters."

"Did you know Cantrell?"

"No, but everybody knows the story."

He said he'd heard from Mr. Riggs at the bank that Adda and I were living in a house not far from the Whitney House, down by the river. He had learned from a Chelsea newspaper that after Chase died, I had become Eldorado's schoolteacher.

He said, "Someone sent us a Butler County newspaper that announced the first marriage in Eldorado between you and Jacob Chase. You know it was Chase and your father who surveyed our claim. In fact, your father conveyed my down payment and details of the claim with the Land Office...I'm not sure I ever paid him for that service."

He asked if Adda was working at the Whitney House now and I explained that she had through almost all of 1859 but that she had married about two months ago.

We had a protracted parting. I asked him what he was going to do now. He laughed and said, "I don't know, but I sure 'saw the elephant' and got that out of my system." Chase used that phrase in the summer of 1858 when he was wrestling with whether he would stay and improve his carpentering or whether he would "go see the elephant." Mr. Woodard use of it made me introspective and melancholy.

"I might go back to the Mountains. The Russells think we haven't scratched the surface, there's so much gold to be taken. At the head of all those gulches we are mining, and there must be fifty of them, nobody has ever found a mother lode, the stuff we get has simply washed down from the Mountains in hundreds of little cricks and streams over the centuries.

"There are some European and California miners out there now beginning to tunnel. When they drive enough tunnels, they will find the real gold, which is locked up in quartz veins and seams.

'Best underground miners are the Welch or the Cornishmen from South West England and among them is a large group of Irishmen that had been brought into the mines of Wales and Cornwall. They are very skilled in what they do and have a culture all their own. They never work Sundays; indeed they get dressed-up and go to church or church services. They are great singers and have singing clubs and competition", which provided the best entertainment we had.

I looked up and he seemed to be scrutinizing me and said, "What are you doing? Are you also a reporter?"

"I'm taking notes of this discussion, which I will rework and put into my journal. I've been keeping a journal since the summer of 1856 when we came out. Some day my ancestors will read my stuff and get a little different picture from what they will get from historians of this period. Oh, they'll cover the important people alright, like the Robinsons, the Lanes, all the appointed governors, but the historians won't know about you and me, our day-to-day lives.

He continued telling me about the role of Cornishmen and Welshmen in Colorado.

He asked if they could call on me, saying they had been in Leavenworth for a few days (he came back using the Overland Trail), that he'd banked his "cabooner" at the Leavenworth bank, like most returning miners.

When I looked puzzled about "cabooner", he laughed and explained that was a Cornish or Welch term for a successful "take home". They have only been around Lawrence for a few days. I should have asked but didn't, where they were staying.

I told him things are very dire in Eldorado now due to the drought. Mr. McCabe is in-town right now or was, maybe he's in Leavenworth or Atchison, trying to get some relief for the people out there. Due to the drought, the grasshoppers are eating their harvest (in 1860)…even the cattle are starving.

We were in the Eldridge coffee shop so long; out of embarrassment he ordered us both a sandwich and more coffee.

I told him I'd better be getting back and we parted company. It's been one of my vanities from which I derive some pleasure of knowing many people, never forgetting them and later, out of the blue often by chance, we meet again, as was the case with Mr. Woodard today.

JANUARY 31, 1861

I woke up during the middle of the night disturbed by an irregular booming racket off in the distance. I lay there wondering what it was and hoping it would stop, but it didn't. I went back to sleep anyway. In the morning, still curious, I got up early and before breakfast, put a shawl over my uncombed head, slipped on my lace-up farm shoes and Father's old "slicker" and went outside.

It was cold but clear. Several small wagons and horses were milling around the front porch of the Whitney House, people coming and going from breakfast, I presumed. So I thought I would mosey over and see if any of those fellows knew what all the racket was last night.

Mr. Burt, the "Famous Mesmerizer", who boards here, but lives elsewhere was having difficulty walking down the steps, waving at people, obviously in high spirits: probably some whiskey in his coffee had aided his elation and affected his steadiness on this particular morning.

In response to my query, he said, with slurred speech, "Didn't you hear? President Buchanan did one thing right in an otherwise miserable career and he started to ramble about Buchanan's many incompetences.

I interrupted him, "Yes, yes, Mr. Burt, but what did he do?"

"Who?"

"The President; you said he did something right. How did you hear about it so soon"

"The Leavenworth "rag" got a telegram straight from Washington, saying that he signed the bill making Kansas a state."

"Well, did that have anything to do with the noise last night?"

"Did it? Frank Swift roused old Tom Bickerton and maybe one other loyal Mount Oread soldier. They dug up that buried old brass cannon, got a hold of a keg of powder and Bickerton fired that dang cannon all night. That was the joyous noise."

As we talked, people came and went, some I knew and some I didn't. "Mrs. Chase, go inside, have a drink with the boys. Frank's in there right now and so's the "cannon master, who said he's almost "deef."

I had never met Mr. Bickerton, but I had remembered his name as the soldier in-charge of the cannon when Lane's company under Colonel Harvey fought at Hickory Point in '56. Father was in that skirmish.

Well, I thought, I'm not properly dressed to go in with these silly work shoes. I hadn't even combed my hair. But I would really like to see Frank Swift after all these years. He was often in-charge of the "Stubbs" Company when they were guarding Lawrence, after the Missourians had burned part of downtown. When their company boarded with Mrs. Gates, we saw Frank, often twice a day. Later he was a co founder of Buffalo, a town site near us in

Eldorado. I wanted to see him but I didn't want him to see me. So I went home. I had satisfied my curiosity. What I was really thinking was, wouldn't Father be having a swell time in there with those two, especially Tom Bickerton, the "famous" operator of "Old Sacramento", the brass cannon. I was surprised at my own elation. Maybe I'll comb my hair, put on the right shoes and go over there to join the celebration.

I was also thinking how close that vote for statehood had been. *The Lecompton Constitution* had been finished and in Washington, waiting to be signed into law…a law that would allow slavery… and, by god, a handful of us, like those celebrants back there, came out here and in a year or two-turned Popular Sovereignty upside down. A victory snatched from the jaws of defeat!

FEBRUARY 12ᵀᴴ 1861

This is one of the nicest days I've had for a long time. Thank goodness both Adda and Graton were at his gun shop. Mr. Preston Plumb, Emporia's young founder, visited me today and we had such a pleasant time. I was so pleased that I could comfortably entertain him in our parlor with some furniture that Adda and I have been purchasing on and off from various families returning to the States. Only a week ago we finished with the inside wall plastering. Now it needs painting, for it's too rough for wallpaper.

The two of us recalled the exciting and dangerous-for-abolitionists early days in Plymouth, just inside the Nebraska line over four years ago, when he, Sam Tappan and Alfred Pierce, men not much older than me, brought in three wagons heavily laden with eastern supplies for our four or five small new abolitionist communities, not much more than camp sites. Their supplies included additional quantities of Sharps rifles and ammunition, a small cannon and several kegs of gunpowder. During the intervening years I never had an occasion when I could tell Mr. Plumb that a few days later in October of 1856 a search party from a temporary Army camp established nearby found a keg of powder that he Tappan and Pierce had recently brought in and buried beneath the very floorboards of our own cabin and three more kegs hidden elsewhere in Plymouth and the problems that caused for us. But that was so long ago that in telling him of the powder affair now, the episode has taken on an air of conspiratorial humor.

Most of their cargo was reloaded and transshipped down to Topeka via a wagon train, which included 300 newcomers that had arrived that same day. Mr. Plumb and his two valiant companions later went back east for more supplies, but that warm summer night they stayed with us talking politics 'til midnight: he was barefoot.

"How's your sister?"

"Adda's just fine. She was married about four months ago: November 6th last year.

"Do I know the lucky man?"

"Well, maybe. She married John Graton, a local gunsmith. He has a shop over on New Hampshire.

"Well, I don't know him personally, but I've heard about his business and I've seen his newspaper ads. I hope they are happy. Give Adda my warm regards.

"Certainly. She'll be disappointed to have missed your visit."

He is pessimistic that we can avoid a civil war and mentioned that he had just returned from Ohio and expects to have a meeting with General Lane in the next few days. I asked if he expected to see the General here in Lawrence. He laughed and said he didn't "rightly know"; all he knew was that General Lane lived in Lawrence. At least he has a house here. Taking a letter from his coat, he showed it to me. It contained a single paragraph notifying Mr. Plumb that he had been appointed aide-de-camp to the General, but the letter was silent as to where he should report. The letter was signed by Major General J. H. Lane. As he put the letter away, he said he supposed that if he couldn't find him in Lawrence, he would go up to Army headquarters at Leavenworth, I offered our parlor, if he and the General needed a quiet place to conduct their business here in town. I suggested he make inquiries at the Whitney House or Cincinnati House before going to Leavenworth. They usually know the whereabouts of people like him.

I made a pot of tea and served some new cookies made from a type of rye wheat that the Canadians call the tan flour they get from it, Graham. He expressed his condolences for Father, saying how he had been looking forward to Father's business prospects, particularly the sawmill and hearing of his on-going activity in the territorial legislature and stood up as though he had been sitting too long, walked over to the front window, looked out, then facing me, still standing, said, "Well Mrs. Chase, what do you make of our complicated political situation now?"

Of course, I'd followed the two main political conventions last summer and for us the great heartwarming election in November, but I said, "Why do you call it complicated?"

He said, "Well, I suppose we *are* in good political shape with Lincoln headed for the White House, and last month, Kansas was admitted exactly the way those of us that came out here from 1854 on, planned it…to ultimately bring us in as a free state, and leaning forward slapped his hands on his thighs with glee. Your father and I were on the committee that helped write our state constitution free of slavery that Congress and President Buchanan approved. So we beat old Douglas with his own stick, * didn't we?"

But the Southern Democrats last summer were too hard on Douglas. He truly wanted us to vote, up or down, on slavery. I don't believe the South ever wanted such a vote. Anyway his insistence on the vote is when Douglas lost the support of the Southern Democrats and split the party…and the Southern Democrats nominated this Kentucky fellow Breckenridge. Remember Douglas did get 1.4 million votes. Between Breckenridge and Douglas each on separate tickets got 2 ¼ million votes. Old Abe would still be practicing law, getting rich, representing the railroads, because he got only 1.9 million votes, which was fewer than the tally of the two Democratic candidates… but he's in and that's that.

* He meant Popular Sovereignty

"But now that he's in the White House, I'm afraid that he's got more than he bargained for. He's got to work with a Democratic Congress…a pro slavery Senate and even before the election in October state leaders in South Carolina in a meeting decided that if Lincoln did get in, they would secede, which we know now, they did. And by Valentine's Day Georgia, Alabama, Mississippi, Louisiana and Florida followed them. Those were the very states that in my opinion caused them to lose the election by insisting on their candidate Breckinridge."

Before he left, he showed me a likeness of Mrs. Barrett (the doctor's wife. It had slipped my mind that after they had moved from Eldorado, the Barretts had settled in Emporia.) He said in the two winters of 1858/1859 and the following year he'd been studying Law in Cleveland but complained that it looked like the war had interrupted his studies. That might explain why on some of my trips from Eldorado to Lawrence, when passing through Emporia, I seldom found him "in town". It never dawned on me that he might be in some Law College back in East.

I remember Father saying that he had been on a committee with Preston Plumb, working on the Free State Constitution and that the two of them had the satisfaction of both being signers of it on August 5, 1858. It was four in the afternoon before we parted company. His flattering visit buoyed me up for days. He left our place walking towards the Whitney House.

His visit not only buoyed me up but was so stimulating that for two or three days, when I had time, I wrote and rewrote my notes about the visit, particularly his political observations, before putting them into this entry for February 12th.

In mulling over our discussion it made me aware of how little I really knew at the time of what was going on in the Legislature after Father was elected to it from our new voting district in Butler County. I checked volume I of my journal and discovered that by October of 1857, before Adda and I had gone out to Eldorado that they had already had one election in District 17 (which then included Butler and Hunter counties). Father got 69 Free Soil votes, which elected him to represent our new voting district. Since we didn't leave Lawrence until November 2nd, Father must have attended the Grasshopper Falls Convention in September and participated in the October election, which is the one that laid Popular Sovereignty to rest.

Father always seemed reluctant to tell Adda and me what he was up to politically and what progress he and other Free-State legislators were making during his many long absences. One of the advantages I have now in Lawrence that I didn't have in Eldorado is almost daily access to newspapers, particularly the editorials. It would have been so educational for Adda and me if he had explained what the Free Soilers were up against in converting a territorial legislature that even after we had a popular majority, remained proslavery but by insinuating new anti-slavery delegates into the Legislature, as more immigrants came in during 1856 and 1857, little by little we finally gained a majority.

That must have finally happened in October '57 while we were still in Lawrence. Of course, I knew that they had already been working on our own constitution banning slavery out here. After October they began the tedious process of getting the U. S. Congress and the Senate to read it, approve it and send it on to President Buchanan for his signature.

Father must have attended all those meetings: Grasshopper Falls (August), the Topeka Assembly in June and July (where they planned the October Territorial elections.) But I sure wish he had said so. (I checked volume II of my daily journals and his absences seem to coincide with those meetings of the Legislature).

As of January 29, 1861 Charles Robinson had taken office of governor now that we are officially a state. The Federally appointed governor has...evaporated. I don't even remember who he was.

There is a rumor in Lawrence that President Buchanan and the Department of War in Washington, D.C fearing for the life of the President-elect and the safety of the city, have requested, of all places, for Kansas, a company of volunteers to act as a guard for the White House and they've asked Father's old "Comrade-in-Arms", Jim Lane (recently appointed Brigadier General of Volunteer Forces *) to organize a military company and to bring it to Washington, D.C. as fast as possible. Mr. Rackliffe says that for some reason Governor Robinson is opposed to Lane's promotion and has written President Lincoln expressing his reservations about General Lane. Governor Robinson has said publicly that Jim Lane is socially unfit to be a Commissioned Union officer, claiming that he is uncouth, exaggerates conditions in his speeches and was unnecessarily ruthless and violent in his 1856 and 1857 military campaigns against proslavery militia in the territory. His atrocities, claims the Governor, brought such violent retaliation that the U. S. Army had to step in and imprison two of Lane's companies, claiming that Lane and John Brown were "two peas in a pod". Robinson also claims that the news of Lane's violent retaliation against pro slavery elements here made it difficult to recruit moderate abolitionists in the east to immigrate to the territory, particularly in 1856, which, as much as I respect the Governor and his talented wife, is simply not the case.

I had asked around town, with all the armed forces available to the President in Washington, DC, what sort of calamity do they expect or is upon them to request help from us so far away. It was no secret that twenty-two carloads of troops under General Lane in recent days mustered at Fort Leavenworth. Whether they would take riverboats to St Louis or not, I couldn't find out. Obviously, President Buchanan hadn't seen fit to clarify the reason why he would call for special troops from Kansas to protect the in-coming President and maybe Washington, D.C. prior to the inauguration.

But if they do choose the river, you can bet your bottom dollar that if Jim Lane with a strong contingency of his old Kansas militia is on some riverboats whose crews are antagonistic toward Northerners, he won't put up with much nonsense from them. Once in St. Louis they can be in Washington, D.C. in a matter of days by using the rails.

* Pending Senate confirmation

I did read in a news article shortly after his visit a few days ago that Preston Plumb, and his old comrade, Sam Tappan, were listed as volunteers on the Wash., D.C. junket with Lane. (That would explain the letter Preston Plumb showed me when we visited a few days ago.) Out of curiosity I scanned the list to see if any of Father's Lecompton fellow P.O.W.s were among General Lane's volunteers for the White House guard duty but found none.

Augusta seems not to have gotten an answer to her queries about why General Lane and a force of 200 well-chosen Kansans was being called so urgently to Washington, DC. Her entries that winter are silent as to the pre inauguration dangers existing in Washington, D. C.

We turned to Carl Sandburg's volume on Lincoln to answer this question, "The Prairie Years and the War Years" published by Harcourt-Brace in 1926.

Lincoln had been nominated on the Republican ticket for president in Chicago, May 1860, and elected in early November, expecting to be inaugurated about four months later, March 4th of the following year in Washington, D.C.

In early February, Lincoln and his family made ready to leave their home in Springfield, IL. There was a gala goodbye on the 6th. In a few days his party of fifteen left Springfield for a complicated railroad route to Washington, DC. He spoke in Indianapolis (Indiana,) then on to Cincinnati on his 52nd birthday, February 12, '61.

Two days later he was in Pittsburg for speeches then on to Upstate New York speaking in Rochester and Syracuse; then down the Hudson with stops before reaching New York, where he knew that their mayor had suggested seceding to declare the city a separate and free sovereign city. Because of this ambition to be free of the war, his reception in New York compared to elsewhere was subdued.

In Philadelphia Lincoln was quickly introduced to a railroad detective, who had some secret but alarming news. The detective had discovered a plot to assassinate him on his way through Baltimore, where he was scheduled to speak two days later. (Pinkerton, the detective, had earlier infiltrated the group of assassins.)

The reader must keep in mind that on the eve of the Civil War, Baltimore and Maryland were for the most part, proslavery; many of them hated Lincoln enough to be involved in the conspiracy. Before leaving Philadelphia, Lincoln learned that though the Governor, T. H. Hicks favored the union over slavery, Baltimore's mayor was an unabashed secessionist. Lincoln was keenly relieved to learn that Pinkerton's evidence had been confirmed by a separate New York detective…all unbeknownst to Pinkerton. President Buchanan was aware of this politically explosive situation, that Washington, D.C. was surrounded by angry secessionists on all sides, which to his credit accounts for his earlier request that Lincoln and the White House be guarded by Kansans under General Lane. He knew he could trust those Kansans abolitionists led by General Lane who by now had a national reputation.

After Philadelphia, Lincoln was scheduled to speak at Harrisburg and he did, three times. That evening he left quietly on a non-scheduled train, passing unrecognized through Baltimore arriving in the Capitol at 6 AM. He checked in to the old Willard Hotel on Pennsylvania Avenue, where it stands today. Within a week, he would be inaugurated.

The would-be Baltimore assassins were rounded up and jailed. Lincoln's train (without him) pulled into Baltimore on schedule to a waiting crowd of 10,000.

It was in the Willard that he made his headquarters during Buchanan's lame duck period prior to the inauguration on March 4, 1861. And it was during that four-month interregnum that the near-term course of U. S. history unfolded.

Prior to and for some weeks after, Lincoln's inaugural, Lane's regiment remained in Wash., D.C. available to maintain peace in the city and to act as a personal bodyguard for the president and the White House. They "bivouacked" in the big East Room until after the inauguration when they were relieved and returned to Kansas.

We know now that while Lane and his Kansan company were stationed in the White House, President Lincoln and he talked daily. The two of them had much in common. They had both been

Congressmen from "Western States." Lane was in Congress from 1852 to 1854; indeed he voted for the Nebraska-Kansas Act in 1854. Prior to that he was Lt Governor of Indiana. Lincoln was in Congress (Whig) before Lane, from 1846 to 1848, which reflected the five-year difference in age. States like Ohio, Indiana, Illinois, etc. were considered then "western", as contrasted to "Eastern States" (Pennsylvania, New York…New England States, etc.) Both men were pragmatic thinkers. Both were leaders of men. Both were lawyers and with Lane's conversion (in Kansas) to the party, both were Republicans. War would soon be declared. Lane had distinguished himself in the Mexican War, so it's safe to assume that the subject of war and its conduct in the Kansas/Missouri region came up between the two of them.

So, it's reasonable to conclude, as have others, thinking about the situation that Lincoln got to know Jim Lane much better. Keep-in-mind, when Kansas became a state three months earlier, Jim Lane was its first Senator, and Lincoln must have decided he could count on Lane's loyalty.

Sometime after the inauguration, Lane and his regiment returned to Kansas. Lincoln then asked him to accelerate recruitment in Kansas.

Lane's execution of Lincoln's request put him at odds with Governor Robinson, who considered all recruitment to be his authority and by now the competition between these two was becoming both apparent and heated.

SPRING 1861

A sad letter from Mrs. Critchett, the prior Mrs. Fiske, who is or has been in Concord, New Hampshire and has visited with Chase's parents: She writes that two of my young nephews (on Chase's side) are both dead of diphtheria.

March 1861

Adelaide Henrietta Stewart "Adda" Taken in Lawrence, Kansas in November 1859 Adda was 18 years old and working at the Whitney House

55.

LAWRENCE, KANSAS
THE EVE OF CIVIL WAR

March 1861

John F. Slack, a gentleman from Emporia, a farmer a little older than me that I've (only) met twice, has written a very flattering…proposal of marriage. Then a few days later a second letter from him, asking me what I thought of his earlier proposal. I suppose I owe the man an answer…and maybe I owe myself an answer. The prospect is so sobering I find it hard to face. I am dreadfully lonely. I continually but quietly compare my state with the happier girls with whom I associate. I've never gotten over losing Chase and I'm not sure I ever will. But the contemplation of that loss makes me so melancholy that to think of marrying anybody now fills me with guilt and fear that I could make anyone else a good wife. Thinking of the marriage bed fills me with such apprehension that, well I just don't think I'm up to it… maybe, never will be.

MARCH 1ST 1861

Julia (Graton's sister) dropped by to say that business at the Eldridge House is bustling and she's heard from Mr. Burt, who frequently boards there that they need help. We were told to ask for Mrs. Johns, so we've agreed to walk up there tomorrow. It's only two or three blocks and I could use the cash.

On Monday midmorning Julia and I presented ourselves to the uniformed hotel desk clerk in the lobby of the Eldridge House, in hoopskirts, lace white gloves, the works asking to see a Mrs. Johns. We took a seat on one of the hotel's elegantly upholstered red velvet sofas and waited.

In time a skinny middle-aged lady, dressed entirely in black entered the lobby from one of the back rooms and approached the desk clerk. He pointed to us.

In a minute or so she was standing in front of us with her arms tightly close to her body and with her hand clasping and unclasping, said with an obsequious voice exceeded in manner and delivery only by Uriah Heep in one of Mr. Dickens currently serialized novels, bowing her head until her chin touched her bony collarbone said in tones dripping with apology, "I'll bet you two ladies just arrived on the morning stage. I am so sorry that our rooms aren't ready. I'm Mrs. Johns, the landlady and before I came out here, I gave strict orders to straighten up two rooms for you. I'm so sorry, if we have inconvenienced you." We both stood.

Julia spoke up, "No, no, Mrs. Johns, we're not guests. We live here. We're here to see you about a job. One of your boarders is a friend of ours, Mr. Burt. He told us the hotel was looking for help"

Her entire demeanor changed immediately. "A job? A job?", she said, as she assumed a new posture. She spread her feet apart, put her hands on her hips; her arms bent at her elbows and scrutinized us while she changed from being an apologetic soul to a domineering, fussy supervisor. And it was obvious that she was going to take it out on us that she had humbled herself foolishly and needlessly.

First, she reminded us that if she hired us, we would be employees, not guests of the hotel and hooped skirts would be out-of-place and unnecessary and in the future we were to use the service entry.

She advised us that, if employed, to dress much more plainly and she proceeded to lecture us about the behavior expected of us regarding the hotel guests including those that take regular meals with them. She warned us about getting too friendly with two female employees that are currently "on probation," for "dubious and uncalled for social contacts" with "our" guests: one a Swede and the other, Irish.

Suppressing a smile I wanted to ask if she'd received any complaints from the male guests that had been "approached" in such an uncalled for manner.

She turned 90 degrees from us and said, "Follow me" and she led us back through the doorway from which she'd entered to a dark dingy corridor, filled with smelly hampers full of dirty laundry. She stopped and began a detailed questioning of me about my domestic skills, particularly sewing. It seems that she has accumulated quite a pile of torn bed sheets and pillowcases waiting to be mended. She seemed (to me) to be unnecessarily put out that we came to the interview so well dressed expecting to be interviewed in the hotel's lobby.

I told her that I certainly knew how to sew, mend pillow cases, etc., but because I'd had kitchen experience at both the Cincinnati House and the Whitney House, that I'd be better suited for that sort of work.

She snippily reminded me that she was the landlady. All kitchen help was hired by the chef and the way she said it implied that neither one of us, looked to her as qualified to work in the kitchen of a hotel of this stature. Presently she excused herself and quickly returned with a bellboy who she instructed to show us the room we could expect to occupy...in the unlikely event that she hired us.

After we saw our small upstairs room with three beds and no windows, no furniture, we went down stairs to continue our interview. I asked if she didn't mind, we'd prefer to room at our own house, but take our meals (board) at the hotel. She said, "What do you mean, 'your own house'? I explained that Adda and I had sold our claims and a sawmill in Eldorado and bought a house here in town. This proposition was very upsetting.

She said, our pay, $2.00 per week was reckoned, based on our needing both board and room. Well, when she heard that that I'm a half owner of a house in a respectable neighborhood and that I had previously worked for their competitors (Cincinnati House and Whitney House) and I let it slip that my sister knew the Robinson family personally. She said she didn't expect to employ people so "well off" or well connected. She said, though she certainly needed the help, she'd need to discuss our case with the proprietor. When I asked about the health of Mr. Eldridge and his extended family, she dismissively raised her eyebrows and chin and said, "Who's that?"

I explained that I presumed Mr. Eldridge and his brother were still the proprietors; both abolitionists, who had built this hotel, then rebuilt it again in 1855 after the proslavery Missouri militia and the local Sheriff Jones destroyed it and part of the town. All that anti-abolitionist history seemed new to her. She sniffed and said that must have been before "her time." Lifting her chin she said, "The hotel is now under new management." Our interview lasted about fifteen minutes and in hindsight I doubted that either one of us would get a job offer.

There is so much unrest, nationally, regionally and domestically. President Lincoln has finally been inaugurated and rather than rejoice about his new administration, all over town, all they want to talk about is secessions, that the Union is dissolving and what is Mr. Lincoln going to do about it. Secession is the current topic of the day having displaced slavery. Senator (or is it General) Jim Lane and his Kansans are still in Washington.

And in this strange household Adda comes and goes and her husband's presence is unpredictable. When Adda and I are home, we are pleasantly sociable. This morning, directly after breakfast, Adda got all dressed up. Mrs. Johnson and Mrs. Lewis (Sarah Goss) called on us and we discussed what would happen to Kansas, if all of the South really does secede.

Those two left before noon. Adda and I had "a bite" together. Then Mrs. Perrine called on us. She is a lady of many talents including that of midwife, who took Adda to one side for a woman-to-woman "talk. " Late in the day the hack driver, who usually parks over at the Whitney House knocked on the door, asking if Adda was ready. She was. She had been since breakfast. She said that I could expect her next Monday. I said, "If I need to find you, where will you be?"

"At Mr. Wrights."

No sooner did she drive off, in an awful cloud of dust, I might add, than Mr. Burdell came by with Mr. and Mrs. Johnson. Their daughter, Jule, who is about Adda's age, has worked on and off at the Whitney House with Adda when Adda worked there and has been Adda's constant chief rival for John Graton's "attention." They have two other daughters and a son, who are all here in Lawrence, when the children are not back East in school. We've known them since the winter after Father was paroled from the P.O.W. camp.

During the three days that Adda was gone I had time to answer some letters, but not the most interesting one, another written proposal from my Emporia suitor, Mr. J. F. Slack.

Then Monday no sooner did Adda come home that she suggested we both go visit Sarah Lewis (Sarah Goss) and we did. Adda asked if her husband had been home while she was gone. Before we left, Julia Graton's intended dropped by to pick up her "things". They are going to be "keeping house" soon. His name is Johnson but he's no relation to the "other" Johnson family.

This morning I went up to Mrs. Killam's boarding house to see if I could help Mrs. Rackliffe and little Ermee settle in. I felt obliged to help them from what happened yesterday.

Mr. Sumner Rackliffe is now in the new State Legislature representing the Walnut River Valley voting district #17 established by Father. He has been attending the spring (March 1861) session in Topeka.

This is our very first Legislative session since becoming a state in January. He is so proud to be part of it and we are so proud that Sumner, our Eldorado neighbor, is part of this historic event.

When Mr. and Mrs. Rackliffe came over to Lawrence yesterday looking for temporary quarters, Adda and I invited them to supper. Graton was home. During supper Mr. Rackliffe inquired if we could provide board and room for Mary and Ermee while he's in Topeka. He thought they'd be more comfortable here than as strangers in some boarding house. Knowing them so well from Eldorado, Adda and I thought we could work things out knowing it would only be for a few weeks. When Graton heard their request, he took Adda into the parlor and demanded that she say, "No! That, there's hardly enough room for the three of us." Adda returned to the dining room table and whispered to me Graton's sentiments.

I asked Adda and Graton to step into the parlor with me. We tried to explain to Graton that the Rackliffes are old friends that they aren't looking for a handout. He is a substantial rancher and is now in the State Legislature representing voting District #17 that our father cut out of open prairie, etc. I said, "It seems to me that rather than being rude to him, it might serve your purposes some day to be able to say you know the gentleman.

Disregarding our explanation, Graton declared that if we invite them in with that "youngster", he will move out!

Well, I thought to myself, that would suit me just fine. But I could see this would only make our bad domestic situation worse.

So I went back into the dining room and explained, as best I could, that as much as we would love having Mary and Ermee stay with us while her husband is doing his legislative duty, it won't work. (I heard the front door slam and suspected that Graton had left anyway.) I told Mary that Adda and I had worked here in town and there were plenty of nice places where we could find board and room for them. Figuring that Graton would be gone for the night, I suggested that Mary and Ermee use my bedroom. I slept in the parlor. Graton did not return.

This morning the three of us walked over to Killam's (a block or so away). Mrs. Killam said she'd be delighted to help. I told her I'd bring her a gallon of milk this afternoon. Little Ermee, who I helped usher into the world, needs her milk.

I'm afraid I've talked myself out of a job at the Eldridge house. Adda has been offered employment at both the Cincinnati House where Aggie Rourke is still running the kitchen and the Whitney House, which the reformed old Mr. Stone is still running.

That afternoon before Graton came home, I asked Adda if she went back to the Cincinnati House, would she, could she resume the previous business with Aggie of bottling and selling Missouri- made Irish whiskey for hotel guests and some river boat passengers, who preferred Irish whiskey over "corn" whiskey. She laughed and said, "If I went back to work, that business and the sociability would be my major reasons."

That evening during supper I related to Adda and Graton our unusual interview at the Eldridge House two days ago. I didn't say that we didn't get a job offer. Graton said, as though he owns me and his sister, that he didn't want us "in hotel service"… that it would make the family look bad, socially. Before he could continue, with a guarded wink in my direction, Adda announced that she was giving serious thought to a job offer she'd had at the Cincinnati House. Graton exploded! "Adda, for heaven's sake, I take some of my noon meals there, I socialize with people who may buy my guns and ammunition or get their guns repaired by me. It would embarrass me for you to be waiting on tables, particularly in your "family" way, serving people that were probably my customers. I don't want them to conclude, because you two are working, that I can't provide for my own family. But Adda, who winked again during her husband's speech, enjoys teasing him and letting him know, in her own way, that she is employable and has enough skill and resources so as not to be totally economically dependent on him. He in-turn finds this independence irritating because it frays his male need to control and dominate everything including, me, his disagreeable sister-in-law.

He brought up the subject again that we buy an extra cook stove, physically divide the house into two separate dwellings and he would have a carpenter build a bunk bed in the kitchen for me.

Well, I recently had the opportunity to buy a medium-sized wood-burning kitchen stove including six feet of stovepipe containing the damper from a family moving back to Indiana. I'll need help in getting it in through the back door and I'll need help hooking-up the stovepipe. I can't get that pipe into the existing chimney, so I'll just have to saw a hole in the kitchen wall some place. But we won't be building a partition to make two kitchens and you won't see any bunks in my kitchen.

President Lincoln was inaugurated March 4th but all hell had broken loose during the four months between his election and inauguration. That's when all of the Southern States seceded and they had time to organize a new, separate government: hard to believe!

It's very dry for March…maybe too early for spring rains. It's dry and windier than the usual Kansas wind. I can stand the wind. I'm used to it, but this wind picks up a fine dust, which just gets into everything.

This house has cracks and gaps between the window and door casings and the walls in which they are mounted. I believe the wood that the Chicago builder used was uncured. It has shrunk in the short time since the house was prefabricated and shipped down here via the river system, so the dust just blows in everywhere.

Graton, who is from Massachusetts and reminds us (regularly) that his state has been building wooden ships for 200 years and they don't leak. He thinks our windows and door jam cracks and gaps can be filled by an old ship building process called caulking and has offered to either do the job or have it done. He explained how irregular space between ship planking is filled by caulking, using a fibrous material (called oakum), which is twisted into loose cordage, lightly impregnated with an oily pitch. A blunt but thin chisel-looking tool is struck to tamp the oakum so tightly into the space between planks that the ship becomes waterproof. The caulking lasts for the life of the ship. He promised that he would send today an order for 100 pounds of oakum and a caulking tool from a ship chandler he knows in Plymouth, Massachusetts.

This is the first constructive suggestion the man has made since he moved in. We'll see if he keeps his word.

In the mail I picked up at the Post Office was a letter from the Critchetts who have arrived in Concord, New Hampshire. They have visited with Chase's family and sent me a report on their status. But she goes on to advise me that I should try not to leave Adda at this time. According to her memory (from a discussion with Adda before they left and her calendar) that my company and services with Adda will be important…that in a few months now Adda should be ready to deliver, and with the war on Kansas will be a "dicey" place for a new addition to our family. Adda has been proudly showing "her condition" within the family for some time.

SUNDAY, MARCH 24TH

A fine looking wagon pulled up out front by our new white picket fence. We had invited the Rackliffes here for a noon meal before he goes back to Topeka this afternoon. Before he left, he shared some of the gossip coming out of the Topeka Legislative session.

It was so pleasant to receive his compliments about our new white fence. He even noticed ours was the only one on our block. Of course there are only three houses on this block! There are more empty lots than houses. In fact, when Adda and I get "on our feet" financially, we are going to buy up the empty lots!

APRIL 18TH

Mr. Rackliffe gave me an editorial he had clipped from a St. Louis paper reporting that the war, which has been impending for months, has been formally declared. Fort Sumpter three miles out in Charleston Harbor was short of supplies. When the North tried to resupply the fort, on April 12th Southern troops fired on it and continued to pound it for two days. After some thirty hours of bombardment, Major Anderson surrendered, which technically commenced the war. All Northern states have been called upon for regiments.

Augusta goes on to tell of a company of Mounted Riflemen being immediately formed in Lawrence. President Lincoln hardly in the White House six weeks, declares Missouri to be a Union State, free of slavery. Ex slaves begin to flock to Lawrence and other abolitionist's settlements in eastern Kansas. Graton tells the sisters that pistol sales and ammunition to whites are "way up" from fear all these Colored might try, in their new freedom to take things that don't belong to them.

With the help of two visiting engineers that Adda and I had known previously off the *Emma Harmon*, a shallow draft riverboat that makes regular "stops" at Lawrence, we moved the extra stove into the kitchen and that's when we began having problems with the installation.

Our original stove's pipe was accommodated by a brick chimney built into the wall separating the kitchen and dining room. There is no good place to locate the new stove because there is no outside wall through which I wanted to cut a hole to accommodate the new stovepipe, although we finally did. Then we had to go uptown and buy two ninety-degree sheet metal "elbows" almost six inches in diameter. The outside stovepipe was fastened along side the eave of the sloping roof and it looked cheap and ugly. When we were finished, which took all afternoon; these fellows simply wouldn't take money for their help. But they did say they'd take a quart of that rye whiskey that Adda used to provide them when they had visited Lawrence and took meals at the Whitney House. They pretended to be disappointed when I told them that Adda was married, but that she's in town.

Just after we got a test fire going in the new stove, to see how it "draws", Adda arrived with a new accordion and began practicing, so she had an opportunity to renew her acquaintance with these two engineers. When Adda agreed to walk them to the Cincinnati House to settle our whiskey obligation, they invited us to their boat for supper; we accepted... and had a grand time. Their riverboat is like a small, rather elegant floating hotel but big enough to carry several hundred tons of cargo. Before we left, they showed us the engine room and their huge, wood-burning steam boiler.

By mid April Graton has won the domestic contest. I agreed to temporarily move out. Adda has enough to worry about (in her delicate condition) without the tension caused by my being there, particularly when her husband is home. I intend to take board and room with our old friend Sarah Goss, now the wife of Doctor Lewis, who lives nearby.

APRIL 1861

Mr. Rackliffe, in town from the Topeka Legislative Session to spend a few days with Mary and little Ermee, had asked Adda where I was living. When he located me at Killams, he said he was aware of an opening for a chief cook at the Pomeroy House over in Topeka, where he and other legislators take board and room while the state legislature is in session. He could arrange for me to get the job, if I was available. It didn't take me long to make up my mind about that opportunity. I packed immediately. He agreed to pick me up on his way back to Topeka the following Sunday afternoon. I asked livery to send my trunk.

TOPEKA
FRIDAY, MAY 3, 1861

I've been working for the Clemenson family, which operates the Pomeroy House here in Topeka, where Mr. Rackliffe and a dozen legislators take their board and room. I'm pleased that I'm getting along so well as an employee (again). I wasn't sure that I would be able to adjust. I've kept mum to my current employer about being a real estate owner in Lawrence, though one so short of cash I've had to seek employment for my daily needs.

I am getting along very well here; I am the Chief Cook with adequate kitchen help. I order the supplies and supervise the fry cook, a kitchen assistant and two girls. We serve three meals a day. It pleases me that my menu plans have never been altered by my employers for...economy. I was a little peeved though to discover that my trunk had been here in Topeka for two days, undelivered.

I've heard again from Mr. J. F. Slack, the persistent gentleman from Emporia. He writes that he will be in Topeka in a few days on his way to Leavenworth to examine a "reaping machine", coming in on the river steamers, which he says he's considering buying and would like to renew "our acquaintance." I've met the man twice in my life!

Two (military) companies of 150 recruits formed-up here in Topeka" will leave today for Lawrence. I wonder what's happened to our old friend and benefactor, D. H. Montague, who was so successful in getting our back pay, from old Mr. Stone at the Whitney House. He had been a sergeant in the Mexican War and seemed to me to have been quite a military organizer.

Tonight I heard two well-known speakers (here in Topeka). General Lane and General Updegraff, an old associate of John Brown (the general owned land in Osawatomie). He too had been elected to the territorial Legislature but I never heard Father speak of him. Well, now that we're a state, he's Speaker of the Legislature. He and General Lane both gave tub-thumping speeches tonight, which of course is what we always expect of Jim Lane, who spoke last. The general was not in uniform. He seems never to comb his hair...maybe that's his trademark. For a man of his position he dresses...or at least tonight, he was certainly dressed not to impress. He did wear a coat or jacket, but he had a checkered blue cotton shirt like shirts we saw worn by loggers in Michigan when we did business with them at the sawmill. But as soon as he begins to speak, what he wears becomes insignificant.

I had learned about the speech at suppertime, from Mr. Rackliffe, so I barely had time to get dressed and up to the (packed) hall on time. Old General Lane is still the fiery speaker that persuaded Father to come out here in the first place.

General Updegraff spoke first to a full house and I had an excellent seat. I would say he was not a remarkable speaker, considering all the significant events going on today, most of which he failed to discuss.

All during General Updegraff's speech the fellow sitting to my left kept making these awful sucking sounds. It appeared to me he was trying to clear something from between his teeth. I had reached the limit of my patience towards the end of the speech and said in a soft voice, "Please stop that noise! It's been so distracting I couldn't hear the General. Just then the speaker finished.

Taking no offense, during the applause he said, "I must have a half pound of mutton lodged in between my teeth. I had a meal of what the menu said was spring lamb. Hah, that cook wouldn't know lamb from a billy goat, but he's a big improvement over the last cook, who was frequently drunk."

"Where did you eat?"

"At the Pomroy House."

I didn't want to tell him I was the chief cook there and had personally cooked and served two legs of lamb tonight, but I agreed with him that lamb was tough: tough but tasty.

"Well, how did you like the gravy? I thought that was pretty good on those boiled potatoes…and how did you like the candied yams?"

"Yes, they were good but how do you know so much about the gravy and yams?"

"Well, I ate there too".

"S'funny, I didn't see you in the dining room. Why are you taking notes? Are you a reporter?"

While he was talking and still trying to clear his teeth, I fished through my bag. During the afternoon break I had purchased a small ball of darning cotton I needed to mend my work socks and still had it with me. I unrolled about twenty inches of cotton string, gave it to him and said, "draw this back and forth between your teeth, bend your head down and nobody will see you.

Presently the hall quieted down. I could see General Lane standing alone over by one of the pillars. Then someone I didn't recognize introduced him.

Big applause. Many stood. On his way to the podium he removed his coat and during his speech he removed his wrap-around tie, unbuttoned his collar. The fellow behind me asked his friend, "Think Old Jim will take his pants off next?"

After General Lane finished, a gentleman sitting close to me jumped to his feet and yelled, "Hey, Jim, how did you find things when you got to Washington?"…And the crowd roared their approval to all that the question implied. Of course, the General saw this as a great opportunity and he began to respond as though he had expected the question.

He said that when his Regiment of loyal Kansans got there, they quickly realized that the Capitol City was surrounded on all sides by slave states: He said our Kansas boys were quartered right there in the White House…in the big "East Room" and stayed there for some time after the inauguration, although, he said from the looks of things fighting could have started any minute…And we were ready!

Big applause.

"Buchanan had not ordered the Navy to blockade Southern ports in February and March. Since I had the President's ear most every day...you know we had both been Congressmen, I recommended that the Navy begin the blockade and you'll note that's exactly what happened."

More applause.

"Arlington (Virginia), across the river had declared for the rebellion. But us Kansans were not alone. Pennsylvania troops, to make a show of force were already parading in the streets. A regiment from Massachusetts slept in the Senate Building after having fought their way through Baltimore to get there. We had cannons mounted in the Treasury Building and the U. S. Mint." And he made a joke about gold in the Treasury that I didn't "catch," because of the instant laughter and I was busy trying to write his last sentence.

He went on to say that New York City had sent a regiment of volunteers from their fire and police department. Before April was over the Capitol had 10,000 troops in place, not only to defend the City but also to lash out and take Alexandria, Baltimore and even Richmond if the President directed it. Richmond's only one hundred miles from the Capitol.

Big Applause—in closing, General Lane said one of President Lincoln's problems, which came to light while we were there, is having to cope with the loss of so many well-trained Army officers, every day going to the side of the South. There were 400 of them at the last count. Three-quarters of that number were West Pointers. His major loss, of course, was Robert E. Lee. The President had offered Lee top command of the Union forces, but to no avail. The superintendent of the Military Academy, followed Lee, the General said, but I didn't get his name.

When I hear gentlemen like these two, speak and I'm in the same hall with them and realize that our lives have touched each other, often with pain and sacrifice, but ultimately with success, the experience reinforces my conviction that what we've done out here was profoundly virtuous and history will remember us, though it saddens me that Father was struck down before he could begin to reap some dividends from all this effort.

As we stood, preparing to seek the exits, the gentleman on my left offered to return my string. I laughed and said, "You'd better keep it."

"Why?"

"Well, with all that left-over lamb, it looks like we'll be getting lamb-hash tomorrow."

But I lost track of him as we filed out. The following day I surveyed the dining room at the Noon meal through the little window in the kitchen door …and sure enough, there he was, my gap-toothed friend from last night. I later learned he too was in the legislature representing Jackson County. He is a farmer from Holton.

In the crowd milling around, trying to get out of the hall, last night who should I bump into but Mr. Stein and Mr. Connor from Eldorado.

It was so good to see them that I suggested we walk back to Clemensons and I would warm up a pot of coffee and we did.

We had so many things to talk about, particularly with Mr. Connor who two years ago was so much involved in our lives. His store was the post office. The Hildebrand trial was held in his store, which at that time was the only store in town. Hildebrand's whipping took place behind his store. Mr. Connor was very helpful and solicitous to me personally during Chase's illness and death.

I asked what brought them to Topeka. Mr. Connor said he was thinking of enlisting. I asked, "Who will run your store?" Apparently he has someone running it and if he does enlist, he will sell it.

I asked Mr. Connor what he's enlisting in…the Kansas Militia or the U. S. Army?

"What difference does it make?"

"Well, I am not an expert, but our state Militia seems much better organized. They have been around in various conditions of organization since General Lane organized it five or six years ago to confront the Missouri Bushwhackers. From what I can tell, right now there is considerable confusion about the regular Army. I suppose you could go sign-up for the Army. But we've only been at war a few weeks and Leavenworth had so many officers and non-commissioned officers with Southern views and grades of Southern loyalties that I hear they are still sorting things out within their own ranks up there, as to who will stay and who will leave to join the secessionists.

According to what I've been reading and from friends that have already...or they plan to enlist...tell me that prior to Mr. Lincoln's inauguration ninety days ago, the U.S. Army only had about 15,000 soldiers and three-quarters of them were scattered out here, out west. Nobody, except the War Department really knows how many enlisted men and officers we really have after those defections to the South.

"On the other hand", I said to Mr. Connor, "General Lane is right here and I would imagine he could rally, in a state militia, if he hasn't already, 3,000 to 5,000 Kansans...and I'm sure that Governor Robinson would join that effort, even though I see those two as political competitors."

It's no secret that hundreds of officers have resigned from the Army to join the rebellion. The Army of the West, which is supposed to protect all our territories west of the Mississippi all the way to the Rockies and north to Canada, is headquartered right here. That is Leavenworth. So I can't imagine that Leavenworth has been immune to this exodus of the officer class.

Mr. Connor asked how I had become so informed about the military situation and that gave me an opportunity to explain Adda's marriage to Graton and the inquiries that Graton has made towards his enlistments. And I explained that Adda and I have been living in Lawrence for over a year and during that time war was declared. We are very sensitive to these military matters if for no other reason than war is so close to us. Local newspapers and Eastern ones as well are full of war news.

Before we broke up, I suggested that they come to Clemensons for breakfast. There's bound to be some state legislator that hasn't gone home yet, who can give you better advice about enlistment than me. We might catch one of General Lane's staff before he leaves and ask him. And I gave them our address and invited them, if they got up to Lawrence. I told Mr. Connor that Adda is married and is expecting in late summer. Well, we talked until the coal oil in the lamp was gone (about midnight.)

The second day after I had taken this job, Sumner Rackliffe (whose full name, I've discovered, is John Sumner Rackliffe) came down to the kitchen at 6:30am and asked if the house would give early birds a cup of coffee.

We begin breakfast service at 7am, so I said, "Sure, if you'll give me a report on what this first-ever Legislature, now that we are a state, has accomplished so far; and I got out my note book knowing that all the tables had already been set. The fry cook, who's also a baker, was already frying bacon, sausages, diced potatoes with onions, etc. He'd been in the kitchen since 4am, when he put dough for the bread, rolls, cinnamon buns in the hot oven, which is kept hot by the night watchman, so everything was already organized.

"Well, the first week we were in-session Governor Robinson took the oath of office…now that we are a state. I came up here the last week of March, you remember, for I needed to get Mary and Ermee located and there was no room for them here in Topeka."

"Yes, yes, I remember and Adda and I were so proud of you and we felt so bad that Adda's husband couldn't have been more hospitable…but that's water over the dam."

He continued, "The first thing the Republican majority did was to unravel all the previous territorial acts on the books by the Democrats, particularly those dealing with slavery.

So far we have debated the qualifications of the two U. S. senators and we've elected two and I'll let you guess who they will be."

"Jim Lane certainly and, I hesitated…Mr. Pomeroy."

"Correct."

"But we spend an awful amount of time gossiping about the conduct of the war since Sumpter last month."

A few minutes before 7am I could hear our dining room fill up, so I asked the cook to give Mr. Rackliffe two eggs – straight up, some sausages, two biscuits with gravy and some potatoes. He did and took his plate out to join his fellow legislators. Two legislators board with us: one Robert Morrow from Douglas County, and an editor. Three of our boarders are senators. The one I like best is Josia Hubbard from Connecticut. He came out here in 1856 with the Beecher's Rifle Company. Most of the legislators are farmers.

Years later I ordered a bound volume of Transaction no. 10 of the Kans. St. Hist. Society, from a bookstore in Lawrence. It has a much better summary of the first Legislature. I noted with pride Mr. John Sumner Rackliff represented our old Eldorado District #17 at that First Legislature.

After that breakfast, I began getting down to the kitchen at 5:30am to put the coffee on and to get things organized in anticipation that Mr. Rackliffe would join me for his early coffee and most mornings he did...and I took notes.

On one of our sessions he said, "Yesterday they voted to sell upwards of $150,000 in bonds to finance the State Government. At that same breakfast he said they were debating which town to locate the permanent capital and had a big laugh by saying, "It sure as hell won't be Lecompton!"

About June 1st he said they were debating terms for representatives and senators. The term for the Governor is bogged down because we can't agree as to when he began. Lane wants to end his term in one year and that has increased the acrimony between the two of them. He said he needed to leave early today because the representatives will meet in the Congregational Church, which is some walk from here.

On one of our "coffees" I asked him "How many are there of you?"

"Twenty-six senators and seventy-five legislators or one hundred all toll, give or take a couple, and he added that's why all the boarding houses and hotels in town and nearby are full."

Summer 1861

James H. Lane

JAMES H. LANE

For several years following the Kansas-Nebraska Act of 1864 James H. Lane was the most powerful man west of the Mississippi.

Drawing on his political experience as a congressman and his military experience as an officer-in-the-field during the Mexican War, he used the anti-slavery cause in Kansas to advance his career. A superb organizer and fiery speaker, he spoke to rallies all over the

North and persuaded thousands to move to the new Territory to out-vote the pro slavery population already there or to donate to their cause. Soon the safest route across Iowa to Kansas was called the Lane Trail, which Sam, Augusta and Adda used in 1856.

Once there he quickly organized the male Immigrants into several well-armed military companies and put a stop to Missourians riding into Eastern Kansas to terrorize the abolitionists.

During the 1861 interregnum, President Buchanan asked Lane to bring a Regiment of Kansans to help protect Washington, D.C. and the White House, which he did, with relish.

While actually quartered in the White House, he got to know President Lincoln better. (They had both been congressman). By the time Lane returned to Kansas (now a state) Lincoln had asked the Senate to confirm Lane's commission as Brigadier General.

Without the Senate's blessing, "General" Lane called up parts of his old militia and took to the field (Western Missouri) with his famous Kansas Brigade to ruthlessly put-down the insurrection. Lincoln asked him to take-over recruitment (in Kansas) and he did including the recruitment of several regiments of ex slaves, while Governor Robinson, his political foe replaced him as Senator. In time he outlasted Robinson.

Lane certainly was one of Quantrill's targets when he raided and almost destroyed Lawrence in August of 1863.

56.

LAWRENCE, KANSAS
THE CIVIL WAR

Summer 1861

JUNE 7ᵀᴴ — THE LEGISLATURE ADJOURNED.

I suppose with the legislators all leaving town, unless I'm asked to stay, I will join the exodus. We do have a few boarders that are not politicians. (Looks like I will miss Mr. J. F. Slack's visit.)

The day after the legislature adjourned Mr. Whitney offered me a ride to Lawrence in his fancy two-horse carriage. I had failed to settle my affairs with the Clemensons, because he was gone for a few days. We left it that he could give Mr. Rackliffe what was owed me. Mr. Whitney helped me with my trunk and drove me directly home and I invited him in for a cup of tea. Instead he invited me to take dinner with him at the Whitney house and we did. While I was there, I noticed that Graton was not at home.

We've known since we came out here in the summer of '56 about John Brown and a handful of his associates occasionally riding south of town, south of Westport, where they could simply cross over the boarder into three or four counties of southwest Missouri to raid, plunder, steal livestock and to bring back slaves. Before the war most of the Colored were secretly conducted north, using several routes but collectively referred to as the Underground

Railroad. All in all I doubt that this effort freed any more than five hundred and gave the Missourians reasons to retaliate with raids over here, for which we had very little defense until the summer of 1856. By the way, I think Governor Robinson took offense at those abolitionist's acts of General Lane and others.

Of course, John Brown, Jim Lane and others who did these things, claimed that it was simply in retaliation for the months of similar behavior by the Missouri Bushwhackers or Border Ruffians, who came over here, voted illegally, burned abolitionists' settlements and killed over 200 free state people almost unopposed from 1854 until 1856. When Jim Lane organized several regiments of well armed free state militia in the late summer from all the immigrants he persuaded to come out that year, he and many of the people, we knew including our own Father fought and put a stop to these Missouri invasions, but I've more than covered all that before.

Since the war this raiding activity by our side has accelerated and the number of ex slaves brought over here has increased considerably. We don't hear anything about the Underground Railroad now. Most of the liberated slaves are staying here in eastern Kansas and are generally assimilating into our society.

Those who are physically fit are recruited for military services but that's become very controversial.

The heavy recruitment of Whites into the Army has left us with a labor shortage, both in the cities and the farms. As a result, many of the Colored, who possessed non farm skills, as blacksmiths, working in the livery stables, grain and feed stores, etc. are filling those vacant city jobs here in eastern Kansas and I hear from my farming friends that have lost sons to the Army, some farm work is now getting done by willing ex slaves, for pay. We see Colored men and women on market day this summer with all sorts of fresh high quality farm produce to sell. And for reasons beyond me, I hear that Indian tribes in this area have welcomed the ex slave.

Sometime after the Legislature adjourned, the Rackliffes dropped in for a visit. They said they were going down into the

Cherokee Land for a visit. I asked them if they didn't think that area was dangerous. I guess not, because that's where they are going.

Mr. Rackliffe handed me the money that the Clemensons (Topeka) owed me. Before they left, they took a walk down along the river. He said he wanted to see how the new bridge across the river is coming along.

I read in the *Lawrence Republican* early July that Ben Van Horn, now a lieutenant, who I knew at Clemenson's (in Topeka), is involved in recruiting Colored for military service. He found enough ex slaves among the Sax & Fox tribes in the northeast corner of the state to form an entire Company (eighty men), which should be three or four squads of twenty-five to thirty men per squad. Why would ex slaves have an affinity for the Indians or vice versa?

That same issue carried an article from Washington, D.C. noting that by the 4th of July the War Department had sixty-four regiments (A modern regiment has 900 men)…And a cadre of U. S. Army to swell the available forces to 225,000. By July Congress had authorized the recruitment of 500,000 but if that fails, plans to draft will be considered.

Graton got a few days off and came home August 3rd. That date coincides with Augusta's first journal entry dealing frankly with marital disharmony between Adda and her husband. Though Graton was home, Adda who is big with child didn't return to it until August 11th. By then her husband had returned to duty. (Adda is only a few weeks from delivering.)

Graton left a note for Adda, saying he had been ordered to move their (Colored) Regiments south, towards the fighting, even though he and other officers felt that their troops needed more training. In Graton's case he is about half way into his six-month enlistment.

James Montgomery, an old associate of John Brown, has a group of Jay Hawkers and has stepped up his raids into Missouri, likewise, Charles Jennison and a new comer to this business,

Daniel Anthony. Of course, none of them are as well known, nor as effective as I imagine is Father's old officer, General Lane.

Then in early July I read in the Lawrence *Herald of Freedom* that the President had appointed General John Pope to take command of that part of Missouri north of the Missouri River, as it flows across the state generally east/west. By then the proslavery administration of Missouri, including the Governor had "fled." It must be a comfort to the president that General Pope is one of few Republican generals.

This article says that the Union is particularly interested in keeping the new railroads mainly the east-west line in Northern Missouri safe and able to transport troops and supplies in both directions.

Oh, yes, I received another letter from Mr. Slack of Emporia.

In just a few weeks after war was officially declared up to 3,000 Union troops have mustered at Fort Scott, just inside the Kansas line about ninety miles southeast of Lawrence on a well-traveled north-south road all under the command of Jim Lane, which was (then) his headquarters. He had returned from Washington, D.C. about mid May. By the end of June he had been appointed Brigadier-General and was asked or authorized to assist Governor Robinson in recruiting.

Rebel generals Price and Raines also had several thousand men in the vicinity, even though President Lincoln had declared Missouri to be a Union state. Lane expected an attack by them into southeastern Kansas.

By late summer General Raines approached within twelve miles southeast of Fort Scott.

The next day Lane sent out a mounted regiment of 500, pulling a twelve-pound howitzer to reconnoiter. This group engaged the Rebels and fought until Lanes men ran out of ammunition. That skirmish cost Lane five killed and twelve wounded.

Believing the Rebels had superior forces, Lane ordered Fort Scott to be abandoned and moved his troops and the town's occupants (about 300) to a fort nearby that he had previously built, called Fort Lincoln.

In the meantime, Raines turned his attention elsewhere and made a march for Lexington (Missouri), though General Price's force, that was about ten miles from Fort Scott, did indeed attack Fort Scott, only to find it abandoned.

Late summer – early fall 1861: A few wounded Kansas Militia coming back to Lawrence report that they were with a Regiment under Lane who within a few days of his return from Washington rounded up his old Regiment and went down into Missouri to do battle. These returnees refer to the enemy as "insurrectionists." That word seems mild to me, as does the other current word, "Rebels." General Lane has said in an interview that his entire intention in going into Missouri was to put down their insurrection.

As Commander, Lane complains in a letter to Lincoln from Leavenworth that Governor Robinson is interfering in his recruitment efforts, and he complains that the Commander of Fort Leavenworth fails to acknowledge Lane's authority. (Many in the "regular" army at Fort Leavenworth thought it was folly to believe it possible to make a soldier out of an ex slave.)

To make matters worse, Lane later complains that when he accepted the commission of Major General of the Kansas Brigade, from the President, Governor Robinson claims he forfeited his seat as Senator from Kansas, whereupon Governor Robinson appointed Fredrick P. Stanton to Lane's vacated Senate seat.

When Lincoln tries to mollify all parties by appointing Lane, Brigadier General, reporting to the senior officer (in the West), General Hunter at Fort Leavenworth, Lane complains that General Hunter is uncooperative in providing military help when he does recruit, so General Lane respectfully declines the commission, saying he wishes to return to his seat in the U.S. Senate.

Lincoln tries to smooth things over by asking (again) for Lane to "head-up" recruiting for the defense of Kansas and Missouri, which he accepts. However, when General Fremont reorganized Lane's Brigade in October 1861 the new organization excluded

Lane, which forced him out of the Union Army and back to the Senate.

Kansas had barely been a state in 1861 when in April war was declared. Jim Lane had, during the Popular Sovereignty period raised and trained several companies of so-called Free State militia to fight, mostly the Border Missouri hooligans. So on and off prior to the actual declaration of war, Kansas was still a territory with maybe as many as 3,000 men-at-arms including the remnants of the Stubbs Company that guarded Lawrence in 1857. Adda and I knew all those fellows, because on and off we worked at various boarding houses in or near Lawrence, where soldiers from some of these companies took their meals.

Others were Preston Plumb, Richard Hinton, A.D. Searle, Joe Cracklin, George Dietzler, Frank Swift, Sam Tappan, Colonel Phillip St. George Cooke U. S. Army, Mr. A. Gates (husband of Mrs. Gates) and Alfred Pierce, including James Redpath, whose names I see from week to week in one military outfit or another. Adda and I met all these men and more from the summer of 1956 and over the next few years. Three or four of these men were co founders of Eldorado: Joe Cracklin, who in 1857 and 1858 was captain of the Mount Oread Rifles, one of the companies guarding Lawrence mostly from Missourians who thought they had some special rights in Kansas…more special even than the citizens of the territory, Joe Cracklin in fact gave Eldorado its name. He visited us on more than one occasion.

Although Kansas had this cadre of trained soldiers and a recently recognized elected governor (Robinson), I think there was some confusion re: these early enlistments, and their military organization. I believe for at least ninety days and maybe a year, many of our boys and ex slaves had enlisted in and fought as Kansas State Militia, not the U. S. Army. It was later as the Army in the West got organized for war that these Companies or Regiments were "mustered" into the U. S. Army.

General Lane, as much as I love him, contributed to this confusion by the manner in which he executed his Federal authority to recruit, train, etc. For instance, the Regiments under Colonel Jenison, Montgomery and others paraded in the early days of the war as Lane's Brigade and General Lane did all the commissioning, often in antagonism to Governor Robinson, who claimed sole authority to commission officers, but I think these were still Kansas Militia, not Regular Army.

The *Leavenworth Conservative* in November 1861 reported on their battles in western counties of Missouri. Lane had, as early as November, a Black Regiment in the field. Those ex slaves had to have some sort of training, which must have started in the summer just weeks after the war "began." That's also part of the current confusion.

The paper reported that one of Lane's Black Regiments in October had a fight very near Wyandotte (Kansas City).

I suppose, but don't know, that these White Regiments initially under Lane, were later (gladly) mustered into the U. S. Army after the defection to the South of about forty officers...many in senior command. What I mean is that what was left of the Regular Army in particular, President Lincoln was glad to have these standing State Militia of the Northern states with military experience available when the rush to recruit commenced.

This practice is not unlike the current situation where the military calls up "National Guards" from various states for active duty.

We had arrived in the summer of 1856 and before Thanksgiving Jim Lane probably had 2,000 trained men with better rifles and ammunition than their Missouri counterparts. Lane's companies "suddenly" became a cadre of trained officers and men available to the Union Army, when the larger war broke out. Every Northern state had their militia. Indeed it was public knowledge that several states that had contributed immigrants and/or money to settle Kansas Territory offered to send their state Militia to defend against the marauding Missourians.

In the spring and summer of 1861, when I was living in Lawrence, we were certain that after General Price had taken

Lexington, and after the Battle at Wilson Creek that, flushed with victory he would invade Kansas and on his way to take Fort Leavenworth and destroy Lawrence. So as a very concerned citizen I was very grateful that we had fellows like Lane, Montgomery, Jenison (Lane's Brigade) available to defend us. But I don't think they were then in the Union Army…but that's just my opinion.

By September Jim Lane has experimented successfully in arming people that he had liberated into a military Company that he affectionately calls his "Irregulars."

All of this accelerated activity in Missouri by Kansans has gained respectability for General Fremont's First Confiscation Act. Whether it's official or not I don't know, but since August 1st, the influx of these people is sharply on the increase and for good or bad, we are going to have the opportunity to get to know, first hand, the very people for who's cause so many of us have sacrificed to champion.

As the war got underway, recruiting Colored troops proved to be an easy assignment. Training them or any other non-military cadre would be the real chore. Most of the training is being done in Leavenworth, Wyandotte and Westport. Of course, my brother-in-law, Captain John Graton, the ex Lawrence gunsmith, is one of Colonel Williams officers in charge of this, although there is a very large group of well-meaning citizens right here in Eastern Kansas, who believe that the Negro is too incompetent to be trained for military service. Others thought that in the end, the government wouldn't really use them in combat and there was a major resistance in the Regular Army claiming that training the Colored for military training was a waste of time.

AUTHOR'S NOTE:

Remnants of that resistance remained in the military through most of World War II. The war was almost over before the military took the first steps to end its segregation.

Adda has been married about ten months and it's obvious that she's in the family way, yet she seems unsettled and is easily irritated. She's happy to have me around to help with the housework and cooking but it seems to me she is not living "happily ever after" as the storybooks promise. Within months of their wedding it was obvious that she and Graton were at odds with each other.

A week or so ago I received a very nice note from Mr. Slack expressing disappointment that he had missed me when he was in Topeka a few days after the Legislature adjourned. He said all that the Clemensons knew was that I had moved back to Lawrence and they had given him my address. His note said he would be in Lawrence on August 3rd and hoped I'd be available...that he had something very important to tell me.

About noon Mr. Slack appeared at our front door. Expecting him, I had dressed for the occasion. Rather than entertain him here and since it was mealtime, I suggested that we walk over to the Whitney House for dinner. In the back of my mind I thought if they are full, we could walk closer to town and take our noon meal at the Cincinnati House. That way, as a distraction from being alone with Mr. Slack, I could introduce him to Aggie Rourke and if Mrs. Gates were available, I'd ask her to join us.

He thought that was a good idea, but he insisted that we drive over in his rather impressive wagon. He does have two of the most handsome horses I've seen since the big Canadian that Father owned.

He is a very considerate man. He had a wooden crate that he suggested I use, as a step-up into his wagon.

As it turned out we were early enough at the Whitney House that we got a nice table by the front window...and Mr. Stone came over and said hello. I also noted that Jule Johnson was still working there (though she rooms at Killams.)

At dinner he said in spite of the drought that he'd have a pretty good year. He farms two-quarter sections...half of it in saleable grain at harvest. The other half in corn, which he feeds to four-dozen head of beef that he also pastures on his place.

Again, he proposed. This time he claims he had some sort of association with both Preston Plumb and Father but he had not been in the Legislature.

I've underestimated the man. He's polite and like most farmers, very practical. He lost his wife the winter of '56 when they moved out here from Ohio. He practiced a short silent prayer before the meal. He may be a Quaker, for there are plenty of them in the Emporia area.

Although he didn't drive me home until well after two pm I never really felt comfortable or at ease in his company. But he is a much more substantial man and much more sociable than I had previously judged him to be.

August 8, 1861

Augusta briefly notes her birthday: she is 22 years of age.

I've read in the newspaper that Frank Swift who had been Captain of the Stubbs Company whom Adda and I have known since we worked for Mrs. Gates and had been our guest in Eldorado has been commissioned a Captain in the Union Forces assigned to the First Kansas Regiment. I've spread the word that if he is boarding in the vicinity, before leaving with his regiment, I'd so like to see him.

The town is abuzz with rumors that Missourians are coming to burn Lawrence and we are concerned that with so many regiments of our men off to war that we will have adequate defense.

August 18, 1861

I hear both General McCulloch and Price were killed in a large battle over in Missouri. I heard also that Caleb Pratt, a boarder at the Cincinnati House was killed along with Lawyer Jones, who was a lieutenant. Colonel George Dietsler and Captain Frank Swift have been wounded.

General Lane has been back in Lawrence for some months since the inauguration. The U. S. Senate never got around to approving the General's Commission that the President recommended. He has been given a new assignment by the Secretary of War, Edwin M. Stanton, to recruit soldiers for the Union Army including Colored Regiments. (He's specifically ordered <u>not</u> to recruit Indians.)

General Lane complained to the War Department that Governor Robinson seems to find ways to impede him in raising volunteers for the Union forces.

†he August 23rd edition of the *Leavenworth News* carried an article about our old Plymouth friend (and friend of Preston Plumb) Sam Tappan. He is now in the Kansas Mountains (among the gold miners) recruiting a military company from the miners and merchants to defend Kansas (Union) interests out there. He claims that the Union Army will need that gold but just as we need it for trade, the Confederates with their regiments in New Mexico and Texas are expected to come looking for it.

That same edition also listed more dead from Lawrence: Lewis Litchfield, Mrs. Litchfield's husband, and Frank Wicker. I feel so sorry for Mrs. Litchfield. More boys that Adda and I knew: Mr. Dyke and Harry Barinian of the Kansas 1st, both wounded.

We heard this evening from Mrs. Litchfield who lost her husband in the August 10th battle at Wilson's Creek in Missouri that Frank Swift and Mr. George Deistler, of First Regiment Kansas Volunteer Infantry were both wounded in the same battle. Colonel Deistler, who with Father was a P.O.W. at Lecompton and a co founder of Eldorado, is in charge of this regiment. Governor Robinson commissioned it.

Considering the likelihood of Lawrence being invaded, early that summer a neighbor suggests that it might be safer for us to go east before Adda expects to deliver. Although we seriously considered that plan and discussed it with Graton, he is adamantly opposed, saying that Lawrence will be kept safe by Union Forces stationed in Fort Leavenworth. He reminded us that in spite of Missouri being declared a Union State, river transportation to St. Louis or Iowa City is still very dangerous for small parties of northerners in general and abolitionists in particular. That would be the fastest way to get on eastbound trains. The other alternative is a series of long rides on stagecoaches across Iowa to the trains at Iowa City. Graton is opposed to the Iowa stage, even if one is available.

AUGUST 24TH 1861

Call me Aunty Augusta. Adda delivered a healthy little seven-pound girl late in the evening of August 24. Twenty hours earlier Adda said her pains were so regular that we all thought she was ready...and so did she. But her labor continued for almost twenty-four hours, but both baby and Adda, who has always been so strong, are both doing just fine.

Dr. Lewis, who had married Adda's best friend, Sarah Goss, was here when she delivered, as was Mrs. Perrine, who Dr. Lewis often uses as a midwife, was here before, during and after her delivery. Graton's sister, Julia, came over the day before and has been both a big help and a comfort to Adda.

Dr. Lewis came by early this morning to see how his two patients are doing. He did say his wife wasn't well. He didn't stay long enough to have a cup of offered coffee, so I guess he thinks all's well with mother and baby. As much as I think the father should have been here, he wasn't, but Adda had all the help she needed, so all's well that ended well.

AUGUST 30TH 1861

The war news is just terrible. Capt. Walker is in town and reports on his men being killed in the Battle of Wilson's Creek (I don't have the foggiest notion where that is.)

Apparently it was very hot and the dead quickly putrefied. Walker said he was concerned that our wounded were left on the battlefield for lack of conveyances and the health risk to those trying to recover them. The Southerners have buried theirs in shallow ditches, he says.

SEPTEMBER 19TH 1861

The widow Mrs. Litchfield came by to pass on the news that there will be a celebration in town to welcome two wounded Lawrence heroes home on sick leave: Mr. Deitsler and Frank Swift. There will be a display of "Flags and Gunpowder" for them, she says. Her poor husband was in their Regiment.

Autumn 1861

57.

GRATON — PART I

While I remained in Eldorado and Adda was working and living at the Whitney House in Lawrence, she had become acquainted with John Graton. That was more than a year before we returned to Lawrence in the dry summer of 1860. Mr. Graton, who was a local gunsmith and sold guns and ammunition at his prominent location between 7th and 8th streets, later named Henry and Winthrop Streets, on New Hampshire Street, had been taking his noon meals at the Whitney House for two or three years. The most zealous of the "Free Stators" including John Brown stayed or ate at the Whitney House, so he probably had a better set of customers there than any other establishment in Lawrence.

That group of "Free Stators" and their visitors including some editors from the east had concluded from observing the violent struggles in Kansas for six years that sermons, prayers, persuasive editorials, all aimed at a national abolition of slavery, had all failed. The Whitney House clientele knew that the economic backbone of the South was cotton: cotton produced so cheaply that, raw or milled, southern cotton was dominating the world market and would continue to dominate it with the use of slave labor and that trade was increasing now that Texas had also become a cotton-producing state.

If cotton was the economic backbone, slave labor was the provider, the producer and with the American invention of the cotton gin, no other nation or state could touch them and the northern mills that prosper from cheap raw cotton for their fabric. They also are complicit in all this.

So if the North and the Free Stators want this country to be free of slavery, and if fifty years of talk has failed, the Whitney House crowd concluded long ago, with John Brown and Jim Lane, it will only come about by force or there will be four nation states in North America: Mexico; a Confederacy of Southern States with legal slavery; the "United States" with slave ownership legal but rare; and Canada.

The Republicans, by and large want the slave free. It was uncertain that Lincoln would commit the North to war over slavery. But the matter was decided for him during that terrible four-month hiatus between his election and his inauguration; when one-by-one those Southern states agreed to leave the Union and they did…and they did more than secede, they agreed to form a separate country, a Confederacy of Southern states. For Lincoln, like Andrew Jackson before him, who in 1832 resisted secession with the promise of force of arms to South Carolina's threat to secede if they weren't allowed to nullify certain new Federal laws.

Secession of Southern States as a block shortly after his election essentially altered the question for Lincoln. Other than commit arms against slavery, Lincoln had to decide if war was his only remedy to hold the Union together.

That issue too was decided for him (but not without cause), when the cannons of the Confederacy "said" that Fort Sumter in the Charleston Harbor of South Carolina would not be resupplied by northern ships, by proceeding to fire on the fort. That, Lincoln declared, was an act of war.

Although I'm not as verbally articulate in debate as my little sister, I enjoy a fair discussion now and then. And as soon as Graton moved into our house (without a single word, asking me if I would acquiesce in his moving in.) when he was in an amenable mood, we debated current issues.

He didn't believe that the South had the constitutional right to secede but on the other hand, he thought if freedom for the slave were mandated and enforced with arms, their economy of the South would collapse. He thinks, yes, Kansas should be free but the abolitionists have been too zealous in wanting the government to take away the South's main ability to earn a living without just compensation and we argue over this. His main reason for coming out here was more for a business opportunity than to out vote the Southerners already here.

He says, however, now that we have a cadre of available talent in the shape of these ex slaves, he is convinced that they can be trained for military service. General Lane and he are in agreement on that one, though they may be in the minority.

It's my contention that John Graton also had more than a running acquaintance with Jule Johnson before and while he was courting my sister. Jule had been a co-worker with Adda at the Whitney House. It's my opinion that Graton had persuaded Adda to delay announcing their engagement to buy time for him to explain things to Jule. "Forsaking all others" was a difficult vow for Mr. Graton.

Shortly after they married in November 1860, Graton moved into our house on Rhode Island Street and I suppose because I was reluctant to move out of what I considered to be my house that amplified the mutual animosity between us. But because blood is thicker than water, Adda and I have remained loyal sisters and true friends through all of this.

In May the new President had called for the various states militia to volunteer for ninety days, some six months. At the same time they asked for three-year enlistments and got 43,000 in the first round.

After making sure that his gun shop could be well managed, mid summer – about the 4th of July- Graton went up to Fort Leavenworth to inquire about enlisting in the Kansas militia (as contrasted to the Army; for six months, which was the custom at the time.) He preferred a job with the quartermaster department purchasing guns and ammunition based on his gunsmith training and experience. He was offered a captain's commission pending the usual approval process. Whether he was accepted during that first visit, I don't recall. I do recall his being here on August 3rd. when he left a note for Adda, saying he had been ordered to move their (Colored) Regiments south, towards the fighting, even though he and other officers felt that their troops needed more training. In Graton's case he is into his six-month enlistment about half way.

AUGUST 23, 1861

We heard this evening from Mrs. Litchfield who lost her husband in the August 10th battle at Wilson's Creek in Missouri that Frank Swift and Mr. George Deistler, of First Regiment Kansas Volunteer Infantry were both wounded in the same battle. Colonel Deistler, who, with Father, was a P.O.W. at Lecompton and was a co founder of Eldorado, is in charge of this regiment. Governor Robinson commissioned it. When these two recover, the City plans to have a big parade and fireworks for them.

On September 19th, three weeks after news that several men from here were killed and wounded, their Regiment has returned. Three other Regiments are here as well. Even though the Union Army was victorious, our General Lyon was killed.

SECOND WEEK OF SEPTEMBER

There was a fine parade in town today with a great display of "flags and gunpowder" to welcome home our local heroes Captain Frank Swift and Colonel Deitsler. Though wounded, they were paraded through town in a flatbed army ambulance. Of course, everyone that's been here since 1854 knows these fine gentlemen. I recalled the many meals Frank Swift took at Mrs. Gate's, when Adda and I worked there.

During the parade, Adda said, "Do you remember that cold night right after New Years, after Father was paroled when we arrived at that terrible P.O.W. camp in Lecompton with a whole wagon load of supplies for those poor men?" We all know that both these men spent months in that P.O.W. camp (with Father.) So this was a fitting parade and the weather was nice. Even Adda and the baby who is almost a month old, could not be kept home for this event. Two weeks after the parade the *Leavenworth Chronicle* said this Regiment would get a six-week leave, and then would be assigned to Fort Riley (out towards Eldorado) and then on to New Mexico.

This Regiment did go to Fort Riley and wintered there. But the New Mexico assignment was cancelled and I haven't heard anything since.

When the baby was three weeks old, Adda, Graton's sister, Julia, and I went to visit Mrs. Spicer. On Thursday afternoon Julia and I came home. We thought it best to leave Adda and her baby there. It would have been too long a walk for her, even though the weather was quite nice. When we got home, Graton was there. He'd gotten a few days "leave." When he inquired of his wife, we explained the situation. He said he would go over to the Whitney House where there is usually a parked carriage-for-hire, and would fetch Adda and the baby. He was upset that Adda would take such a young baby out.

SEPTEMBER 22ND 1861

We hear that Lexington (Missouri) has fallen and 4,000 Union Forces have been taken prisoner. Graton came by in his uniform to tell us that he will be leaving with his Regiment in two days. They have been ordered to defend Kansas City. Adda, Mrs. Lewis and several other Army wives and I are going to have a big send-off dinner for Graton and his fellow officers.

Some men at the dinner think they will actually be ordered to join other regiments to retake Lexington. One way or the other I certainly hope Graton has trained these darkies to fight, follow orders and not scatter in the face of the enemy! We'll see!

Abraham Lincoln has recommended Lane to be Commissioner of Recruitment and suggests a commission of Major General. He has asked Lane to muster at least two regiments.

The Leavenworth paper had an article disappointing to me that the President has replaced General Fremont with General Hunter. I've followed Fremont's career and held him in high regard. I remember Preston Plumb and Father both thought he'd win when he ran for president. The paper says he's tolerated corrupt suppliers and after the President declared Missouri to be a Union State, General Fremont issued an edict on August 30th that all Missouri Slaves are Free. Democrats and some Republicans say that this edict exceeded his authority.

Apparently General Fremont's declaration offended Lincoln who sees the war mainly as an effort to thwart secession, rather than freeing the slave. Of course, abolitionists and Republicans are very pleased with General Fremont's action...but the President is boss.

Christmas Day: Lawrence. It's been a lovely day. Mrs. Killam invited several of us to dinner...Mr. and Mrs. Graham, Sarah and her handsome husband, and a few others...a very nice gesture on her part.

In the afternoon I went home. Poor Adda had been home alone all day, just her and the baby. Had I known, I would have gone home early. Her husband is in town but chooses to spend his time elsewhere.

Adda says she's having as much trouble as ever with her husband. He told her that just as soon as he gets his commission, he would not trouble her any longer. After that she can go to "grass".

THE NEW YEAR — 1862

Captain Graton came home about noon and stood erect in the bright sunlight coming through our front room window. It had snowed overnight and the ground was nicely covered with fresh brightly reflective snow. He announced that he had just completed his six-month Kansas militia service and had enlisted in the Regular Army for three years. He was particularly proud that he had been issued his new uniform, which includes a regimental sword. Governor Robinson had approved his Captain's commission.

Upon enlisting last July he was immediately appointed to recruit and train a Company of Colored soldiers. After about ninety days his group would be organized into Company C of the First Regiment of Colored Troops. He was among the first volunteers to recruit ex slaves who have been flocking into our eastern cities since Lincoln declared Missouri a state of the Union…even though all state officials over there openly defied the President's order.

His new uniform, which includes a fancy belt assembly consisting of a brown leather strap that crosses his chest diagonally from his right shoulder, connecting to the belt at his waist on which is suspended a short but fancy, flat braided flexible metal strap, from which hangs a huge sword, maybe 2 ½ feet long in its shiny metal sheath.

I'm afraid I failed to show proper respect for Graton's sword, which I knew was a symbol of command and ceremony by saying, "You better hope that any battle that you are in, you aren't reduced to 16th Century hand-to-hand fighting with that thing. This is 1861. You and your troops will be better served by a modern pistol side arm and if you are mounted, you should carry a Sharps carbine in its leather sheath. Are you familiar with that rifle?"

Graton shot me a dismissive scowl and said with contempt, "You seem to forget that I am a journeyman gunsmith, trained in U. S. armories, I own a shop, I sell all kinds of guns including Sharpes, when I can get them."

Yes, yes, but have you ever fired a Sharpe rifle?"

"Certainly, have you?"

"We were issued Sharpes rifles over in Tabor when we were coming out here, when the territory was controlled by pro-slavery militia, who harassed us and tried to oppress us from the day we arrived. Within weeks our father joined one of General Jim Lane's abolitionist militia…and received military training, mostly from officers with Mexican War experience. This included the use of the Sharpes rifle. Some of that training was extended to the two of us, so both Adda and I had several opportunities to shoot that rifle. Adda, haven't you told your husband about taking off a turkey's head at 200 yards?

"One of these days, when you are home long enough, the three of us should go down to the river for some target practice. Bring a couple of Sharpes rifles from your shop and a tin of ammunition. I'll bet Adda can hit the bull's eye more often than you. Is the U. S. Army issuing Sharpes to its troops yet? It can shoot ten times faster than the muzzleloaders…you can be sure that every member of General Lane's troops have Sharpes."

But to concede some respect for his rank, I said, "You do look very impressive in you new uniform. Congratulation on your assignment."

The three of us had a quiet supper together. Adda, put little Alice to bed, said she was tired and wanted to go to bed early, but Graton seemed intent on telling us in more detail than ever just what it is he is doing with these Colored troops.

General Lane had reported to Washington that cities in Eastern Kansas, like Lawrence, Topeka, Leavenworth, Atchison, even Fort Scott, had become a magnet for ex slaves, mostly from Missouri, some from Southern Iowa, taken all together, he thought he could form-up two regiments of basic infantrymen. According to Army "regs", one regiment was about 1,000 strong including the command, which was a full colonel, a Lt. Colonel, a few majors, a captain for each of six to eight companies and numerous 1st and 2nd lieutenants: all white. Officers will number between 12% and 14% of the regiment.

"Three months after enlisting we had a staff meeting of company commanders, all captains, like me, and I along with other captains was invited to present our plan as to the best way to train these Colored soldiers. Part of our problem is we hardly speak the same language. I said that it was within Army regs to have three or four squads of 21 to 27 men in a squad. And each squad would be three lines of seven to nine men. Four squads make a company and six to eight companies will make a regiment to be commanded by a white colonel."

"Our job is not so much to recruit, for that was easy. The job is to select from the available supply those who will make the best fighting soldiers. The others will be organized as support personnel from those selected. The first job was to teach these ex slaves military commands and to obey them. But first they must understand them. They must comprehend what an officer wants done in response to a simply command like forward march; that they don't move on the yelled word "forward," but on the word "march"...and they must all move forward together in step, which means when the quad leader's left foot hits the ground, all left feet in the squad hits the ground in unison. These simple acts, called close order drill are the beginning of their military training. That will quickly get more complicated as we begin to teach commands used in battle.

"I explained how we organized a sample squad with which we intended to experiment in the command process. All of this training, in the end, is to teach the company to fight in unison, to load their rifles in unison, to fire when told to fire and to survive by listening to battlefield commanders and obeying them. Failing to obey could lead to confusion or death. Few of these people have ever handled a firearm so, separate classes must be arranged to teach the rudiments of the guns, and finally marksmanship.

All of these ideas, I and four 1st Lieutenants tried to explain to our Colored charges. In general, we fail to communicate with these new troops. To make matters worse, these new troops are willing. They've all volunteered. There is little or no resistance from them. The failure is with us, the officer-teacher group.

Beyond rudimentary English, like hello, good-bye, yes, my name is _____, what's your name? Beyond that it was obvious that barked commands as complicated as "to-rear-march" or "present arms", "squads right" were incomprehensible to an ex slave.

So I explained to the other staff officers, including the colonel of our regiment, what I had been trying and what, from my experience, I thought would work.

Looking for potential squad leaders, I interviewed about thirty ex slaves. All of these had come from Missouri and crossed over the state line into Kansas a few miles south of Westport, where they had no river to cross. (The south flowing Missouri River turns generally east-southeast and flows across Missouri at Westport.)

I discovered that only half of those I chose to interview were field hands. To my surprise the other half had vocational work experience. Gabriel had been a low level bookkeeper on a large apple orchard and cider press operation near Blue Springs in Jackson County.

Gabriel can read and write about equal to a white youngster's ability (he had no formal schooling.) He can count, do his sums and most multiplication. He was taught that by his owner so he could do that work. And he had bossed others, he told me with confidence. Gabriel brought four ex slaves with him, including his brother, Emil, who ran a hardwood kiln on a neighbor's place that cures select hardwoods: oak, hickory, maple and makes charcoal for forges. He knows as much about wood as I do about guns. And he, like Gabriel, in their own way can articulate with the enlisted Colored soldiers better than us white officers. Another escapee had worked in a dairy handling his owner's herd. All of these men had wives in the physical sense, but I won't go into that except that it's interesting socially and they are now all over here rather than in Missouri.

There were carpenters, stonecutters, bricklayers, blacksmiths, and horse handlers and so on among the thirty or so I interviewed. The purpose of the interview was to determine how well white officers up to company commanders can communicate orders to people who basically don't understand military English and what that English is indented to accomplish...often immediately.

I came to these conclusions:
- Each squad needed to have a black leader.
- His job would be to convey commands to his squad from the company commander. This Colored squad leader would command those 21 to 27 men.
- We will draft some simple specifications or requirements that must be met before a Colored will be appointed squad leader.

The most important requirement is that the volunteers; i.e., ex slaves must be willing to follow the commands of their Colored squad leader, which in the beginning will consist of their own willingness to be trained.

To achieve that I allowed Gabriel and his brother, who will both be squad leaders, to move around with me and talk to each of the 180 to 200 ex slaves here at Leavenworth, though dozens are coming in weekly from Topeka and our other eastern cities. Gabriel, his brother and two others each chose the twenty-seven men they want in their squads and simply rejected all others. Those four squads will be our first Company "C" in our all Colored Regiment. Four other Captains have practiced the same form of Company organization. Those not chosen for fighting Companies but are able bodied will take care of horses; work in the kitchen, etc. ... What the Army calls "staff jobs." About one-third of all those that volunteered were too old and/or had physical disabilities that made them unfit for service. They will not be enlisted but since there is a labor shortage in Kansas, both on the farm and in the cities, these people will be gainfully employed.

"My guess is that from the thirty-six Colored men that Gabriel picked, is that he will get a full squad...maybe twenty-eight men that he and my 1st lieutenant will train into serviceable soldiers, but all the communication with the Colored soldiers will be done by Gabriel. I expect the other three Colored leaders will do the same and that will give us a good company of eighty to ninety soldiers to be trained for battlefield duty.

Graton said that when they finished explaining this experimental training procedure to the Colonel, he was skeptical but he conceded that this is an "Army First." We need to try things to see what works. He gave us the "go-ahead."

The colonel also said that although we've got ninety days to teach these basics, if the war in Western Missouri gets worse, we should expect to have these troops moved closer to the action.

Graton says one of the unexpected problems he's encountered at Fort Leavenworth is that prior to secession; most of the personnel there were Southern pro slavery. They thought most of the Kansas abolitionists were nuisances and that we are wasting our time with these ex slaves. They are unteachable.

Graton was home only two days and most of that time was spent elsewhere, and I don't mean his gun shop.

A little after the first of the new year Adda sent me a note as soon as her husband left, and the two of us are alone again, in our own house, with the baby. Although they had quarreled about a domestic issue, she said, "Graton left in high spirits to join his troops in Leavenworth. They have been ordered to take riverboats on the Missouri River to the vicinity of Lexington and have been assigned, he told Adda, to retake the city.

Shortly after he left, we invited Sarah Lewis, Mrs. Killam and Mr. and Mrs. Johnson here for "pot luck", but after supper, the weather wasn't nice and they left early.

I'm so glad Adda and I bought this house. It gives us the freedom to be as hospitable as we were in Eldorado, that is, when her husband is absent. It's interesting that people here in Lawrence are of a higher degree in their abolitionist zeal than our Eldorado neighbors. But we aren't as safe here in Lawrence, as we have the various battles raging near us. With soldiers many of whom we know personally coming and going and the newspapers are full of war information we are made aware daily of our situation.

In just a few days Captain Graton returned unexpectedly and immediately asked what I was doing here. I replied that I was doing what normal people do in their own home. "What are you doing here," I asked him. "I thought by now you'd be in Lexington. Did you get drunk and fall off the boat or have you deserted."

Ignoring me, he said to Adda, in tones of frustration and self pity, that "at Leavenworth, our whole regiment in full uniform, mustered smartly into companies, marched on to our assigned boats and went down river but he and their entire regiment had to get off at Wyandotte to accommodate a regiment of mounted troops with their horses, howitzers, commissary wagons, ambulances, etc. We made camp nearby to wait for the next group of available boats. I have a leave-of-absence until the boats can return. I took the Leavenworth stage part way back…but missed the Lawrence stage connection, so I walked the rest." It surprised me that a simple change in plans could affect him so. He seemed demoralized and discouraged by the realities of war and not quite so belligerent and irritable.

He reported that Rebels had 40,000 troops in the vicinity of Lexington. General Fremont had 30,000 troops, including several companies of Cavalry. He expects a fierce battle at Lexington and he and his troops will be forced to miss it.

I asked if General Lane was in the area.

Graton said yes and that General Lane had captured an entire trainload of Rebels by blowing up a bridge in front of the locomotive and blowing up the tracks so they couldn't back up. He carried away all the supplies he could and burned the boxcars and was more ruthless than he needed to be in handling captured troops and blowing up the locomotive even when it was no longer useful.

Before Graton returned to his regiment I agreed to keep peace in the family. I proposed that whenever he was going to be in Lawrence, I would leave the house to them and stay with Sarah Lewis (and the doctor.) I seem to be welcome with them, though the doctor is not as agreeable as he has been in the past. Sarah says that he's working too hard and many of his patients are so slow to pay, that she has trouble making "ends meet" in running her house from his allowances. The Army has approached him to join as a surgeon. There is a shortage in the West of trained surgeons.

Someone has set the prairie on fire. It's burning on three sides of us! Several of us must go out and take care of it.

Mrs. Rackliffe has delivered little boy and they named him Tom.

LATE FALL - 1861

November 4th Dr. Lewis stopped in and with visible agitation, asked if I would go with him.

"Sarah is sick again."

"Oh, I'm so sorry. Is she with child?"

"She has Diphtheria, the worst throat I've ever seen. She can't swallow and can't talk. It's even affected her vision."

I wonder why it is that she is so sickly. She seems to "get" everything that comes along. We bought old Mr. Low's place out there on the edge of town, thinking it would be healthier for her but she's been so listless and weak, she hasn't been of much help on the place."

"Can't you hire some help?"…But he didn't answer. I excused myself to get ready to go with him. On the ride out to their place Dr. Lewis continued to complain about his wife in particular and conditions in general.

I found poor Sarah pretty much as her husband described, except in my opinion that, in addition to Diphtheria, I think Sarah is with child, but has been reluctant to tell her husband, for fear it will add to his depressed feelings.

I stayed with Sarah Lewis almost two weeks, until she was able to get up, eat soft food, but noticed two things: she has lingering morning sickness and doesn't have her 'monthlies". Before I left, for my job waiting for me at Mrs. Killams (expanded) boarding house, I whispered to Sarah that she had better tell her husband about her condition.

It wasn't until November 14th I was able to begin work with the Killams. (Sure enough, March 15th Dr. Lewis came by the boarding house and asked if I could get two or three days off to help Mrs. Perrine, the midwife. He thinks Sarah is ready.)

When I approached Mrs. Killam on the subject, she wasn't pleased, but simply said, "Don't be gone any longer than you need to.) Twenty-four hours after I got there, Sarah delivered a beautiful little baby girl. I took the Doctor to one side and asked him if he saw any signs on the child from Sarah's Diphtheria in November. My Gunn's *Book of Medicine* says this disease can have effects on the "unborn". Apparently all's well.

Before I left them, Mr. Burt drove up. It was a fine spring day. I teased him about his mesmerizing tricks, saying that Sarah had delivered yesterday. He said that's why he was there. He intended to mesmerize the baby to be free of any signs of Diphtheria. As much as I like the man, I think he's a little "coo-coo."

58.

GRATON — PART II

Mrs. Killam, whom I've known here in Lawrence for a long time, has taken a much larger house and has opened it for board and room…and has asked me to come work for her in a job similar to my employment at the Cincinnati House and for Clemensons in Topeka. I run the kitchen, plan the menu and order the supplies. I can't seem to stay in my own house for reasons I've described before. But Mrs. Killam is a strange one. She tells her boarders that if they get sick, they'll just have to move out… that she's not running a field hospital and she has ordered me not to allow the girls to take meals to anyone sick in bed. That seems awfully hard-hearted to me but it's her house and her business, so, she's the boss. I've never seen anyone so lacking in sympathy for sick folks.

Adda came by Killam's place shortly after supper. I wondered who was taking care of the baby.

Jule Johnson, who works here now, and I were doing the dishes with Mr. Thompson, a young man in town, who was thinking about joining the Army. I think Adda was surprised when she walked into the kitchen to see Jule here. Perhaps I had failed to tell her that Jule's two sisters board here when they are not in school. Mrs. Killam had told Jule that the family is in arrears for their board and room, so Jule, who hadn't been working, offered to work to pay off what was owed.

We invited Adda to help, if she cared to and she did, but before we were finished, she said to me, "Couldn't these folk finish up? You and I could walk home together." It was a little "nippy", so I put on a shawl and we walked the few blocks to get home.

Adda was simply lonely and still disturbed that whenever her husband comes home, he immediately finds something that upsets him. He gets bossy and there is a heated quarrel. She says she just doesn't know when this will ever end.

EARLY SPRING 1862

There are three or four regiments in town: the Kansas 1st regiment is back from Fort Scott. We've taken as many of the officers as we can handle here at Mrs. Killam's but she won't accept any wounded or sick with some disease they've picked up while fighting elsewhere.

One of the advantages of working in one of the better boarding houses is being able to meet a more interesting clientele. Colonel Jennison, a well known Jayhawker, now in the Army in charge of the 7th Regiment of Volunteer Infantry, gave me a personal invitation to a program last evening featuring two speakers: himself and a Captain Hoyt. I wondered if the Captain is related to Benjamin (Hoyt) who also frequently boards here and has offered to be more social with me than I care to be with him. Both speeches were patriotic and tried to tell "our side" of the story.

Col. Jennison distributed a small "tract" with his speech, which together with the speech, I'll condense into today's entry.

One of the goals of enlisting and training the ex slaves was to afford them an opportunity through military service, to earn an honorable position or status in a free society. Ex slaves, liberated by Lane, Montgomery, Jennison and other "Jayhawkers" by their recent raids into Missouri have followed their liberators into cities of Eastern Kansas. Leavenworth now has a Colored population of 1,500 with two churches and a school. And there was a large population of ex slaves in Lawrence and Topeka, for some reason all called "contrabands."

Col. Jennison announced last night that General (or is he still a senator?) Jim Lane was officially appointed Commissioner of Recruitment for Kansas. He in turn had commissioned Captain James M. Williams to aid in recruitment and to begin training the ex slaves, which would be no easy task. Captain Williams is now Graton's commanding officer. The Colonel said that many in the Union Forces, particularly those at Fort Leavenworth, who believe training these Colored recruits for military training was a waste of time because they were simply an inferior people... incapable of being trained for the complications of military duty. Obviously plenty of well-educated people, who are in positions to do the training, disagree. It was a stimulating meeting and I was flattered by being invited. Captain Hoyt's speech was needlessly technical but it was a well-attended lecture.

On and off since the first of the year I've been staying with Adda when Graton is drilling his regiment in Leavenworth.

Since they were still meeting resistance to training Negros there last fall, the regiment moved down to Wyandotte (Kansas City) and he has been gone so regularly that I've simply moved back into (my) house with Adda and little Alice, even though I come home late and am obliged to get up early to make breakfast for the boarders at Killam's.

APRIL 1862

Adda walked over to Killam's midafternoon saying she'd like a few words with me. It irritated her that we had to chat in the kitchen because I was as usual busy preparing for our evening meal. Adda says that she and Graton continue to feud whenever he comes home. Poor Adda needed someone to talk to, but I had work to do. So, she took an apron and pitched in helping me in the kitchen while we talked.

She's not sure she can hold her marriage together. I asked her if it's the fault of the war and she says, "It's very complicated. On the one hand he is very patriotic, so he feels it's his duty to be in the Union Army and now that he's in, he is very proud of his commission and assignment. He is also convinced that ex slaves can be trained for military service. Yet he has the usual bigotries that most of us who have never known a Colored family as neighbors or worked with them, has. At the same time he resents giving up his growing business, even though we've got Mr. Wheeler running the shop, but Graton really doesn't trust his judgment and I think he takes all this out on me, because when he does get leave and can come home to see me and the baby, for some peace and quiet and warm meals, he's in the house five minutes and he wants to argue and fight about something. My opinions are of little concern to him. I've failed as a wife, he says, to meet even his minimal expectations. My contribution to our home life is trivialized by him. One way or the other he insists on reducing me to a nothing. He seems to need to dominate, control...there is this constant humiliation. I just don't know what it will take to keep peace in the family.

"Augusta, I've never been treated by any man the way Graton treats me and it's dreadful beyond words that I don't seem to be able to handle it."

Knowing of my sister's good-natured temperament and her ability to get along so well with all the men we had previously known and worked with in Eldorado, it pains me now to see her in such a wretched, helpless situation.

She continued, "The first time I thought it was safe to leave the baby, I asked Mrs. Spicer to come over so I could get out of the house for two or three hours. I walked over and surprised him at his shop and suggested we take a noon meal together at the Cincinnati House. At first he said he was too busy, but he had no customers and I finally persuaded him. Mr. and Mrs. Gates both joined us at our table.

Speaking to Graton, Mr. Gates recalled how resourceful father was in rounding up food for the prisoners during the winter of 1856 while he and seventy more were still in the P.O.W camp, that Sara Robinson had just been released but not paroled and how I later left their employ and went to work for their family.

Many of these older men, like Mr. Gates, knew Father either as a P.O.W., a legislator or from his days with General Lane in the militia and when they mention Father to us, Graton resents that and never fails to tell me about it later. I think he's afraid that in the eyes of many of the men here in Lawrence, as Sam Stewart's son-in-law, he might not measure-up.

To my utter surprise, while we were eating, two of the Mount Oread soldiers, who we knew two or three years ago, came over and wanted to know where I'd been "hiding", how was my sister and we had a short, pleasant reunion. I thanked them, as did Mrs. Gates, for coming over and she introduced them to Graton. They knew of his store, if they didn't know him personally. And Mrs. Gates filled me in on the whereabouts of several others. Well, all this simply made Graton more uncomfortable. Just as soon as it was sociable, he excused himself and said we'd have to be going.

No sooner were we outside and he started up. He saw no point in these circumstances that I arrange where we are always dredging up how great your father was or how well we were politically connected. He accused me having been unnecessarily friendly with all those soldiers and told me to go home. I said I thought I'd visit the bookstore first. He exploded again, saying that I fail to show him proper respect and I shouldn't continually resist his orders.

He has so many resentments bottled-up that when we are in town together, which is rare, he resents that I know so many of the men. I've tried to explain to him that half the men in this town take two or three meals a day in boarding houses and for variety and maybe to be more sociable they change from one place to another. Sooner or later they have all taken meals at the Cincinnati House or the Whitney House and my association with most of these fellows is as a little sister or for the older ones, a daughter. But Graton accuses me of having practiced such unseemly familiarity that causes him to suspect that I've been promiscuous with some of these men and he won't tolerate it. He asked me out there on the sidewalk if any of these old flames of mine visit me in his absence.

Augusta, he has these terrible rages. He has even threatened to kill me." Knowing how strong and independent Adda is, he might have his hands full, if he tried that. I listened carefully to my sister. I agree with her that it's complicated but I think Adda is reluctant to face up to the main element of the problem between them, or maybe she doesn't want to discuss it with me, so I thought I'd work up to it gradually.

"Don't you see? He's bullied you. He's bullied me and gotten away with it. I'll move out, but only to accommodate you. I'll live elsewhere if it helps in your relationship with your husband but my guess is that all our appeasing only confirms to him that he can get away with this because…he has."

"Adda, these complaints are not the whole story. They are symptoms. Add them all up and you still don't get a reason for a man to threaten to kill his wife. There is something much more involved here. 'There is another woman, isn't there?'

We were now in the empty dining room. Adda was leaning against the chiffonier, where we had put all the clean dishes and bowls. Flailing her arms she paced across the room, and then back to me, as though my last remark made her more agitated than before.

"All right, all right! I didn't think it would come to this, but yes, there is another woman and what's very hurtful and humiliating to me, is that it's Jule Johnson. We've known that whole family since we've come out here…and Graton is so shameless in carrying on with her right under my nose. At first, of course, he denied it. He said he was just being friendly with her, that he had known her as long as he had known me. Then when I pressed the confrontation, the fact that I knew about Jule, seemed to increase his anger with me."

"You knew? How did you know?"

"Jule simply approached me several months after our wedding, presuming on our old acquaintance, wanted to explain things. Her self-serving explanation revealed the whole thing and she thought somehow I would simply understand that things had not worked out for Graton and me and maybe I would take my baby and go away. She's convinced that Graton doesn't love me any more, because I think that's what he tells her."

"Augusta, I think this is the first real problem I've ever had and it really disturbs me that I simply don't know what to do. I've coped with Father's death. I would have handled Hildebrand by just shooting the old bastard but with Graton, I'm at my wits end. I seem to be defenseless." I suggested that we sit down at one of the empty tables.

"Adda, you not only have some excellent defense, but a remedy. Your best defense is an offense and in the end the offense must threaten this huge self-esteem of his."

"Defense? What defense do I have other than either leaving him, which I have no intention of doing...or raw physical defense, if he takes action beyond his threats?"

"Adda, you simply need to remind him that Father knew General Lane personally, served under him. General Lane commissioned, then promoted, Graton's Commander Williams. So if Graton's commander doesn't report directly to General Lane, he reports to someone very close to him. General Lane knew of Father's work in the legislature. You need to remind him that you know Sara Robinson, the Governor's wife. She knows Father was a P.O.W., like her. She knows he organized the founding of Eldorado and a whole new voting district, which meant more votes for her husband. She knows Father was on the Legislative Committee working on the constitution banning slavery. I know it might be distasteful for you to think about using these political contacts, but in the framework of what's happening to you, your baby and your home…caused by a citizen of this town, commissioned by her husband the governor, if you threatened to write or contact either of those people, explaining the whole tawdry affair, he'd lose his commission over night. He'd be lucky to be a private in the Union Army. That Adda is your defense."

"I have been so upset with all of this, I've stopped thinking, and of course I've been worried sick about the baby. You've explained the defense…and I think you are right about putting his commission in jeopardy, but where's the remedy?"

"Tell him that if he doesn't drop Jule, you will explain all this in a letter directly to General Lane…and you'll tell it in person to the Governor or his aide or his sister-in-law, who you worked for. She could arrange an audience for you with the Governor this afternoon. If you like, I'll go with you. You must make it absolutely clear to him that you will not tolerate any longer his infidelity and his crude behavior to you. His response to your threat, Adda, is your remedy. Otherwise, you are just complaining and things will get worse. In fact, you should tell him that I know about it, and you might not be able to restrain me from writing anyway, since I'm still offended for the way he has dispossessed me of my half ownership of the house." As this discussion wound down, Adda seemed relieved that she could, if she so chose, take control of this situation. Toward the end of our discussion other girls came in and she began helping us set the tables.

I asked her to stay for supper but she said she'd better get home so the neighbor girl, who's been watching little Alice, can go home. I walked with her to the front door.

"Before you go, when will Graton be home next?"

"I don't know. I never know when he gets a few days leave. Why?"

"Well, you mustn't let this fester. You need to plan what you are going to say, so you can say it the first opportunity you get and you must deliver this speech with such conviction that leaves absolutely no doubt in his mind that you mean business. You've never lacked for courage and you are very articulate, so now is the time to put all all those God given talents of yours to use."

Before Adda left, she promised to send a note that whenever Graton leaves, I should come down and stay nights with her and baby Alice. And I do, but by the time I finish my work at Killam's, it's usually pretty late and I need to get up early to make sure we are all ready for breakfast.

On and off through the winter, that's what we've been doing. When he's not in town, the two of us get along much like we always have. We are both relieved that he is off at some military post drilling his company. As much as I detest the man, I must give him credit for what he's doing for the Union Army, not to mention that he's making such good use of all of these ex slaves that keep coming in. They all seem to know that the Union Army wants them, will feed, clothe and train them to fight the old system that kept them in bondage.

Those who are deemed unfit for the military seem to fit in. Many of them are skilled workers: blacksmiths, carpenters, bricklayers, etc., since Missouri is not all that agricultural and raises no cotton at all, many of the slaves over there that have learned these skills can do the same jobs that Whites normally do. Here in Lawrence we now have a Colored blacksmith; two people who work at the livery are Colored. I now send our laundry to a nice old Colored lady, who solicited this business several months ago. I heard about one old fellow who Colonel Jennison brought back, who had been born in the Caribbean, where he learned to roll fancy cigars. Well, I suppose if he can get tobacco, and it is raised in Missouri, he will be very gainfully employed because tobacco in all forms is very much in use.

Yesterday a company of them paraded here in Lawrence, then on out to their camp north of town on the road out to the Gates' place. They had been fitted out with the strangest uniforms I've ever seen: baggy, bright red trousers with an extra fancy jacket. I heard later that these uniforms with a gold stripe that runs from the waist to the boots had been purchased from France and are the same uniforms worn by French soldiers stationed in North Africa (Algiers). They are known as Zouaves.

Mr. Rackliffe invited me this summer to visit with them for a few days and I did, intending to stay two or three weeks, but their little Katie took sick. After I had been with the Rackliffes a week, Mr. Killam came after me and persuaded me to come back to help with a surge of new boarders at their place.

I was hardly back at work and Mary Rackliffe sent a sorrowful note, saying that their little Katie had died. She didn't tell the cause.

Since I run the kitchen and direct the girls, I found a plausible reason to dismiss Jule Johnson. I couldn't stand my own required hypocrisy in needing to be nice to her just because she worked here.

Two anniversaries: I'm twenty-three this August and this is the first anniversary of the battle of Wilson Creek (which officially was the battle of Springfield, Missouri, August 10, 1861.) For us, this was the first major engagement of the two rival armies in Western Missouri, though it was so close to Kansas, we all felt it wouldn't be long before major battles will be taking place over here. The Confederates not only prevailed but also flushed with victory, they went on to Lexington (Missouri) and a month later forced a Union garrison to surrender. President Lincoln can't seem to get and keep good generals out here on this front.

Mr. Rackliffe is in town, bringing a letter from Tom and Elizabeth Cordis. They plan to come to Lawrence this fall and I'm looking forward to a reunion already. Old friends are the best of friends.

It's now official that the Union intends to draft Kansas's males beginning August 15 (1862). Draft eligible males will not be allowed to leave the state. This has been rumored for several months.

Mr. and Mrs. Watts owners of the big boarding house in Eldorado, who incidentally still owe us money for the lumber, are visiting and report that the Schaefers still live there as well as the Martins. Dr. and Mrs. Weibly have moved to Humboldt. Mr. Watts said that in spite of the drought and terrible harvest someone offered Mr. Little $800 in gold for our three claims. He turned it down but said he would consider $1,000. (That's a little over $2 per acre.) Mr. Carey has joined the Union Forces. Dave Upham is a corporal in one of the outfits from there; oh yes, Mr. Conner, our old and dear friend, the Irish grocer is with Dave Upham in the same company. The Watts reported that Augustus Johnson, his brother, two more men and their wives, who were on their way from Eldorado to Arkansas, were all murdered. Mr. Carey had reported evidence of it out on the open prairie. Mr. Watts speculates it was a Rebel group from the Cherokee Nation out on patrol. He thought it was foolish for a northern family to be in that area in the first place. It's a mystery who did it.

We are losing some of our younger male boarders. They leave almost daily for the war...poor boys: two of them left Wednesday morning for Fort Scott (Missouri.) But in the boarding house as soon as there is a vacancy, it's soon filled. We are really quite busy. Every room upstairs now has an extra bed, which puts an extra burden on my girls, who not only serve food but also make beds, carry out the slops, etc.

While Graton was in Wyandotte, Jule Johnson dropped by after I was finished with the noon meal; we walked downtown for some refreshments. She said she hoped that by being frank with me I could offer her some "big sisterly advice." Of course, we've known their family for maybe five years. She is considerably younger than me, and even Adda (in years) but is a very attractive youngster... very naïve...yet she knows she's been able to "turn" Graton's head. It's obvious and annoying that because we've known her and her family that she can trade on that relationship that our association somehow provides an excuse for her behavior. She seems to think I can find a way for her out of this triangle but it's my opinion that the only outcome that will satisfy her, will be if she gets Graton. My take on it is: Graton wants his cake and wants to eat it too. He knows he is married and is enough of a professional to want the world to think his marriage is stable, but he also wants this "adventure" with a younger woman, who encourages his attentions. But contrary to Jule's thinking, given the opportunity, I don't think he would divorce Adda to marry her. For him this is just a dalliance, but in my opinion Jule's availability to Adda's husband and his response to her "generosity" is the root cause of the serious discord between my sister and her husband.

She said she was so grateful that as Adda's sister that I was available to her and that I was not hostile to her. She said, "Augusta, I've never told anyone this but what has hurt me the most in this are two things: that Graton chose to marry Adda over me and that he's never given me a satisfactory explanation. The promises that he made to me when Adda and I worked at the Whitney house right up until a month before their wedding, clearly led me to believe that it was his intention to marry me. That he chose Adda has been so humiliating. He didn't reveal his decision until two weeks before the wedding. I was devastated…yet I love him and would marry him today, if he were free."

"Have you ever asked him why he chose Adda as a wife? This has been going on now for two, maybe three years and I know and almost everybody else knows that when he's in-town he continues to see you."

"Yes, of course. But his answers just put off my questions. He knows that my feelings have been deeply hurt, but he says we'll find a way out of this and for me to be patient. My only comfort is that he does visit me every time he's in town."

"Yes, I know."

"You have been very frank with me this afternoon in explaining the situation between you and Captain Graton and I have been frank with you in explaining what I think all this is doing to Adda's marriage. Now let me be so frank as to possibly terminate our acquaintance. In your affection…or passion, as you call it… you need to take every precaution to avoid allowing yourself to get in the family way, because if you do, and if you think that will be cause enough for the Captain to divorce my sister to marry you,

you are sadly mistaken. As soon as you start to show, he'll drop you like a hot potato. You'll have to move away or find a man here who will marry you under circumstances known to all. He's a bounder, rude and mean, but he's a Yankee and he's not the divorcing kind. He has been raised in a very conservative, stable family that would never forgive him if they knew he was "carrying on" with you while his wife and little baby, their granddaughter, is at home. If word got up to Army Command of this affair, his commission wouldn't be worth a nickel and the captain is well aware of the jeopardy he...and you indirectly...are in!" I stood up, signaling that this discussion was over. "Jule" I said, "'Tis better to have loved and lost than never to have loved at all."

"Yes, Augusta, I have loved, but I just can't believe that I've lost." We parted as amicably as could be expected.

Jule has two sisters, Ruby and Eliza. When they aren't back East in school, they board with us at Mrs. Killam's. They have a brother also here in Lawrence. Joe Mader came up from Shawnee to report that the Rebels have burned some of their towns down there.

On a fine September afternoon, Mr. Hoyt invited me to go riding in his wagon, but I declined. I had gone with him previously and I thought he presumed certain liberties that were socially uncalled for. He said other young widows, that he had known, were not so "stand-offish" and more "accommodating." I suggested that he remedy that situation by simply spending more time with them.

SEPTEMBER 1861

One of the many controversies re: Capt. John Graton, Adda's husband, is: whether or not he was ever a prisoner of war during the Civil War and if he was, when?

Pro: In a letter from Adda to Augusta, while Augusta is in a remote Colorado gold-mining camp, in her August 22, 1863 entry she extracts from Adda's letter, "Had not heard from Graton for three weeks, except a report that they had been ordered to Fort Gibson and all had been taken prisoners." Keep in-mind it takes about six weeks for mail to get from Kansas to a remote Colorado gold mining camp, so the news of Graton being a P.O.W. must have reached her in very early spring of 1863. It is possible that her husband was a P.O.W., which could mean that he had been captured and released well before September 1864.

There were three battles fought at or near Fort Gibson from spring to summer of 1863. Any one of them could have been the battle that Adda referred to when Graton and some of his troops were captured:

March 9th near Fort Scott, Kansas

July 2nd   Cabin Creek, Kansas

July 15th   Honey Spring – Cherokee Nation

Con: We find no military records that Capt. Graton was a P.O.W. We did find among Civil War Archives a handwritten report by him about troops of his regiment that were known prisoners in "the hands of the enemy" in September 1864". Although the report is undated, Capt. Graton does report the dates of capture to be September 16th though September 18th 1864, almost a year and a half after Adda tells her sister that her husband is a prisoner.

Graton reports, "Return of officers and enlisted men, who are prisoners of war in the hands of the enemy, belonging to the 1st Regt. Kansas Colored Vol. Infantry." In tabular form he lists by names: one captain, two 1st lieutenants, all three white: one sergeant, two corporals and five privates: all eight colored troops all captured on September 16 through 18, 1864. One corporal at the Battle of Poison Springs, Arkansas in April '64 and seven of them in the Cherokee Nation September 16, '64 seven miles north of Fort Gibbon.

Army Records *
Of Company C First Regiment Kansas Colored Volunteers: 108,
officers and enlisted

Capt. Graton, John R. in Command:

1   1st Lt,
3   2nd Lieutenants
3   1st Sergeants
4   Sergeants
11   Corporals
86   Privates - all Colored

Of them:

1   2nd Lt   killed in action in 1863
1   1st Sergeant   killed in action in 1863
1   Corporal   killed in 1863
3   died of "disease"

Of the 86 Colored privates:

7   killed in action
12   died in-service, most of them of pneumonia, most at Fort
Scott
3   deserted.
16   were promoted, some several times. 6 of them were
promoted to Sergeant.
64   mustered out with their regiments with honorable
discharges on Oct. 1, 1865...

Vindication
They suffered a 25% casualty rate...unusually high for any
service.

Contrary to the skeptics at Fort Leavenworth in the early days
of the war, these ex slaves proved to be capable of being trained
for combat and capable of being combat soldiers.

* From a report from the adjutant general of the State of Kansas
1861 – 1865.

Regimental History:
First Regiment Kansas
Colored Volunteers
Including Company C;
Captain John R. Graton in Command

Battles Fought

Fought on 9 Nov 1862 at Island Mound, MO.

Fought on 9 Mar 1863 at Fort Scott, KS.

Fought on 2 Jul 1863 at Cabin Creek, KS.

Fought on 15 Jul 1863 at Honey Springs, CN

Fought on 6 Oct 1863 at Baxter Springs, CN

Fought on 17 Feb 1864 at Horse Head Creek, AT.

Fought on 13 Apr 1864 at Poison Spring, AT.

Fought on 15 Apr 1864 at Poison Spring, AR.

Fought on 10 Sep 1864 at Flat Rock, CN.

Fought on 19 Nov 1864 at Timber Hills, CN.

Fought on 18 Jan 1865at Piny Ford, AR.

Fought on 25 Mar 1865 at Roseville, AT.

Mustered Out on 1 Oct 1865. CN = Cherokee Nation

Source: American Civil War Regiments, Kingston, MA

A MILITARY TALLY OF THE ENTIRE 1ˢᵗ REGIMENT OF SIX COMPANIES.

(Which later became the 79ᵗʰ Infantry Regiment U. S. Colored Troops)

A military tally of the entire 1ˢᵗ Regiment of six companies:

Killed or mortally wounded	183
Wounded	97
Officers killed or mortally wounded	5
Missing	106
Enlisted died of diseases	165

Many of the missing are presumed killed... others wounded and taken prisoners.

Many of these men were recruited under General Jim Lane's orders and cognizance, often in regions (in Kansas) sympathetic to the rebellion (pro slavery elements.)

There was in many parts of Eastern Kansas an "intolerant prejudice against the Colored race."

There were genuine loyalists who believed that enlistment of the Colored soldiers would not be approved by the War Department.

A large class believed that the Negro did not possess the necessary qualification to make an infantry soldier combat ready.

At one time this public resistance was so strong that these early recruits were moved elsewhere from Leavenworth for their training.

As early as October 1861 some of these troops were in the field fighting. Six companies (of 1ˢᵗ Regiment Kansas Colored Volunteers) were mustered into the U.S. Army. (Prior to that we must assume they were in the Kansas Militia.)

Source: search ancestry.com, Amer. Civ. War Rgts

59.

LAWRENCE AND THE EARLY MONTHS OF THE WAR
RUMORS OF A NEW SCOURGE: QUANTRILL

Summer 1861

By June Lane had authority to raise two regiments of volunteers but William Weer (an unfamiliar name) and James Montgomery, who is well known, will each be given command of one of these regiments organized as a brigade. According to the local *Herald* Lane has, they say, "stretched his authority, which can usually be expected of him. He intends to take to the field personally with his two homegrown regiments."

Governor Robinson was in my opinion too quick to exploit this situation by appointing Frederick Stanton as our Senator in Lane's absence.

Lane moved these regiments south to Fort Scott. We learned later that one of his (and his superior's) concerns was gaining control of the lead mines in and around Osceola for the Union. On a "bee line" march from Fort Scott it would be close to sixty miles, mostly due east to Osceola. There were smelters in that area reducing lead ore to metal, which was coming in, as ore by wagons and being shipped out on riverboats. Lane's concern was that this lead not fall into Rebel hands.

By September Lane had about 1,200 men distributed in various strategic locations in Southwest Missouri. By September

111

22nd Montgomery and Weer attacked Osceola, first with artillery, then the infantry.

They were, of course, resisted by Rebel forces defending the area, and probably interested themselves in lead for their own ammunition.

While Lane and his Jay Hawkers were in the vicinity, he burned the Vernon County Court House. That county in Missouri abuts Bourbon County (Kansas) about one hundred miles south and slightly east of Kansas City.

There were known pro Union people in the vicinity as well, and some non fighting Union officials thought our troops behavior should not be so offensive; i.e., confiscating property (slaves) etc. to drive the sentiments of those people toward the Rebel cause. Likewise, in these early days of the war the Border States, like Kentucky, Delaware, Virginia and even Missouri had yet to declare either for the North or the South. Lincoln obviously wanted those states to stay in the Union and he didn't want atrocities committed in Missouri by Lane and his brigade to prejudice the decision of the Border States to favor the Rebels.

On the other hand Lane and his Jay Hawkers were in the field, carrying the battle to the insurrectionist enemy. These became points of contention between non-fighting moderates, like Governor Robinson and the men in the field doing the fighting, like Jennison, Weer, Montgomery and Lane.

To add to the overall political confusion, General Fremont headquartered in St. Louis, had ordered his troops, which included Lane's to liberate slaves whenever they could, which we learned later irritated the President…that and the fact that Rebel General Price was able to take Lexington led the President to relieve General Fremont of his Western Command, giving it to General Hunter who had been headquartered here in Fort Leavenworth.

Late summer and through the fall weeks eastern newspapers have been quick to get the facts from the battles out here close to our border and equally quick to express opinions as to how these results are "playing" in the political North. Our local papers from the *Leavenworth Conservative, The Emporia* and the Lawrence *Herald of freedom*, Topeka *Tribune* reprint these articles, many taken verbatim from the *New York Times*. But I'm learning to be skeptical of military news in the local Herald: because the editor, George W. Brown*, who is no relation to the "Old Captain" nor is he any comparison, writes his editorials slanted in-favor of Governor Robinson's moderate views and seems prejudiced again Lane, the Jay Hawkers and the abolitions' cause.

Two Leavenworth papers, *The Daily Times* and the *Daily Conservative* owned by D. E. Wilder, who father once said was the only gentleman in Leavenworth, favor Lane's strategy and his actions but a letter to the editor by Sara Robinson is critical of General Lane. I like the new but smaller paper *Lawrence Republican* owned by John Speer. In one editorial Mr. Speer compares Jim Lane to one of those old Roman Senators that could debate until he recognized that debate was futile and he would take to the Field of Battle leading the troops.

Added years later, I learned in 1864 or 1865 that Quantrill burned Mr. Speer's newspaper with one of Speer's sons in it. Many years later Adda sent me a book written by John Speer on the life of Jim Lane.

When in 1857 I was able to get a copy of Sara Robinson's book and read it, three or four year ago I was so impressed by the simple fact that she had written it at all. That the subject matter was so significant that it was published not only in Boston; by Crosby, Nichols and Son, in Cincinnati as well and in London. And the volume I bought was the seventh edition, which tells me how interested people are in our affairs out here. She seemed so accurate and indignant in describing the many acts of brutality, fraud, and illegal voting over here by Missourians directly after Congress had created the new territory. Of course, I realize now that her criticisms and like-minded, well-intended abolitionists, incarcerated mainly for their opinions, which were considered treasonous.

* Later he was a co-founder with Preston Plumb of Emporia. Father surveyed part of Emporia

But that was typical of Southern thinking at the time, that if you are against slavery, you are a traitor. Now four years later I think I'll reread her book and try to figure out why she and her husband so often oppose General Lane, when in my opinion they could prosper by endorsing his ideas, particularly his military action in southwest Missouri.

By early October ('61) Lane has written his friend in the White House suggesting that he be put in-charge of the Army west of the Mississippi River with about 10,000 troops. Instead the command went to General Hunter of the "Department of Kansas." The President seemed to be on the horns of a dilemma. He recognized that Lane is a fearless leader…a man of action…but Lane's political enemies also have had the President's ear.

Obviously General Lane believes that the best defense of Eastern Kansas is to take the offense to the enemy nearby and Lane knows where that is and how to do it. Yet, there is always someone to criticize almost everything he does. I guess we are still in the transition to war, where those who initially opposed force, now that we that we are at war, believe there is a moderate way to fight that war. None of them have lived in Kansas for the past six or seven years. If they had, they'd realize that Missouri showed us no moderation or mercy in their form of war and they were, in general, simply proxies for the South. I'm just appalled that the Governor (Robinson) and his wife have joined this "moderate camp", considering that they too, for months were prisoners of war of the "United States" in Lecompton and neither one of them has ever fired a shot either in anger or self-defense.

Among General Lane's lieutenants are Col. Dietzler, Father's old political friend and mentor. He has been active in the Missouri military campaign, as has a Lt. Col. Blunt, another favorite of the General.

By February of 1862 Colonel Blunt has been promoted to Brigadier General. I wouldn't have known about it, if a boarder had not given me a copy of the *Emporia News*, which to my surprise attacks the promotion. It seems to me to be too early to make a judgment.

SEPTEMBER 1862

Mr. Francis, the editor of the Olathe* newspaper was in town today, staying with us at the boarding house. He reports that a band of 200 well-armed and mounted men sacked Olathe yesterday. They took the entire commissary stores, destroyed the printing press and shot two men who resisted them. Mr. Francis says the raider was Quantrill who is also known as Charley Lenhart. I've never heard of Quantrill. The Quantrill raiders captured a Federal (Union) major in the Olathe raid. A Mexican wagon train headed for the Santa Fe Trail was intercepted but not molested by them. Mr. Francis is on his way up to Leavenworth looking for military help.

Several of us asked Mr. Frances, "Who is this Quantrill?" All he knew was that he and his riders are either guerilla fighters, on behalf of the Confederate or they are some sort of Special Force authorized by the Confederates. This editor says they know now it was Quantrill who raided another little town, Liberty, which is east of Olathe in Missouri.

He goes by several aliases: Charlie Lenhart, Charley Hart and Captain Clark.

Mr. Francis believes that Quantrill fought Union soldiers at Wilson's Creek last year and that he was involved in the early skirmishes around Independence. Some say that it was Quantrill, who "took" Independence and captured a company of Union soldiers under Col. Buell. This item he hopes to confirm when he visits Fort Leavenworth this week. Mr. Francis thinks he (Quantrill) is a very young man, maybe as young as twenty-five and must be a very competent leader for his age, even if he's on the wrong side.

* Olathe is about ten miles west of the Kansas-Missouri line and about the same distance south of the Kaw River.

Although I respect his zeal, it's very interesting that it's a newspaper editor going to Fort Leavenworth, looking for military protection. Don't they have a sheriff in Olathe or a mayor to perform this chore? His visit here is disturbing and has upset our housekeeping routine. All the boarders want to hang around and commiserate and gossip with the Olathe editor and the girls keep serving them coffee until it's time to set the tables for the noon meal.

The Olathe editor is back with us for a few days after his call on Fort Leavenworth for help. At breakfast I asked him how things went up there for him. He said he was able to file the facts with the military, as he knew them, They said they would try to send a company down or notify a Kansas militia company in the area to patrol around Olathe.

I said, "General Lane is back here someplace in Eastern Kansas. He's the best person to see, because he's so well connected politically and when he puts on his general's hat, he gets right into the field with old hands like Montgomery and Jennison. Before you go south, why don't you try to see him?

I also suggested that while he's in town, why not visit Governor Robinson's office and "ask the Governor to intercede on your behalf." His response was very strange and sobering. He said, "Governor Robinson was having such problems of his own that his political influence has become compromised." I mentioned that through Adda's working for the Governor's brother and my father's founding of Eldorado that we had held the Governor and his wife in very high regard.

"Well, that may be so, but he's got his own trouble now. The 1861 Legislature authorized the state to borrow several hundred thousand dollars through the sale of bonds. The Governor had contacts with New York Banks and sent the State Treasurer, Mr. Dutton, to New York to negotiate. A friend of the governor, Mr. Robert Stevens somehow got involved with Mr. Dutton. The long and the short of it is they had such trouble selling Kansas State bonds during the war that sizeable discounts, like eighty-five cents on the dollar and probably bribes were resorted to. It's very complicated. There is some reason to believe that with all the people involved, some cash receipts may have been skimmed off by these middlemen. The state accountants are trying to unravel it now, but Governor Robinson is not coming out of it with clean hands. Part of the complication is that our two Senators were needed to approve the terms of the bond sale, so they were asked to look into it. It's turning out that maybe Senator Pomeroy knows more about this than was previously thought."

"Has it been settled?"

"No, but if it isn't by election time, the Governor might not fare too well, because of this bond-mess and the fact that he's been such a public thorn in the side of Senator Lane, who has emerged, so far, clean as a whistle. This is turning out to be an excellent opportunity for Senator Lane to even-up a score or two with his old political adversary."

Well, this was certainly news to me. After we had cleaned-up from the noon meal, I walked over to Mr. Willmarth's bookstore. He sells local and out-of-state newspapers. Maybe he'll have some more clarifying information. At his store I was able to read a few news clippings and political editorials but it's been very complicated. Apparently it's been going on for some time. Though I'm simply not "in" with people who are current with state politics anymore. I'm sure Sumner Rackliffe is familiar with all this but I haven't seen him since the Legislature adjourned this spring.

When the elections heat-up this fall, all this will be front-page news. Speaking of news, Mr. Willmarth has heard that some Republicans in town want Lane to run for Governor... but he thinks Lane's role will be to choose who should run on the Republican ticket against the Governor. We both shared a chuckle when he said, "Well, Mrs. Chase, in this election we won't have any of "them Missouri Pukes" over here voting illegally, will we?"

By November the newspapers lined up along party lines, as well as those that have been pro-Lane, like the Topeka Tribune. The Leavenworth Times favored the Republicans but backed the new candidate, Thomas Carney, who won. As much as I favor General Lane for all he's done for Kansas since it became a territory, I also feel a little sorry for Governor Robinson.

I received a polite note from Jule Johnson thanking me for my time and attention during our visit last month and hoped that she was not a bother in seeking my "good will". I'm afraid that she has taken little heed from my long-winded, but verbal rebuke and advice.

One of the advantages of working in one of the better boarding houses this summer is being able to meet a more interesting clientele. Colonel Jennison, a well known Jayhawker, like General Lane, gave me a personal invitation to a program last evening featuring two speakers: himself and a Captain Hoyt. I wondered if the Captain is related to Benjamin (Hoyt) who also frequently boards here and has offered to be more social with me than I care to be with him. Both speeches were patriotic and tried to explain "our side" of the story.

As the Colonel was getting ready, a stranger sitting next to me said, "In Missouri after Mr. Jennison swept through a county, they called the chimneys standing in the smoking ruins, "Jennison's monuments."

I said to him, "Well, remember Jennison's acts are retaliations for similar raids over here by Missourians from those counties. "I can tell you, from living in Lawrence in 1857, those Missourians and local pro slavers left a few "monuments" over here, as well." Col. Jennison distributed a small "tract" with his speech, which together with the speech, I'll condense into today's journal entry.

He writes: one of the goals of enlisting and training the ex slaves was to afford them an opportunity to live in freedom or through military service earn an honorable position or status in a free society. Ex slaves, liberated by Lane himself, Montgomery, Jennison and other "Jayhawkers" and their raids into Missouri in recent years followed their liberators into cities of Eastern Kansas. Leavenworth already had a Colored population of 1,500 with two churches and a school. And there was a large population of ex slaves in Lawrence and Topeka, for some reason all called "contrabands."

This was a perfect background for General (or was he still a senator?) Jim Lane this year (1862) when he was officially appointed Commissioner of Recruitment for Kansas. He in turn commissioned (then captain) James M. Williams to aid in the recruitment and to begin training the ex slaves, which would be no easy task. Many in our own Union Forces believe to train these recruits for military training was a waste of time because they were simply an inferior people…incapable of being trained for the military.

Authors' note: we've covered this training process in Chapters 57 and 58 since Adda's husband, Captain Graton, was personally involved.

Through August I've been staying with Adda. Graton is with his regiment drilling a company of those ex slaves in Leavenworth.

Adda reports that Graton and his regiment has moved down to Wyandotte (Kansas City.) He has been gone so regularly that I've simply moved back into (my) house with Adda and little Alice.

In mid October two lady friends came by with Mrs. Killam's horse and buggy this afternoon and proposed that we go out towards Wakarusa to a large stand of timber to see if we can find some Hickory nuts. It's late in the fall and we've had some sharp frosts that usually knock down the nuts and make the outer shell come off easily. We found some, but this must be their "off year" They bear more heavily in alternate years. Maybe the big rusty-fluffy-tailed squirrels in that area beat us to the few that the trees bore this year…but by accident we found some excellent, fat, Black Walnuts. Father loved these "hardwoods." He often said that Hickory is hard but resilient, is excellent where strength is required and as for Walnut, he thought Walnut was the most beautiful of wood. That's why furniture and cabinetmakers love it.

We had so many walnut trees up and down the valley at Eldorado that we collected the nuts by the bushel in the fall and ate them in one form or another particularly in candy all winter. Most of the hard wood we cut in our sawmill was walnut. All of the framing, rafter, floor joists, etc. in the big Watts boarding house all came from walnut trees, Jerry Jordon and others cut north of us along the river.

OCTOBER 25ᵀᴴ

Three or four companies of Colored soldiers marched into Lawrence today about 150 of them. They were led by several white officers, two of them on horseback. We believe they are from southwestern Missouri and have been recruited for either the Kansas Militia or the Union Army.

NOVEMBER 9, 1862

In the middle of the night, Wheeler, Graton's employee came down, woke us up for the keys to open the ammunition locker at the shop, knowing the town's people will want it to defend themselves. He said many of the town's men were up and standing guard. A gun salesman from the east reported that a week or so ago Quantrill raided Shawnee about twelve miles east of us, near the river. They killed two men but mainly burned several buildings. General Blunt has authorized our military to seek and kill these guerillas. There was a warning that the Quantrills were coming, but they didn't show up.

Graton came home a few days ago and will return the end of November. His regiment is stationed in Fort Scott…about ninety miles southeast of Lawrence…just inside the Kansas line, though Graton says General Lane wants to move them over to Butler, in the middle of Bates County, Missouri.

Persistent Mr. Slack dropped in on us unannounced two days before Thanksgiving. He said he'd been in Topeka on business and thought he'd come by to see me. It was mid morning. Graton was in the parlor working on some Army documents, at an ugly roll-top desk that he really should have installed in his gun shop. I thought I could entertain Mr. Slack (who is several years older than Graton) in the parlor if we didn't speak too loudly.

I asked him if he ever bought the new threshing machine that he was looking at in Topeka in April and yes, he had ordered it and was here to take delivery. He was mildly upset that he missed having it for the fall harvest.

But we did disturb the Captain and he gruffly and rudely suggested we continue our conversation in the kitchen, where he said, derisively, giving my guest the impression that he owned this house and was the master of it, "where you usually entertain your…" and he let his voice trail off. Mr. Slack suggested we walk over to the Whitney House for a cup of coffee, which we did. But Graton's behavior spoiled what might have been a pleasant call… at least pleasant for Mr. Slack, because I have no romantic interest there. Nevertheless, I was offended enough by Graton's rudeness that I felt a need to explain that my sister, who was married to the Captain, and I bought this house free and clear before their marriage and that Captain Graton was home for a few days on leave from his regiment. It was important to me personally that Mr. Slack know these facts. I guess I didn't want him to think that I was living in my brother-in-law's house at his indulgence.

The day after Mr. Slack's visit, while Graton was still on leave, I asked Adda if she'd "had it out" with him yet. I was referring to her warning him that if his threats didn't stop and if he wouldn't stop seeing Jule, every time he's in town, she would use her political contacts to inform those in control of his Army career of his sordid behavior.

She said they had started to have a gruff exchange over Mr. Slack's visit because I had brought him into the parlor while he was writing his reports. Adda said she thought that this would be as good a time as any to tell him of her intentions. "At first he was incredulous, that I could even think of hatching such a humiliating scandal that would cause his superiors to reprimand him, possibly demote him or to perhaps question his moral right to command, considering his sordid behavior towards his wife and child.

It was obvious that he was concerned that what I might have to say to Governor Robinson might put his commission in question. I don't think he ever doubted my resolve to get this put to rest, once and for all.

Then he sat down, became very quiet and conceded that we should stop the quarreling, etc." Adda said that would be a good start, but that the core cause of their trouble was his brazen, shameless carrying on with Jule Johnson and the effect it was having on the stability of our marriage. This absolutely must stop, she told him. She said she wanted his solemn promise that he would end, terminate, stop this affair with Jule. And if she found the slightest evidence that it didn't end, she would do as threatened and swiftly.

On the last day of November Graton left to catch the stage back to Fort Scott. Although he had been back about ten days, he hasn't spent all that time at home. Two or three days before he left I noticed a change in him He seemed to be less abrasive with me. I wondered if it was from my sister's ultimatum. Adda told him about the Quantrill scare and that Mr. Wheeler had come by for the shop keys to the ammunition locker.

After he left, Adda showed me an undated note she found in his uniform pocket as she was ironing it. The note was from "Jule" to her husband and it is full of rather immature romantic ideas about herself and Graton. This situation is particularly upsetting, since we've known this family on and off for several years. We've considered Jule a friend. She has visited us irregularly ever since Adda and I moved back here two years ago and bought the house, and we had stayed in-touch with her while I was in Eldorado and they worked together at the Whitney House, and until I dismissed her, she worked for me at Killam's.

Adda asked me if I thought Graton had deliberately left Jule's letter in his jacket pocket to taunt her.

She added, "After our discussion, I don't think so. I think he simply forgot that it had been in his pocket for some time." We both speculated whether he had received this note in the mail while he was in Fort Scott or whether she had given it to him during this recent visit. He has been home almost two weeks, so he had plenty of time to explain to Jule, Adda's demand.

Of course, I've known about some of his dalliances before they were married when he was taking his meals at the Whitney House (here in Lawrence.) Jule was a part-time worker and a cute little employee. But I had never passed this information or my suspicions on to Adda until last April when the two of us had our long talk about her deteriorating marriage and the cause of it.

I said to Adda I had to get over to the boarding house, "Tuesday is laundry day, but before I go, let me give you a suggestion to think about. You have your husband's address in Fort Scott. Consider returning Jule's note to him that you found in his uniform jacket. Tell him where you found it and when, but that's all. It will certainly be a cause for him to worry as to what you are up to. He has made your life miserable for a year and now his knowing that you found this note, after your talk with him, will cause him no little concern." Father used to say that when you discover that your politeness and consideration has been interpreted as weakness and has eroded respect for you, you need to change your tactic to regain that respect by creating enough fear to serve your purposes. It wouldn't hurt your inconsiderate husband to experience a little fear and uncertainty from a source more personally threatening than his Rebel enemy. Your husband's self-esteem derives from what he has done professionally and who he is, or who he thinks he is, or who others think he is. If his moral authority to command a Company in the U. S. Army were put in question by his superiors or worse, threatened, it would be such a blow to his self-esteem, he'd never get over it. Your ultimation is the first step in all this and he knows it."

Well, now Adda knows a lot more about her husband. I suspect that Jule has been more of a source of tension between the two of them than his personal conflicts between duty and business.

Since the last of November, Graton's been gone and when I'm not working, I'm home with Adda. Working or not, I sleep here.

123

Mr. Killam, my employer's husband is chronically ill and Mrs. Killam really resents having to take care of him, which seems strange to me. He was originally from Concord (New Hampshire), the same city where Chase's family lives. He plans to go back there and see if he can recover his health. He hasn't looked well for months. I have my doubts that he is strong enough to make the trip.

I've written a long letter to Mother Chase in Concord, bringing her up-to-date about Adda and myself and will ask Mr. Killam to carry it back to her with him.

We are getting up a party to go over to Shawnee to spend Christmas with friends, some who have moved there from Lawrence. Jule's two sisters, Ruby and Eliza Johnson, both friends of ours, had been attending school in the East, have just returned for the holidays and will go with us. I gave some serious thought about the wisdom of visiting Shawnee. Just a few weeks ago (October 26th to be exact) Joe Mader came back from there to report that raiders the day before, killed at least two people and burned houses there. I asked him if he thought the raiders were Quantrills. He said he didn't know. But in the end I decided to take my chances. I knew I'd be lonely on New Year's Day in Lawrence.

I persuaded the Rackliffes to join our party. I rode the entire nine miles... horseback on Old Kate, which we've been keeping in a local livery.

NOVEMBER 26TH 1862

Graton's home and is rather pleased with himself. He reports that Union officers have "reviewed" his Colored troops and their records. As Kansas's militiamen they will be "paid off" and will be mustered into the U. S. Army. Some of them have been in the militia for a year, since their recruitment. He considered their acceptance by the U. S. Army to be a personal vindication as well as a credit to his troops.

Another letter arrived from Jule Johnson just before we left for Shawnee, asking that I pay her a visit. She wants my advice about going to California in the springtime. Hmmm? Maybe she is tiring of playing "second fiddle" to Adda. Or maybe, just maybe, Graton has decided that his family stability and the respect and self-esteem that comes with his commission are more important than Jule's company and he has finally, under that pressure, explained all that to her. If she has an ounce of conscience, it must bother her that she's been "dabbling" with the husband of an old friend. Maybe my frank talk with this young woman is having/has had some effect on her behavior.

In Shawnee before Christmas we all went sleigh riding. The men hired a sleigh so big it required four horses. The snow out on the prairie and down in the little draws was marvelous. It was a little cold but we had buffalo robes, etc. Got back in the afternoon. Then we took the sleigh four or five miles down to the Alexander's for supper. There was a very large turn out, mostly people from Lawrence that Adda and I know. We didn't get back to Shawnee 'til very late.

Those of us from Lawrence hired a hack and headed home New Year's Day (arrived at 3AM), but we couldn't leave before celebrating the New Year's midnight with the Shawnee crowd. It's a strange new 1863 with the war swirling all around us with Shawnee much closer to Missouri than Lawrence.

On the way back to Lawrence we were stopped and questioned by a squad of camped Union soldiers guarding the road. They had built a large bonfire. They searched the hack and questioned the driver. These were young soldiers from back East, so they really didn't know much about Lawrence and they couldn't identify any of us. Actually their questions were rather stupid but they had the guns and their orders and they were not going to let us continue on the road north. Our hack driver, about Father's age, normally drove stagecoaches. He got down off the wagon and speaking politely, but with authority, persuaded the guards that we were all abolitionists...pro-Union, some were wives of soldiers currently fighting in Missouri and that we had all been living in Lawrence for some time. Finally they allowed us to pass.

When I got home, Adda was there. For some strange reason she had moved many of her things into my room and had obviously been using my bed. I asked her why in the world would she move out of her bedroom, but got no answer, but strange behavior.

I said, "If you moved out of your room, I'm curious to know what use you are making of it and where do you expect me to sleep, when I'm here?"

She physically resisted me when I wanted to "inspect" her room. Finally I got her door open and saw a man in her bed and it wasn't her husband...it was Mr. Frame from Eldorado. I asked Adda for an explanation.

She said the poor man arrived a day or two ago on "death's door" and asked if he could stay with her 'til he got well. "Of course," she said, "but I had to put him somewhere. We've only got two beds, so I decided to do what I did and I hoped you'd understand."

All the while she worried that her husband would return and fly into a jealous range upon finding Mr. Frame in "our bed", never mind that he's old enough to be her father.

The neighbors keep chickens, which supplies the neighborhood with eggs. We trade them milk for the few eggs that Adda and I use. I asked one of them if they had two old hens that haven't been laying, explaining that we had a sick man on our hands.

She "rung the necks" of two rather scrawny White Leghorns. We all pitched into pluck, but since we were going to make soup, I said it would go faster if we just skinned them. With a few pulls here and there chickens skin very easily and old hens make the best stew or soup, though it would have been tastier if we'd saved the skin.

Well in a few days with some nice homemade chicken soup and boiled vegetables, we got Mr. Frame on his feet. On Wednesday he left for Shawnee. He didn't say what was over there for him. We had so many visitors I really didn't get a chance to get a report on the status of Eldorado from him before he left. But thank god he left before Adda's husband returned.

Well, the old year went, and good riddance. We'll see what the New Year brings.

The Leavenworth *Territorial Register* says in headlines that it's official. President Lincoln has issued a decree to free all slaves: called the Emancipation Proclamation. I find it rather interesting that the President has now made official what General Fremont did some months ago and was rebuked for it. I guess in politics it's a matter of *who does it as well as when it's done.* We've been expecting the decree for some months now, but it's my opinion that any slave in Southern Iowa or Missouri who wanted freedom only needed the ambition to run away, get across the Missouri River or walk across the border south of Wyandotte into Kansas, as did hundreds of them.

A few days before Valentine's Day a soldier in uniform came by, said he was delivering mail from Fort Scott and insisted on hand delivering a letter to Adda. Until she opened it, she said she feared it was bad news. It was a two-page letter from her husband dated January 10 written in or sent from Fort Scott, Kansas. She read it quietly, and then handed it to me, saying in a rather puzzled voice that perhaps the change that we had hoped for in her husband is slowly happening.

I read the letter, looking for an affectionate word or two, but instead, the letter sounded more like he was writing to an old business partner, but his letter was at least free of animosity or acrimony. It was also totally free of affection or tender regards for his wife, the mother of his child...In fact, he didn't even inquire as to how the child might be.

Adda and he have speculated in property here in Lawrence and had made an offer to buy a vacant city lot next to the Cincinnati House, using Mr. Burt as their negotiator. The amount they offered was less than what the owner wanted, which was $1,200. In the letter Graton didn't think the lot was worth that but "authorized" Adda to continue the negotiations; that any reasonable offer she made would be all right with him.

Graton writes that he expects to get paid soon, that his Company is down to seventy men due to casualties and desertions and he is looking for another eleven to get his Company to full strength. He said he was relieved that his Colored troops are getting $13.00 per month, the same pay as a White soldier. This was an earlier source of grievance but General Lane has championed equal pay for all ranks. He says that General Blunt had reviewed his Company (on January 8th) as they marched in the pubic square someplace over in Missouri. He presumed that scene must have been very galling to the local (Missouri) inhabitants to see Colored troops in full uniform marching smartly, obeying commands, all the while being reviewed by a general of the Union Army in a rabidly pro slavery state. Indeed, he writes, some of my soldiers, probably in previous months, were slaves in these very counties.

During the review, Graton writes that a soldier, obviously a White one in the Regular Army, was overhead by Colonel Williams to have made a disparaging remark about "Nigger soldiers have finally figured out which foot is right and which foot is left." Graton says that soldier will spend a few days in the guardhouse.

Graton reports that General Blunt at dinner gave a speech, praising the performance of the Colored troops of their regiment. He says he received a New Years gift from Governor Robinson in the form of an engraved document, his formal commission.

He says he doesn't know how long it will be before he can come home and straighten up his business. He wishes he could send Adda some of their coffee in that he has at least thirty pounds more than he needs. He's been selling his surplus (food) supplies locally to raise money to help his sick and wounded troops.

In closing he promises to write a love letter next time and signed it Captain John R. Graton 1st Reg. C.T (Colored Troops.) The letter had been dated January 10th 1863. He probably doesn't remember leaving the note Jule gave him that Adda found in his jacket pocket a few weeks ago before he left for Fort Scott.

Early Winter 1863

*Adda at 40 years of Age (1881- She had been widowed nine years)
Taken while she was visiting relatives in Rochester, NY. Husband:
Captain John Graton had organized a company of Colored Soldiers
(ex slaves) and fought twelve Civil War battles from November
1862 to March 1865. He died the summer of 1872 of a lingering
illness contracted during the war.*

60.

GOING TO COLORADO

Spring 1863

Mary Rackliffe and her two children have been staying with us here in Lawrence. They came up with Tom Cordis, the blacksmith not long after Mary's husband, Sumner died. The last time I saw him was the Monday before New Years here in Lawrence. Though he looked too bad to travel, and I told him so, he left nevertheless for Eldorado on a cold and windy New Years Day. So he must have died some place west of here on the California Trail. In February Mary had written to say she had sold their claim in Eldorado, which increased her "nest egg" from the proceeds of the cattle sale they made two summer's ago. She said that she'd been offered a job as chief cook for a mining camp near Pike's Peak.

While Mary has been here, she's been busy packing, planning and buying last minute stuff. According to her, Tom Cordes' blacksmithing has been so slow (in Eldorado) that they too are planning on going west; it's either the Rockies or California. Mary has suggested that four of us "old abolitions" all go out together in early spring.

Mid March Elizabeth Cordis arrived. With Mary and her children here we didn't have room for them, so they have been staying at a boarding house nearby. Tom is very busy making arrangement for going west. They've decided to try their hand at ranching, hoping to stake a claim on the high plains east of the Rockies, though Tom will let his neighbors know that he's a blacksmith. Several of our evening meals, when Adda and I could entertain our old friends were just delightful. Adda seemed to be her old self again with Mary and Elizabeth.

I'm ambivalent about such a trip, though Lord knows other than (my share) of our house here in Lawrence, there's not much holding me here. Two men have persistently plagued me to marry them, but I'm unimpressed with either, though Mr. Slack is the more substantial of the two. Only lately has Mr. Benjamin Hoyt revealed that he'd been married before. His wife died not long after their wedding, so he was in the same fix as…yours truly, except he says his major reason that I should marry him is that I resemble his dear departed wife. I've told him repeatedly that that is an inadequate reason for him…yet he persists.

I guess I finally made up my mind to go west on April Fools Day. Oh, I made plans and actually packed things I'd need out there, but I waited 'til the last minute to decide, yes. Father always said, "Don't make a decision 'til you have to."

But Tom Cordis and Elizabeth are certainly going and have been staying with us on and off while making their preparations, which included an arrangement for us to travel with a west bound outfit. Some of them are Colorado bound. The train will be a mix of Midwesterners including several from Eastern Kansas that have the gold fever…Tom claims there will be twenty-five or thirty wagons.

He had purchased a heavy-duty wagon and two horses, which meant we had to carry grain for them. If he had chosen oxen; yes, they would have been slower, but they graze, unyoked early in the morning and evening, and can subsist entirely on trail grass. The problem is they all want to leave before there's enough grass for oxen, so we'll use horses.

Ten days before we were to leave Mary Rackliffe's children took sick.

We called in Dr. Lewis, who said both children had whooping cough. I took him and Mary to one side and said we can't leave these children here with Adda and her baby. Dr. Lewis agreed. He said he had built a one-room cabin to use as a clinic at their place and he offered to take Mary, Ermee and the little boy (whose name I don't know) with him.

Before they left with Dr. Lewis,, Elizabeth volunteered to go out in Mary's place if she could "catch" the coach, which she did, though the driver complained about her "excess" luggage. The arrangement was that she would only cook until either Mary or I arrived to relieve her.

Mr. Hutchinson agreed to drive Mary and the children later, using his two oxen, since oxen can get along without grain, so long as there is plenty of grass. After the children recovered, they waited until they were sure that there would be available grass all the way, which would be late spring. They too, came out with an organized train.

While I was deciding what I would need in the Mountains, Adda said that she thought she would try to get down to Fort Scott to be able to visit Graton more often. Even though his regiment had been ordered off to some battle south of the fort, she thought he'd be able to get off occasionally, much the same way he was he was able to get away from his duties at Fort Leavenworth on and off all last year. Adda said that Mrs. Bowles, the wife of Colonel Bowles of Lawrence and her children, are there and she would be good company.

"Adda, where is Fort Scott?"

"It's about ninety miles southeast of us, just inside the Kansas line."

Tom Cordis and I left Lawrence on April 2nd for the Colorado Mountains. Driving past Fort Leavenworth we went through Oskaloosa to Atchison, where we bought some grain for the horses and other last minute supplies, and waited. Where Lawrence has always been a headquarters city for the Free-Stators and abolitionists, Atchison and the personnel at Fort Leavenworth have always been the settlements for those favoring slavery and other Southern sentiments, so I wasn't too anxious to spend much time there. It has in recent years become a place where westbound outfits stop, reorganize, buy supplies and take on more wagons (like us.)

Tom had made arrangements for us to rendezvous in Atchison with a west bound wagon train made up of Kansans as well as an eastern outfit that had crossed the river at Council Bluffs, intending to meet us in Atchison. In this way three days were consumed.

We estimated that we had a load of 1500 pounds, including two trunks of mine but most of the load was Tom's blacksmithing equipment including his forge, anvils and the tools of his trade.

We traveled generally west until we dropped into the deep ruts of the Platte River Trail, which is part of the Overland Trail, day after day crossing the flat, slightly undulating Nebraska prairie, where the blue sky melds with the horizon. We were usually within sight of the muddy, shallow, snake-infested Platte River in which flows absolutely undrinkable water; well, I guess the horses and oxen can drink it. Thank goodness we had plenty of water with us! The trail was littered with cast-off junk, mostly, I suppose, from the forty-niners and all those other thousands that have used this trail, particularly for the last fifteen years.

When those of us Colorado-bound reached a spot near Julesburg, in Nebraska territory, we picked up a southwest-bound trail and followed it until we arrived at the two communities of Aurora and Denver separated by Cherry Creek...exactly where my darling husband was five years ago, the summer of 1858.

When Chase was here, this was a small tent city of miners. Since then over 100,000 adventurers have flocked to Colorado with one-fourth of them remaining in this area on one side or the other of Cherry Creek. Now in 1863 Aurora is well developed. Streets are all laid out with commercial buildings or houses on both sides and is competing for growth and prominence with

Denver on the other side. I understand that the local population is 3,000.

I told Tom before we moved on that I wanted to visit the spot where Cherry Creek meets the Platte River's South Fork. Chase said that was the most active and productive-of-gold area when he was here.

We arrived in the Denver area a month after we started and we looked for the Cherry Creek settlement, to discover that the locals call it Aurora, which I know now was named by four professional gold mining brothers after a town in Georgia, where gold had been discovered and mined until it gave out. They were not farmers or merchants but I was to learn in the nine or ten months, while I was in Colorado, these were very clever and successful miners. By the time they got to the Eastern Rockies, they had already been among the thousands, mostly Southerners, in the California Gold Rush, starting in 1849. They spent at least two successful summers there.

When the Russell party reached the intersection of Cherry Creek and the Platte in 1858, they had 104 people, 19 Georgians, 27 from Missouri. The largest group was from the Cherokee Nation (due south of Kansas Territory.) By July no gold to speak of was found and the Cherokees voted to go home. Soon there were others of the party who wanted to go back. The Russells were down to thirty persons. Before the summer was over, they were down to thirteen. That very day they found gold in a gravel sand bar. Green Russell knew placer gold had its source in the mountains. Six of them spent ten days at or near the headwaters of the Platte River.

Now that I know more about this famous mining family, I can connect the events when their party came up from the Cherokee Nation and into Eldorado in the early summer of 1858, and leaving on May 22nd, using the Santa Fe Trail part way. At that time I was more concerned about losing Chase to these fellows than I was about their enterprise but that was the summer that Chase stubbornly ignored my pleading and came out here anyway, though I believed at the time he had traveled with a group, not intending to mine but to layout a city and prosper by selling town lots, what many of them stupidly called, "seeing the elephant".

Once we arrived in the Aurora settlement, Tom and I made our "goodbyes" to our traveling outfit and found lodging in a boarding house, bought a few supplies and asked around for the best route to the Tarryall area.

With all the people coming and going it didn't take long to get instructions from two miners we met with claims on Snyder Creek and Jefferson Creek in the Tarryall area in town for a day or two. Their suggestions turned out to be as interesting as they were complicated.

First we were told there are three different trails to Tarryall, all leading generally southwest into the eastern slopes of the Rockies. But going there from Denver/Aurora they all come together as the canyons get deeper, unless, as they say you want to go "way around" to the southeast and arrive at Tarryall from the south. These three trails or routes all come together at the beginnings of a generally south-west high pass in the eastern most mountain range called Kenosha Pass.

According to these miners Kenosha Pass is the most direct, but difficult route.

They told us that we are actually going to an area called South Park, which contains several small gold mining settlements that aren't as active now as they were "before." Tarryall is just one of them. Como, founded by some Italians, is nearby, as is Hamilton on one side of Tarryall Creek. Buckskin Joe, Fairplay…these are all close by and reachable after you negotiate the famous pass. They said streambed mining is "going out". Maybe 50% of this year's gold comes from streambed gravel. The rest is all coming from tunnels going deeper, using drilling techniques and blasting power. Miners from the old country have emerged as leaders of that work.

When I told our informants that our first stop would be the Kenosha House, one of the miners scrutinized me more closely and asked why I'd be going there.

I said I had a job-offer to cook there or nearby for some miners. "Why do you ask?"

"Well, Kenosha House is sort of a first rate road house, right on the trail. It's where the Denver to Pike's Peak stage stops, gets fresh horses, if needed and stage passengers can get a good meal and a night's lodging.

Harriman's place is known for its good meals, fresh butter, and fresh milk. They even serve Rocky Mountain trout, when they're available. These two miners said they'd had supper there a few days ago on their way up here, adding that several local miners take board and room there. In fact, one outfit is digging a tunnel or mine shaft almost directly under the hotel.

It was built by George Harriman…from Kenosha, Wisconsin. He built it and he owns it. He's an "all round fella: miner, builder, hotel operator, rancher who's been purty successful."

These fellows warned that we'd better make sure our horses were well shod. The trails would be rocky and hard on both the animals and our wagon. We were also warned that if we saw Indians camped on one side of the river on our way to Tarryall, not to be alarmed. They were usually peaceful. In fact, our informants said they would probably want to do some trading with us.
They have a right to stretch a net across the stream or river and since it's summer, if you want fresh trout, they'll have some in a little pond, they've cleverly dammed up to keep their fish alive.

The morning after our session with the two Tarryall miners, Tom said he wanted to find a blacksmith. He was concerned about the iron tires on our wheels and he wanted to take a good look at the shoes of the two horses.

I said, "Good, I'll mosey around Aurora this morning and if I can find a way to get over there, I'll go inspect Denver. You know, Chase was involved in naming that town and they didn't do it here. They did it over dinner in Lecompton with the new Territorial Governor, James Denver. Maybe I'll pick up some newspapers at that Rocky Mountain News office, so we can catch up on the war back East. I told Tom I'd like to find a market and buy as many bushels of fresh vegetables that we can comfortably carry. We agreed to meet for supper at our boarding house.

In the back of my mind, I was mildly curious to see if I could bump into Mr. Eastwood. I wondered if he ever got our sorghum mill up and running out here. I also understand there is a sawmill here abouts. I wouldn't be surprised if he wouldn't be bossing that. It would have to have a boiler.

I easily located the Rocky Mountain News, which is run by a local character, Bill Byers. I spoke to one of the young writers there from Brooklyn, New York, who had written a several page tract on the history of the Green Russell party. I bought two of them for ten cents each. It turns out he's also written a tract on John Gregory, who made the big strike at Central City, due west of us some forty miles. I bought two of those also. Gregory, a Georgian, he said was with the party of Green Russell in '58.

I asked the young editor if a Mr. Eastwood with a Scotch accent had ever placed ads for local whiskey and I explained our transaction.

He said he didn't handle advertizing but when he saw that I was interested in the Russell party, he invited me inside a little enclosure where two or three people were either writing or standing setting type.

They had a pot-bellied stove, warm and he invited me to a cup of tea, even though I thought it was a rather warm day for tea, and proceeded to tell me things he said may or may not be in the Russell tract.

When I told him my husband had been in this very area of Aurora and that he had come out in '58 in a party that had joined the Green Russell group, when it came up to Eldorado from the Cherokee Nation. He asked me for particulars about Chase and his party and began leafing through sheets of papers containing names that he's collected from the various groups that have come out here annually since 1858. He has a list of over 150 names.

"The same summer your husband was out here, the Russell boys with their two or three successful years of mining in California, had surveyed enough of this area and were experienced enough to realize that almost any of the stream-fed gulches that had a mountain source, was likely to bear gold. But they also realized that this mountainous area, stretching from (today's) City of Boulder south to Pike's Peak and inland to at least the first range, needed a population of 50,000, maybe 100,000 people to explore, exploit and develop...some of them miners and others to service the miners and the mines...and the Russells intended to prosper from both.

Late in the summer of 1858, intending to give the impression that gold was so plentiful that they could be generous to one of their kind who was returning to eastern Kansas, the Russell Brothers gave John Cantrell a small pouch of gold gratis and enough cash to cover his expenses to the Missouri.

In the Leavenworth area Cantrell bragged about so much gold in the Rockies that the Russell boys had given him a pouch full of it.

I said, "That name is vaguely familiar. I remember first reading in our papers in the fall of 1859 about him, then articles about him were carried in the St. Louis Democrat; even the New York Times." The young writer said that news and a few others sparked the rush out here that year and every year since then. The results are, we accommodate one hundred newcomers a day.

That and tales of other returning prospectors began the rush out here to the Kansas Gold Fields and the Pike's Peak area, as the area was then called. Gold was the "pull". By 1858 the U.S., particularly the northeast, was suffering from an economic "panic". So, the depression of '58 helped create the "push". The young editor said he got "laid off" in the summer of 1858 when advertising revenue at his New York newspaper dropped sharply. That's why he was here, he said.

The railroads had expanded too fast and too far.

Their stocks and affiliated businesses had become priced so high their profit could not sustain them. The bubble broke and many transportation companies and enterprises that supported them went bankrupt, as did scores of eastern banks. Unemployment soared. Many of those unemployed responded to the call of gold in the Rockies. That depression lasted until 1862 when war preparations or enlistments soaked up the unemployed.

When the Russell boys went back to Georgia in the fall of 1858, they brought their Rocky Mountain gold to a local mint in Dahlonega, which was in the county where they lived. That was the first Colorado gold to be minted as U.S. coins and it was minted in Georgia.

I told him of the Osage Indians in Kansas and asked who were the original Indians out here. He said in Eastern Colorado, including these mountains it was, it is, the Arapahoe and the Cheyenne, and White men are viewed as squatters by them. Some early miners, realizing their presence might not be appreciated by the natives, immunized themselves from Indian threats by marrying Indian women. In that way they could validate ownership of their claims by passing such ownership through to their wives. A Mr. McGaa of Aurora did exactly that. (Early Aurora honored him by naming a street after him.)

It was his theory that the gold "bubble" based on streambed panning and general placer mining has burst, but gold is found in such abundance that it's only worth $20 an ounce. He said that, what you'll see now on the slopes of every mountainside in these parts are tunnels. The miners now are mostly looking for quartz veins by digging back into the mountainsides and chiseling into hard rock and blasting their way to gold It's a lot more work than mining the streams and…in his opinion…so far seems to be just as productive.

"The people making the money today are the blasting powder salesmen".

He asked me if I knew Messers Clark and Gruber from Leavenworth. I said, "No, I hadn't heard of them."

Well, they came out here two years ago, first to broker and freight gold, but soon began their own mint, using dies from Philadelphia. And he handed me a copy of their newspaper article telling about the Denver ten dollar and twenty dollar gold pieces minted by this private Denver mint. It was his opinion that they bought and minted about half the gold discovered here since then.

He said other areas are now or have also minted Colorado gold: one in Tarryall, where you're going, and another one in Gregory Gulch near Breckenridge also, not far from Tarryall.

Last year government sources said, "Colorado produced over 200,000 ounces and they are predicting about that same amount this year."

When I asked what happened to the Clark and Gruber mint, he said the U. S. Government bought them out last year.

I thanked the gentleman from New York and said I'd try to get someone to row me across to Denver.

He laughed and said, "You'll find the creek so low right now you'll be able to walk across on several logs of varying size lying in the creek. You'll see others using that as an easy place to walk across without getting your feet wet. It's only a few yards from us at the end of this street."

I found several grocery stores near us, made my purchases, which they promised to deliver to our boarding house. I got back before Tom, which gave me time before supper to digest the two tracts I'd purchased at the Rocky Mountain News. and read several editions of their papers, which I intend to keep and use as journal entries dealing with local information.

It's my impression that there is much more business and organization on the Aurora side of the creek. They had had a serious fire in the business section of Blake Street last month.

I hadn't realized that Colorado was now a territory, well twelve counties anyway. They'll have their problems with statehood, but slavery won't be one of them.

The Russell boys annually returned to the Eastern Rockies from '58 to '63 in the early summer always bringing with them a traveling contingency. Some were experienced miners, some journeymen carpenters, blacksmiths, lawyers and tradesmen of all stripes. Many of the Russell volunteers, as they came out in 1858 and subsequent years had become unemployed by the economic depression in the East.

The May 17th edition of the Rocky Mountain News announced their return in 1859. They had seven wagons full of supplies, oxen, mules, etc.

More miners were enticed here when Eastern reporters visited the mining sites and wrote about it. Horace Greely, editor of the New York Tribune came out himself. He saw the fortunes (a few) miners were making. He gave well-attended speeches in 1859. Not all in the audience were impressed. Greely was an out-spoken abolitionist. Many in the audience were Southerners with their own prejudices.

At Gregory Gulch in 1859 there were seventy-five sluices in operation and individual miners working their claims, panning, often in the water. It wasn't unusual to take $5.00 per pan. One in five men were taking out $125 a day…a little over six ounces.

That September Dr. Levi Russell with a companion went home by stagecoach. He had studied medicine in Philadelphia and had a practice in Aurora in the summer, as reported by the Rocky Mountain News.

According to this tract, one year, when they went back to Georgia, Green and his brothers used a boat to go down Cherry Creek to hook up with the Platte, hoping to go on it all the way to the Missouri with a current of six miles per hour. They've been called the Green Russell outfit. The oldest and most experienced of them was named Greenberry, which was shortened to Green. The Russells had intermarried with Cherokees, a tribe that was originally in Georgia. Green Russell was married to a Cherokee woman.

Freight rates on supplies into the Rockies were $6/100 wt. (or 6¢/#). Rates on the plains were one-fourth that. When the railroads came in, rates fell to 12¢ to 24¢/100 wt.

In 1859 with the news of gold in the Rockies and unemployment in the East, 100,000 scurried to Colorado in 1859 (K.T.)…only 25,000 did any mining.

This immigration continued through to the eve of the Civil War. By then there were 300 to 400 gold camps in the Eastern Rockies…all within a western semi-circle with a radius of 35 miles, radiating out from Denver.

The Russell Brothers had invested in sawmills and by 1860 there were two: one in Downeyville and the other in Franktown, but the lumber wasn't very good, almost lacking in hardwoods, like maple, oak and walnut, which was available in Kansas and Eldorado.

_____ 0 _____

Last year Oliver and Green decided to take float boats down the Platte River to where they hoped to catch a stage coach for Fort Leavenworth. They had a quantity of gold, some of it hidden in quills of an Arapahoe costume they had purchased from the Indians intending to take it home as a souvenir. They changed coaches uneventfully in Fort Leavenworth; pressing on for St. "Joe" where Green Russell unbraided his whiskers to look more like a Northerner, maybe even to be mistaken for an abolitionist. At St. Joseph, Missouri, they hoped to get passes through Union lists (by then Missouri was declared, "Union" and Union troops were generally in control. They transferred their gold into some bags containing spare horseshoes. They reached Tennessee (through Kentucky) and on to North Carolina.

When, with a Kentucky guide, they arrived home, they discovered some of their kin had enlisted with the Confederates. Georgia had suffered terribly during the war, but the Russells had been careful, quiet and frugal with their gold. They decided to leave the state.

Green and his wife wanted to return to Colorado to their claims, their investments and get back to placer mining.

_____ 0 _____

Leaving Aurora/Denver, Tom and I traveled south-southwest in the foothills being careful to pick up the correct well-traveled trail. We asked other travelers going in both directions to make sure we were on the right road. In that area there were several, all well marked and some were "licensed" toll trails. We followed our chosen trail maybe thirty miles to a little camp called Platte Place on a small lake and marshy area and spent the night there in a rather humble but adequate boarding house. Turning generally west we continued on the same trail along the south fork of the Platte with steep mountains on both sides. We continued to climb on a fairly well traveled but rocky and rough road.

Bare mountain cliffs were rising almost vertically on our left with other snow-covered peaks a short distance to the north of us. I used the word peak. This general area is called Pike's Peak (after Zebulon Pike). Actually we are some distance from Pike's Peak Mountain, which is southeast of us maybe twenty-five to thirty miles.

We continued to gain in elevation as the trail turned west and into a deep valley with clear swift water running in the creek on one side of us. Every half hour or so we stopped to give the horses a rest.

After about eight to ten miles the trail winds southwest through ever-steeper mountains whose bare, stone cliffs seemed to be closing in on us from both sides. We continued to climb on a fairly well traveled but very rocky road with no alternative but to bend and climb southwest again. (We learned later this was the famous Kenosha Pass. And we were successfully navigating it.)

We speculated without realizing it that this might be the headwaters of the south fork of the Platte River.

As we began to go down hill but still in the very heart of these high mountains, we arrived at a rather impressive two-story building. Tom parked his team in front of a wide porch of a fairly new building. Hanging from a heavy beamed lintel high above the steps was a sign, "Kenosha House-Elevation 10,000 feet." Tom had hardly gotten the horses tied to the rail when a gentleman came out and asked him to move our rig to make room for the Evening Stage Coach, which they were expecting.

At the Kenosha House, Tom's wife, Elizabeth, who had left Lawrence ahead of us by stage, when Mary Rackliffee's children took sick, was cooking for a company of eleven miners. So, we had a fine reunion.

The "House" furnished the provisions and paid her a dollar a week for every miner that "sits down" at the supper meal. Of course, she gets her board and room (though the "room is simply a small area separated from the kitchen by a canvas flap.) There was no furniture in her room. A washbasin sits on a two-foot high cottonwood stump. That's it, and no windows.

In an establishment as large and impressive as the Kenosha House, I was surprised to learn that Elizabeth had furnished her own stove and dishes. (Where did Elizabeth get the stove, I wondered. She sure didn't carry it on that crowded coach.) When Tom and I left Eldorado, we bought Mary Rackliffe's fancy stove, the new one with the little Izsing glass window in the door that I admired at Christmas over four years ago, when she delivered little Ermee. Elizabeth Cordis was the skilled mid-wife on that delivery and I was her apprentice.

Elizabeth said if I stayed, I could have most of her dishes, but I'd have to find my own stove. (I wished then, if I'd known about this strange custom, I'd brought out that second stove that I bought to keep Graton happy.)

Although she and Tom had planned all along as soon as he arrived, to leave and locate land for a cattle ranch on the high plains east of here, she had given Mr. Harriman, the owner; notice that she'd be leaving as soon as I arrived. But she warned them that I might not stay for these paltry wages.

I seized that opportunity to say that I'd stay, but not on a head-count basis. The miners said, since they paid the bills, they wanted to be in on the negotiations, so I figured I would need to bargain with these fellows, but I would wait a few hours before supper when they would be good and hungry. I let it be known that I had with me several fresh buffalo tongues packed in snow, which when boiled, is the best part of the buffalo. They all knew that because they saw Tom and I unload all the fresh vegetables, including several bushels of potatoes, Irish and sweet. carrots, onions, 50# of white corn for hominy, etc., I brought all I could reasonably carry, which I had purchased in Aurora.

Just before supper, while the meat and vegetables were cooking and you could smell it, the negotiating group came in. Mr. Harriman, who's about one generation older than me (37 years) was with them. He wanted to meet me and intended to take supper with the miners and a few overnight coach passengers. He had heard about the vegetables.

We quickly arrived at $40 per month independent of the number of boarders with a (mutual) term that I'd stay at least until fall when several of the miners will leave for the winter, which I understand is a custom in this area.

A few days after our arrival, the Cordises decided they would move on to find a ranch site before it got too late in the summer to put in seed corn. Elizabeth and Tom intend to buy or homestead for a ranch, to begin buying very young calves to fatten up …much like they had been doing in Eldorado.

I learned today that the territory already has an organized legislature and a delegate to the U. S. Congress. Although the area has plenty of Southerners, the territory has pledged that when admitted as a state, they will be pro Union.

What a contrast. In Eastern Kansas, before we left, beyond earning our "daily bread", all talk was about the war or the politics of the war, what General Jim Lane was up to, what cities in Missouri had been taken by the Confederates or held by the Union and I was concerned about Adda's troubled marriage to Captain Graton, who was fighting his war with ex- slaves he had trained.

But out here, oh, they are curious about the larger battles back east, but I'll bet there's not a miner out here, who even knows the Governor's name or about the guerilla fighting led by this fellow Quantrill. All they care about is their claims, how many ounces they "took" today, local Indian threats, the price of gold down to $20 per ounce. The younger miners, down on their luck, trying to decide whether to join the military or move on to California, Oregon or some new gold strike in British Columbia.

August 1863

Tom Cordes (Eldorado Blacksmith) In the spring of 1863 Augusta and Tom left Lawrence for the Gold Strike in the Colorado Rockies. His wife, Elizabeth, and he began ranching south of Denver. They were driven-off by Indian uprisings two years later.
Allan Reingold, Illustrator

61.

KENOSHA HOUSE-TARRYALL, COLORADO

Early May 1863
The morning after our arrival

"You must be the new cook"
"I am"

"Well, we shore have been waitin' for you. Mrs. Cordis said some time ago she wanted to leave but we persuaded her to stay 'til you arrived but we've been on "tender hooks" that she might leave before you'd get here or you might not stay. What's yore name?"

"I'm Mrs. Chase. Elizabeth Cordis is an old friend. We were settlers together in Kansas."

"Where in Kansas?"

"Eldorado"

"Sure, I know Eldorado. We come through that town on the Cherokee Trail and picked up a few prospects in the summer of 1858."

"A Missus, eh?"

"Yes."

"Where's yore husband?"

"He's dead. I'm a widow.

Pause

"Who are you?"

"I'm Thatcher...Charlie Thatcher from Georgia, way up in the northeast part of the state. I was with the Green Russell outfit. I live in the same county as the Russell clan...you've heard of the Russell brothers, haven't you?"

"Yes."

"Where'd you say yore from Mrs. Chase?"

"Eldorado, Kansas. My father and a few of his abolitionists friends founded Eldorado"

"Hmmm? So that makes you an abolitionist, don't it?"

"It does."

Pause

"When I asked you where yer from, I expected a different answer. I figgered you'd be from Aurora, mebbie Dry Creek or Central City"

"I'm not familiar with those places".

"Not familiar? Hah, those were the real gold strikes. A big strike in Aurora in '58 and mostly '59 quickly petered out. But a bigger one in Dry Creek and the biggest one on Clear Creek, where they built Central City."

"Do you mean 1858?'"

"Yep, why?"

"Well, although we married in 1859, my husband left Eldorado in May of '58 for Cherry Creek and what's now Denver."

"In '58 eh? He musta come with the Russell party. We came up from the Cherokee Country to Eldorado in May '58""

"I don't think so. An outfit from Lecompton, the territorial capital came through the same week. He joined that smaller group as a carpenter. They intended to lay out a city and did.He returned to Eldorado in August. He was gone less than three months."

Well, don't you remember? The Russell party came through Eldorado that same week of 1858, I was with 'em. From the Walnut River we all traveled together, for our common safety... used the Santa Fe most of the way...yore sweetie, come back with a big poke, I suspect?"

"No, as a matter of fact he came back and went back to building houses and helping with our sawmill. We had a sawmill in Eldorado."

"Too bad he didn't stay with the Russells. I was with the Russell outfit that summer...the summer of '58. For the Russells that was their second year...for me, the first. Only a few of us found anything over at Aurora. I did my best over at Central City. If that man of your'n had stayed out here that year and learned a little mining, he'd probably done pretty well, especially if he had staked a claim at Dry Creek. For most of us Dry Creek was the best.

"What main trail did you use to get out here?"

"The Overland. We left from Lawrence the first week of April. The war along the Missouri River Valley into southwestern Missouri State and south into the Cherokee Nation was becoming very threatening. Lawrence is very close to the fighting going on in southwestern Missouri.

We went up to Atchison near Fort Leavenworth for some supplies and joined a good-sized outfit...then went west, picked up the Overland Trail on the Platte River and followed that to the Julesburg Cutoff, which as I'm sure you know leads down into Denver.

"I remember Eldorado the spring of '58. We followed the Santa Fe Trail to Pueblo, as I told you, and then picked up a trail that goes north more or less along the east face of the Rockies. I'm surprised, if you lived in Eldorado, you wouldn't have used the Santa Fe to get here."

"Well, this spring when I decided to come out here, my sister and I were living in Lawrence, which is 120 miles northeast of Eldorado, rather close to the Missouri River, so that makes connecting to the Overland Trail along the Platte more convenient. Have you ever visited Lawrence, Mr. Thatcher?"

"Well, no. My town in those parts would be Atchison, maybe Leavenworth. The people in those two towns are friendlier to people, like me, than...Lawrence, if you get my Southern drift.

But I went through that area twice on my way home in the fall of '59 and '60. In '61 I was roughed up by some Jayhawkers, who took me for a Missouri Bushwhacker. They didn't know I was a miner, so they didn't look for my poke. Last fall I avoided Kansas entirely. I crossed the river at Omaha to Council Bluffs and went down along the eastside of the River to Sydney, Tabor and into Missouri. I had no trouble catching the River steamer across Missouri."

That night I tried to figure out what it was that Charlie Thatcher does here. I know he supplies me with wood for the kitchen and he helps with the stagecoach passengers and the horses. Once or twice a week if the weather is nice, he takes the house rig and goes prospecting alone. But he seems to have so much time on his hands. He's not nearly as old as his beard makes him look. I'd guess he's about fifty, maybe not that.

On July 18th Mary Rackliffe arrived a month and a half after me. She had been detained. Both her children had come down with small pox. She brought several letters. Two were from Jule Johnson. Why does that girl pester me so? Mary came by way of the Cordis ranch. I'm just amazed that she could first locate Tom and Elizabeth in this wilderness and then find me up here in Tarryall. She said they had no problem crossing Nebraska and brought a welcome letter from my little sister, which informs me that we have a cousin on Father's side who is a captain in the Union Army. Adda writes that poor Mr. Killam has died.

A few days later I had another talk with Mr. Thatcher who, because he likes my cooking offered to take me out on one of the streams and would demonstrate how mining is actually done. He said, first we'd pan for gold. Then he said, "We'd graduate to a "rocker".

When I asked him to explain the rocker, he said it was such a "complicated contraption"; he'd simply have to show me when we get there.

"Do you own a rocker?"

"Certainly. If we find color," he said, "We might file a claim together"...that sounds exciting.

Many, but not all, of the miners here get what gold they do by placer mining. That is by using water to wash constantly agitated sand and gravel taken from the streambed and banks. The shaking separates the gravel and sand from the gold. They use sluiced water or they hand carry it to their rockers. Shallow corrugations in the bottom shelf of the rocker collect the gold dust and nuggets because gold is so heavy it settles in these small grooves. They also use a device as simple as a large round pan, much like a deep metal pie pan but the process is the same, using water and a rocking motion to separate sand and rocks from the gold flakes.

A few of the miners are professional underground miners, financed by Eastern money. They tunnel deep into the rock looking for quartz seams, which are most likely to contain gold. The quartz rock carried out (by man or beast) from the mine is mechanically crushed into small granules. This breaks away the gold from the quartz. Some quartz crushing is done with a stamp mill, which is simply a heavy metal arrangement of several mauls or vertical hammers that by some contrivance are lifted a foot or so, then released to pound and crush the quartz. The products from the crushing or stamping are collected, then constantly washed, which separates the stone waste from small nuggets and flakes of gold. According to Charlie Thatcher, a cubic yard of quartz containing ore can have anywhere from no gold to several thousand dollars worth.

When miners pan...often working right in the stream...they occasionally pick up small nuggets that had been melted by nature eons ago and carried, often miles down stream.

I immediately began asking the more experienced miners if they knew Francis Dempsey, the Irish miner, who had learned mining in the deep tunnels of Wales, who dug our well through a rock ledge in Eldorado, while his outfit was repairing their wagons before pressing on for these gold fields. They didn't, but they suspected that if he had had Welch mining experience, he was most gainfully employed, probably within just a few miles of where we were.

After supper, while I was cleaning up, I had a chat with Mr. Harriman, who came out from Kenosha, Wisconsin in the summer of 1860 (though he said he had lived all over.), but worked in mining only about a month, in Central City getting there in the middle of their big strike. He built a large boarding house, ran it for a year, sold it at a profit and came down here at the peak of Tarryall Creek strike and built this place, named it the Kenosha House.

"I drove stages both direction between Pikes Peak and Denver. I've been over Kenosha Pass, both ways more times than you can count."

"So you named the pass, eh?"

"Well there have been other names, but when gold was discovered in Tarryall, Como, Fairplay, Buckskin and other places down here, we began running scheduled stages between these camps and the Denver area, or using the longer Southern Route from Pueblo to here. Kenosha Pass was the best way in and out. So, yes, I guess I named it.

I asked him where he lives, when he's not here. He said almost due east of here maybe twenty-five miles on a ranch a little north of Fort Logan on Bear Creek. I asked him if he had a family and he said, "Yes. We've had four children…lost two when they were infants. The children are in school up in Denver most of the year, where we spend winters."

He said, "We found so much gold around here we minted $2.50 and $5.00 rectangular gold bits as well as $25 gold pieces right here in Tarryall. The first gold taken out of Tarryall Creek were little nuggets the size of watermelon seeds. By 1860 we had 300 log houses scattered along the creek and had a town laid out by the following year. By 1861 both sides of the creek had a population of over 5,000, In addition to the north-south express stagecoaches, twice a week we had four-mule coaches out to California and back! By 1861 we had thirteen hydraulic operations, each with its own stamp mill. One operation alone had 150 men.

"You know," he said, "that creek from its headwaters to where it flows into the South Platte is twenty-five miles long and we had claims solid…every fifty feet on both sides. The main stream is also fed by upwards of fifteen little streams and cricks that come down from their area of the mountain and there were and are claims on those as well. Miners on the other side of Tarryall Creek thought themselves so important and independent that they copied Aurora and Denver. They formed their own town and called it Hamilton. That creek is only fifteen to thirty feet wide but wider in the spring when it swells from snowmelt. From 1859 'til last year we took over two million dollars out of the Tarryall streambed."

"You know I've operated some rather nice hotels and boarding houses and have always tried to serve first rate meals. What are your specialties, Mrs. Chase?"

"I make an excellent Chicken stew with a dumpling recipe that comes more or less from the Old Testament."

"I thought I knew the Old Testament pretty well. Where do you find a reference to dumplings?"

When the Jews left Egypt, having been down there for 430 years, they left in such a hurry they had no time for bread-dough to rise, so they baked it, unleavened. What they didn't eat, they took with them. I use a meal of unleavened bread for my dumplings. It's all there in several verses: chapter 12 of Exodus.

"I begin with a meal of unleavened bread to which I add some fresh rendered chicken fat and two or three eggs, depending on the batch size. These dumplings go best with chicken stew or soup. Any trouble getting fresh chickens?"

"No, plenty of chickens and plenty of wild turkey."

"In many ways, those of us, who have been moving west, first to the "Western Reserve", then the Northwest, then the prairies of the Midwest and Kansas, and now Colorado this movement resembles the Exodus, but when Moses left Egypt with 600,000, not counting children, I wonder if in our fifty year Exodus we've even equaled the immigration described in Exodus?"

"What else?"

Boiled Buffalo tongue. I serve it hot with a light horseradish sauce or I slice it cold for sandwiches. I also bake pretty good bread. My pan-corn bread is best with yellow corn meal to which I've added coarse ground well-rendered ham rind.

"I make a good boiled ham or large ham hock, but I want three to five pound hocks and I serve those with Navy Beans boiled with lots of onion or for a change I'll serve boiled ham with boiled potatoes.

"I don't like to roast buffalo, but in a pinch I'll serve it. One of my specialties is soup, rather rich soup in that I start from stock that has simmered with meat bones, bacon, and ham rind and vegetables for several hours. My test for my stock is that when cooled, it must gel. I separate the strained stock from the bones, meat, bacon and ham rind and vegetable pulp, take off the fat and add fresh vegetables with small chunks of meat. Of courses this stock is excellent for various bean soups. I have probably a dozen bean soup recipes.

"I make Baked Beans the way they are made in the Parker House Hotel in Boston with molasses and a little chopped onion. When it's available, I can roast whole joints or racks of beef or venison. There ought to be excellent deer in these mountains, if they haven't been hunted out"

"Ever cook elk?"

"No."

"How about trout? Now and then we get a dozen or so trout, not big, maybe one and a half pounds. The Indians net them out of the streams and bring them in for sale."

Well, little ones I'd fry, but, if I'm going to be too busy to fry, I'd bake them...but not too long. I've also poached trout, and then served it cold with mayonnaise, which I can make, if I can get fresh eggs."

Two days later a Mr. Ferren and his wife came by. They are friends of Mr. Harriman. And they chatted with him. They have a boarding house nearby at a place called Laurette Buckskin with ten miners plus their family. After supper away from Mr. Harriman they quietly offered me $60 a month on the same terms as I have here. I figured if they thought so little of Mr. Harriman's friendship as to beat his offer to me behind his back, I could probably expect the same sort of loyalty if I joined them…but I had made a deal with these Tarryall folks and so I declined. The Ferrens went on to say that with Tarryall gold in decline, the county seat has been moved to their town, Buckskin, but they prefer to call it Laurette.

One afternoon, a week or so after our long talk about mining Charlie Thatcher and I took a ride up one of the gulches to pan for gold. It was a beautiful sunny afternoon and quite warm, considering our elevation. On the ride he wanted to make conversation.

"You say that sweetie of yours was out here in '58, eh, and returned that summer?"

"Yes, why are you scrutinizing me so carefully?"

"Well, you must be one hell of a magnet to get a carpenter to leave this area for you."

I smiled and asked, "How's that?"

Well, look at the opportunity around these parts for an experienced carpenter in 1858. He could build houses or commercial buildings. If he had the equipment, he could survey the settlements. By surveying he could establish claim bounds up in the gulches. There was a big demand for cradles of all sizes to rock the streambed gravel, which separates the gold nuggets and dust, allowing it to settle on the corrugated floor of the cradle. They are much faster than the pan. They are best made by carpenters and in several varieties, big and small.

And there are several tricks in making a good rocker. First it must sit comfortably on all sorts of rocky surfaces along side the stream, so the curve of the rocker must be just right. If the curve is too flat, it takes too much gumption to push it. If it's too round, it may tip over easily. The contraption must get rid of the heavy gravel very quickly and easily, which the rocking motion takes care of, but not carry with it sand, because all the flake and dust is in with the sand. Finally the slots toward the bottom must be placed to allow sand carrying gold and small nuggets to pass through to the ridge plate or corrugated plate at the bottom. The best bottom plates are metal, like Yankee scrub boards...and it needs to slide out easy, because that's where the gold is.

Very soon after a team of miners found pay dirt, they needed sluices to carry water from high elevations down to their sluice boxes. There was no end of available work for even the dumbest carpenters.

"So yore man was either lacking ambition...or a source of female companionship...one or the 'tuther.'"

His nosey inquiry was cut short when we pulled up along side a small, shallow, fast running stream that came down from the south slope of the mountain, which, he said, fed into Tarryall Creek, maybe a half mile below us from where we stopped. He wasn't going to prospect the main stream.. Charlie lifted off the wagon a box that looked a bit like a child's cradle. In that there were two rockers on the bottom of this contrivance and placed it close to the stream. He explained I would have two jobs: one, I was to bring buckets of gravel and sand dug from the streambed to the cradle. He reckoned a bucket of gravel to weigh ten pounds, give or take.

"That means I'll have to get my feet wet?"

"Yep."

"Well, why didn't you tell me that? I would have borrowed some boots."

"I wanted you to get a feel of real streambed mining"...and I was to carry buckets of water to him, which he poured over the sand and gravel. For every bucket of sand and gravel he wanted a bucket of clean water, and in that order. He joked and said if I had any spare time, I could rock the cradle.

When I asked him what he did in this partnership, he laughed and said, "I supervise until you get tired, and then we'll see how well we've done. The main thing you'll learn from me is to be careful with the final sand. That's where the gold is, unless we get lucky and find a nugget or two. The rest is just plain hard work and for you, wet hard work."

Mid afternoon, after I was good and wet, and cold, I said I thought we'd better be getting back, so I could start supper. He took a little shelf or drawer from the bottom of the cradle. Pointing to what looked like a metal corrugated washboard containing sand and no gravel, he said, "That's the money maker. Gold is about ten times heavier than gravel or quartz, so it settles to the bottom of these little grooves. Let's see how we did."

Using his finger or thumb Charlie pushed the remaining contents of all the little grooves into his mining pan, maybe two teacup's full. Then he went closer to the stream, splashed some water into the pan and carefully swilled the water over the sand in a way that little by little he washed the sand out of the pan. Then what little was left, he put in a thin metal box with a gaily-decorated top that once contained fancy playing cards, small enough to fit in his shirt pocket.

Walking to the wagon I asked, "How'd we do?"

"We didn't do very well."

He said my water was all right but my pay dirt was lousy.

"You didn't dig deep enough."

"Well, Charlie, if I go any deeper, I'll be wet up to my waist."

"Yore not out here to stay dry. Yore out here to make money. The deeper you dig, the more we make."

That evening after supper several of the boarders were having their evening "smoke and spit". I was in the doorway about to bring a tray of milk and cookies to them when I overheard one of them ask Charlie how he did today with his helper?" He bragged, "Well, actually purty good…maybe an ounce… maybe an ounce and a half, all thin scale stuff. I might stake a claim up there."

What crick were you on Charlie?" One of them asked, "What makes you think I was on a crick?"

I heard that and I walked into the dining room and said, "Charlie, you old fraud. I'm entitled to half that gold. You said that we were partners, and you said to me we didn't do so good. Now you tell these fellows we took out one and one half ounces."

"Oh, we are, we are partners but you're the junior partner."

"Well then, tomorrow morning when you order two eggs, you'll get one. When you ask for three flapjacks, you'll get one and it will be the size of a silver dollar and probably burned and no syrup." Even I know an ounce and a half of gold is worth $30 and I want my share. My shoes and stockings are still wet. I can hardly lift my right arm from carrying all that gravel and water."

The spectators all had a good laugh on Charlie. One of them told Charlie it was a big mistake to take on the camp cook as a partner.

Two days later, when I withheld bacon from his one, over-cooked egg, he paid up. I fried him a steak at noon and we "made up." That afternoon we went back to "our little claim." This time I wore some borrowed boots. I dug at least a half-foot deeper than before and it paid off. We took at least two ounces this time. My god, I work all month long, ten to twelve hours a day for forty dollars, a little more than a dollar and a quarter a day, and today for two hours of work my share is twenty dollars!

TARRYALL

In a letter of August 22, 1863 Adda writes that during a battle at Fort Gibson, Graton and his Company had been taken prisoners…must have been a spring or early summer battle. * She is thinking about taking the baby and going back to Michigan. Well, I'll certainly encourage that.

A second letter tells that Lawrence was burned again on October 11th by Quantrill and 800 men.

Augusta begins her third and final volume of her bound journals in late August 1863. She had obviously owned the blank journal for some time. It was identical as the others, manufactured by Frances and Loutrel, 45 Maiden Lane, New York City.

In her second letter Adda explains a little more about the problems between herself and her husband with Jule Johnson as the "other woman" and in Jule's letters to me she writes that Graton tells her that his wife lacks warmth and understanding and that Adda's sister has been a constant interference in their marriage (isn't that an old male ploy in the novels?) But she tells Adda a slightly different version. Well by now Adda knows about Graton's unfaithfulness. Much to my utter surprise is a second letter from Jule trying to explain her side of the story. But she writes in "past tense", as though it's mainly over. Maybe Adda has won, but if she's won, Graton will bear her a grudge for a long time for threatening his position in the Army and his self-esteem.

But I don't have time to deal with Jule now. Later this winter, if I'm still here, I figure I'll have more time and I'll give Jule Johnson and her role in my sister's marriage her due attention. Adultery and temptations from the "other woman" have always been with us. Remember David and Bathsheba

---

* Given the time for mail from the battle area to reach Lawrence, then from Lawrence to Denver and Kenosha Pass in the mountains, the battle that Adda mentions could have been one they fought on March 9, 1863 near Fort Scott, K.T. or at Cabin Creek on July 2nd the same year. Source: American Civil War Regiments, Kingston, MA.

from the Old Testament book of Samuel II; but I don't have time for that now.

Another letter from Adda arrived with nothing but more bad news. Her little Allie has been sick (near death), but like most children, she has recovered. She writes that she hadn't heard from her husband for so long that she was getting very worried. Finally, she said, she got a letter explaining the situation.

In the summer of 1863 Graton and his regiment had been ordered to Fort Gibson at Cabin Creek and were involved in two battles nearby. According to Adda, during the second battle* there he and some Colored soldiers from his regiment were taken prisoners. He is in a Confederate P.O.W. camp together with some of his Colored troops but he doesn't reveal the camp's location...many of his troops were killed. She understands, that, although the first battle a little north of Fort Gibson at Cabin Creek went in the Union's favor, a second battle, that she thinks was on July 17th involving the 1st Kansas Colored Regiment went bad for them. When one of the Commanding officers was killed or wounded, Graton was put in command of his regiment of Colored soldiers. Prior to that he commanded Company C.

Question: how could Graton be put in command of his Regiment if he's in a P.O.W. camp, unless he escaped or was he released shortly after being captured?

Adda says that Cabin Creek is in the Cherokee (Indian) Territory ten to fifteen miles south of the Kansas line and maybe five miles west of the Arkansas Border. All this, according to Adda is another fifteen or so miles north of Fort Gibson.

Initially Graton was serving under a Colonel James Williams, who not only commanded the 1st and 2nd Kansas Colored Infantry (Regiments) but other Colored Regiments of varying size, including a Cavalry Company from Wisconsin, and two more Cavalry Companies. Colonel Williams' forces also had five or six

---

* This must have been the June 2nd battle referred to in the Civil War archives

major canons and about 1,000 troops. They were up against 1,500 Confederates, no canons, all under a Colonel Waity.

Adda has decided if it's all right with me she plans to rent our place. She will take a larger house in Lawrence and run it as a boarding house until Graton is released. Adda writes that our house needs constant repair and war or no war; the county wants their taxes.

My response will be, pay the taxes and the repairs out of the rent receipts and send me half of the balance.

Adda says that Benjamin Hoyt, the man I had "driven crazy" by declining his marriage proposals in Lawrence has joined the Army "to forget you". Included in her envelope was a sarcastic note from him, saying he hoped I would not drive anyone crazy in Colorado. I guess I hadn't realized how serious he was about marriage with me.

Adda reported that business in Lawrence is thriving due to the war. They are building a bridge across the (Kaw) River heavy enough for railroad traffic. She estimates that this summer and fall there were 700 to 800 freed slaves milling around Lawrence. The Army can't recruit and train them fast enough. She says that Graton's gun shop is doing a brisk business in pistols, as protection if Quantrill comes back and if the Negroes begin to cause trouble. She thinks that's unlikely, because they are so happy to be free. All those that are able-bodied want to join the Union Army and get one of those fancy French uniforms and thirteen dollars a month.

According to officers who we've known, who come back to Lawrence on leave, report that the Colored soldiers are about as good as the white, particularly if they are fighting in an area where some of them had been slaves.

However Adda says, there's an interesting racial thing going on. The Confederacy has recruited Cherokee Indians south of us. When they fight our troops, it's reported that the Indians are particularly ruthless when they come up against Colored troops fighting for the Union.

After I got settled in, but before moving to the Harriman ranch, from talking to the miners and stagecoach travelers staying over plus the Rocky Mountain News and Eastern newspapers, I began to see how unstable this mining area has recently become. Many of the miners who have been here for some time and haven't found a profitable claim, or their claims are "giving out", which includes the Tarryall camps, are either leaving or they are being recruited by one side or the other for military duty. Our old friend, Sam Tappan, and Kansas pioneer, now an Army captain, is the area's principal recruiter (for the Union). He offers about $45.00 a month. Lately he has been sent with John Slough to Central City to begin recruiting there, where he can expect trouble, because the Confederate sympathizers broke up his previous meetings by offering $11/week, about $45/month.

I intend to write to Sam Tappan and tell him about Preston Plumb and Alfred Pierce. He might not know that his two partners were with Jim Lane in Washington guarding the White House just before Lincoln's inauguration.

The camps have been solicited for soldiers on both sides... pretty successfully. Tarryall miners down on their luck could make $45 to $48/month from either.

Covertly the Confederates are here, quietly doing the same thing. They probably do well, since so many of these miners were originally from the South. It's common knowledge that the Confederates want the gold that they might seize from 300 to 400 local camps to help finance their war...and the Union is just as determined to hang on to it.

But south of us we have New Mexico Territory, right next to Texas...both pro slavery and Confederate. Northerners coming to Colorado via the Santa Fe Trail have been arrested and detained by forts south of Pueblo.

The *Rocky Mountain News** reports that Sam Tappan has trouble controlling his recently sworn-in troops. They've looted

---

* Augusta was talking at the *Rocky Mountain News* office shortly after it began publishing but it was sad to see that on February 27, 2009 it had to close its doors.

Denver, bartered their guns, ammo, blankets, etc. for whiskey. They've stolen chickens, pigs, etc. from the locals.

Government agents are buying up lead from miners (for bullets)...Governor Gilpin issued "drafts" redemption, the Feds wouldn't honor them. Gilpin had no authority to "print his own money" and Governor Gilpin has been relieved.

To make matters worse for those recruiting for the Union, 10,000 Mormons have pledged their support for the South.

Summer 1863

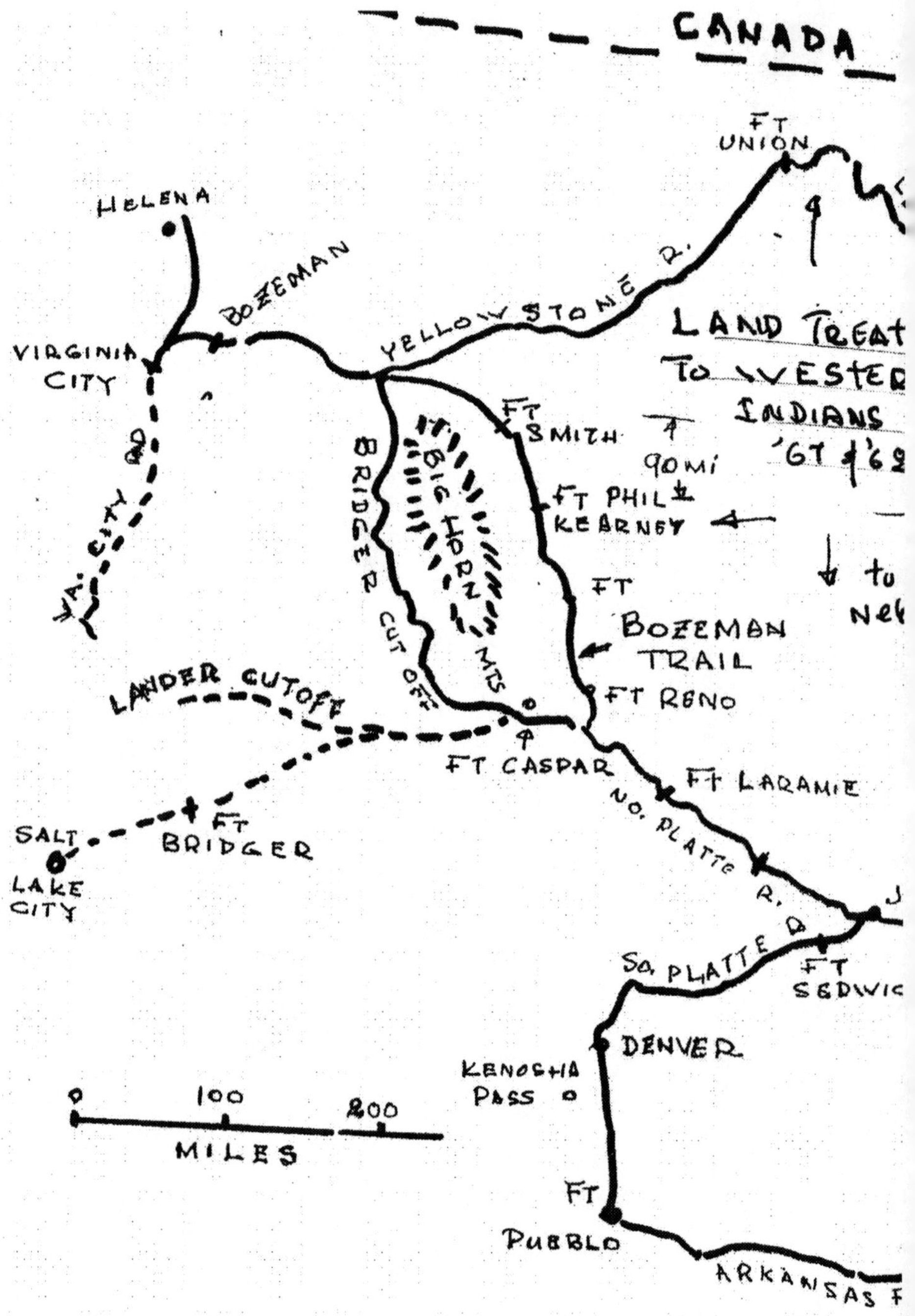

CANADA

HELENA

BOZEMAN

VIRGINIA CITY

YELLOWSTONE R.

FT UNION

LAND TREAT
To WESTER
INDIANS
'67 & '6

FT SMITH

90 mi

FT PHIL
KEARNEY

FT
BOZEMAN
TRAIL

FT RENO

to
Ne

BRIDGER CUT OFF

BIG HORN MTS

LANDER CUTOFF

FT CASPAR

FT LARAMIE

SALT LAKE CITY

FT BRIDGER

NO. PLATTE R.

So. PLATTE R.

J

FT SEDWIC

DENVER

KENOSHA PASS

FT PUEBLO

ARKANSAS R

0   100   200
MILES

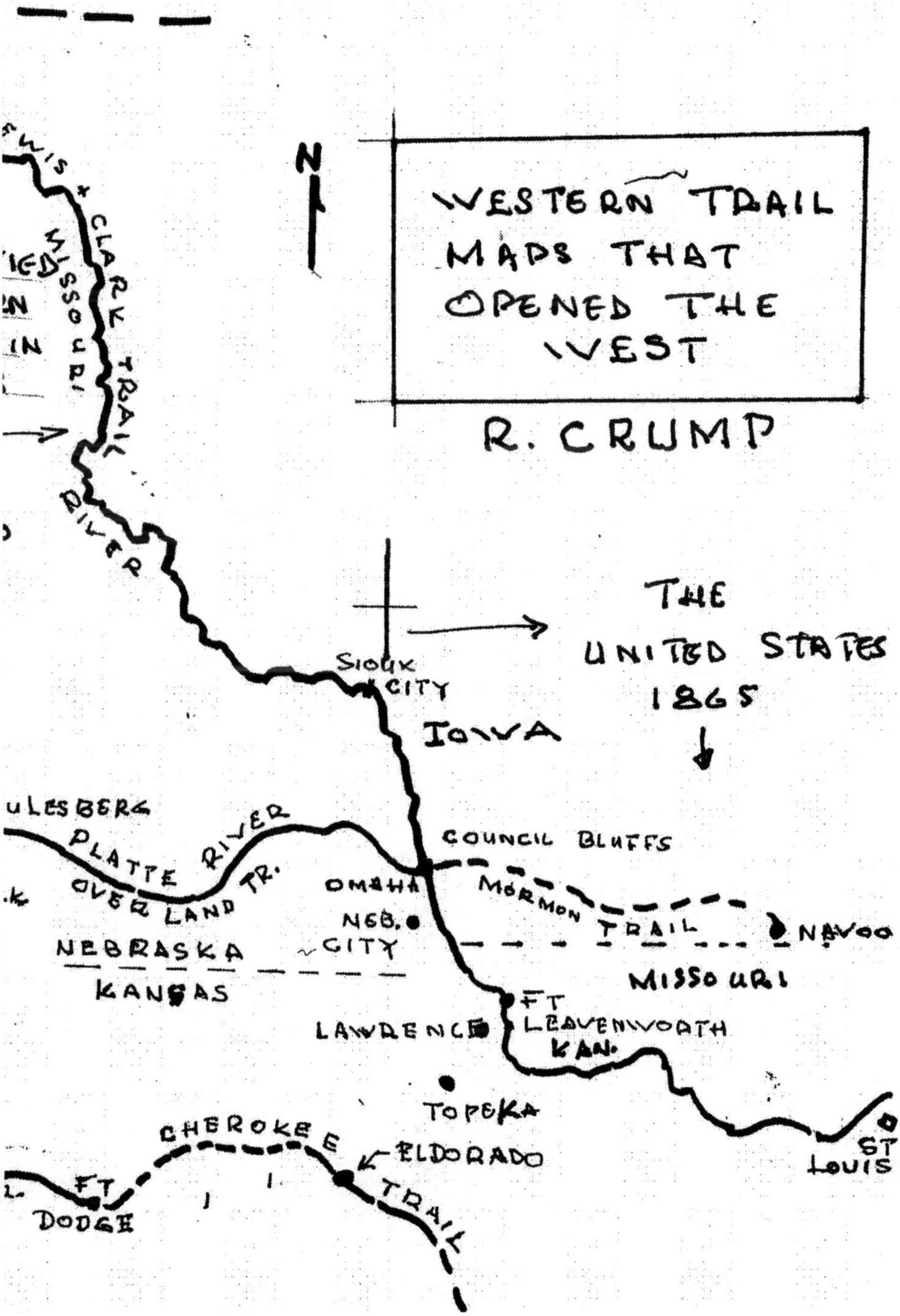

N

WESTERN TRAIL
MAPS THAT
OPENED THE
WEST

R. CRUMP

THE
UNITED STATES
1865

SIOUX CITY

IOWA

JULESBERG
PLATTE RIVER
OVERLAND TR.

COUNCIL BLUFFS
MORMON TRAIL

NAVOO

OMAHA
NEB.
CITY

MISSOURI

NEBRASKA
KANSAS

FT
LEAVENWORTH
KAN.

LAWRENCE

TOPEKA

CHEROKEE
ELDORADO

ST LOUIS

FT DODGE

TRAIL

LEWIS + CLARK TRAIL MISSOURI RIVER

62.

HARRIMAN RANCH
TARRYALL, COLORADO
August 1863

I was invited to a party the week before I left Kenosha House. It was the first real party I've attended since I've been out here, with dancing and singing and everybody having a really fine time, as did yours truly.

Then, lo and behold, the following Sunday two miners with their wives from claims nearby were here Saturday night. We served them supper and they asked for an early wake-up and breakfast, which is not unusual for people on the stage. They explained that they wanted to get away by 8AM to get to church on time…and invited me. We had a fine time. It was the first time I ever heard a part time miner/part time preacher preach. I intend to go again. They sang all the hymns we sang in Michigan.

AUGUST 8, 1863

I can't believe it! This is my 24th birthday, and I have moved physically and financially. I was making about $40 a month at the Kenosha House in Tarryall, but as several of the miners have drifted away, many of them joining one army or the other, or they were simply going home as is the miners' custom before it gets cold, Mr. Harriman had asked me to cook for the cowboys and ranch hands at his place down on the high plain. The Kenosha

House still does about same business from stagecoaches but as winter comes on that will diminish and maybe stop.

I said to Mr. Harriman, "If I have a choice, I'd rather stay here. By mining, even irregularly with Charlie Fletcher, I'm able to save more from that than from what I make cooking."

"Of course, you have a choice. Maybe I'll need to sweeten my offer. But keep in mind that in less than two months, there will be too much snow for you and Charlie to get up on your claim… and if all the miners leave here, I will probably close this place. In October the stages stop running through the Pass. Think it over; we can talk again in a few days."

His offer guaranteed me $50 a month no matter how many people I feed, except if the number exceeds ten, I would get an extra $1.50 per week for each boarder. Mr. Harriman owns both places. He also warned that if the number I cook for drops way off, I should expect to earn less.

At a party I was invited to at Mr. McLaughlin's I met Mrs. Harriman, who certainly seems pleasant, and Mary Rackliffe was there. Other than my time with Mary, there were too many at this party to allow for pleasant conversation.

After Charlie Thatcher and I became "partners", I managed to get him to go with me two or three afternoons a week before I moved down to the ranch. Then, while it was still quite warm, Mr. Harriman had asked me to go back to the Kenosha House with him to cook for a special occasion twice, once in late August and again in September. I was there long enough to persuade Charley to go up on the crick again. He was so lazy, but he also liked to tease me or he'd say, "I'll go, if you make me a batch of taffy." It was nice to hear this rough old miner say that he had missed me when I had moved to the ranch.

On average, we took two ounces each time we went up until it finally dawned on me that when Charlie kept nagging me to dig deeper in the stream bed, that he wasn't playing tricks on me or just trying to see me get more wet. I figured out he was right. He kept saying, "The deeper you go, the better the pay dirt." Prior to that he seemed to take some particular male delight that now and then I'd get water in over my boots or I'd get the bottom half of my dress wet. I thought that's what he wanted and he did enjoy seeing me irritated, because I was getting more wet…but the old rascal was right (as usual) and we had three or four days when I got good and wet and we took out three to three and a half ounces. But I always had to keep my eye on him. As a distraction, when we were done panning, he'd ask me to put the rocker back on the wagon, so I wouldn't see what he was up to. He had this sneaky habit of running his thumb down the grooves of the corrugated collector (that's where the gold is), as he pushed the sand and gold dust into his pan, then he'd put his hand in his pocket, saying his hand was cold and wet.

The first time I saw him do that I smiled and said, "Charlie, give me your trousers tonight. I'll wash them out for you. They are filthy anyway." I figured that pocket must be worth $25.

"Thank you, Augusta, but I only have this one pair, an' my legs would git cold, while you're doing my laundry."

The next time we went out, Charlie drove the team another twenty-five feet up our little stream to where it made an easy bend to the north. He said, "I'm going to show you another old-timer's trick and he took the shovel and began digging a ditch for a new stream bed maybe fifteen to twenty feet long, straight down from where the stream began the bend. He motioned that I should take the other shovel and help him even though I wasn't sure what he was up to.

Finally, when he thought we had it deep enough and wide enough, we broke through and diverted the water down the new straight ditch to below the bend where the detoured water flowed into the original stream. Then we built a little dam to stop the water from going down the old curved section. In a few minutes, twenty feet of the old curved streambed was almost dry…then we both took sand and gravel from a depth of two to three feet. That afternoon we took three and a half ounces home and two days later did the same thing and we've only dug up maybe five feet of the old curved streambed.

On the ride back Charlie asked me if I was dry and I said, drier than I was when I was digging in all that water. But I sensed he just wanted to talk. Pretty soon he held out his right hand. In it was a flat but thick nugget the size of a watermelon seed, gloriously shining in the late afternoon, clear Colorado sunshine. He said, "Yore first bucket turned this up. We used to get these up here all the time"…and he gave it to me.

The next morning I made his favorite breakfast of corn meal mush but it must be made of rather coarse-ground white corn and cooked for almost an hour. I served it with cream that Mr. Harriman brings up from his ranch, so thick you can "spoon it." Charlie calls this dish, "Georgia Ice Cream." He's the only Southerner I've ever met that I could like. The only time I ever heard him express a Southern prejudice was once when he said, "Indians are better than Niggers, any day." Well, that makes sense. Charlie's wife is a Cherokee Indian.

One evening before I moved to the ranch, when he didn't want to play cards with the others, I asked Charlie with all his skills and experience why he needed Mr. Harriman as his partner. He explained that the two of them knew each other up near the Central City "find" in '59 and '60. Charlie stayed in Mr. Harriman's boarding house there. They came down to Tarryall together.

He said, the year he came down here, he was broke. Mr. Harriman gave him a job at the Kenosha House and let him use the team to prospect in the Tarryall streams and gave him board and room until he found something. "And that's reason enough for me now to split my earnings with Mr. Harriman", he said.

Some days later Mr. Harriman was teasing me about my prospering partnership. He knew I was prospering because I was selling him my share of dust for $19 an ounce, paid in coin, so he also knew we had had several sixty and seventy dollar afternoons. I said it was very nice of him to have "grub-staked" Charlie when he was down on his luck. Mr. Harriman gave out a big laugh. He said, "Did Charlie tell you that?"

"Yes, why?"

"Well, because Charlie Thatcher is the biggest liar to come out of Georgia. All those Georgia miners are liars, especially the Russells. When they are doing well, they say they aren't making $2.00 a day. When they do get a dry spell, they'll lie and tell you that even on a slow day, they taking out $100 and try to sell you their no good claim.

"Why if I had all the money that Charlie Thatcher has stashed away in Leavenworth, Atchison, St Joseph, Council Bluffs and St Louis…and if they had a bank in Aurora he trusted, he'd have an account there; if I had Thatcher's money, I'd burn mine. They tell me his house in Georgia is second only in size to Green Russell's. You know he's married to a Cherokee Indian and so is Green Russell."

I thought, both these men enjoy spoofing others, especially outsiders.

In late August Charlie Thatcher drove me down to Mr. Harriman's ranch. A handsome young man helped Charlie carry my trunk and boxes in. I would be cooking for about ten ranch hands and cowboys, that is, until real winter sets in.

The stage, which also stops here, brought terrible news! In a long letter posted in Lawrence Adda writes, "that Lawrence has been burned to ashes!" It was that Quantrill again. This time he had 400 mounted and armed guerillas. They spent half a day riding here and there up and down the streets and between houses in the neighborhood, slaughtering people, looting shops, burning businesses and houses.

SEPTEMBER 7, 1863

By a very strange coincidence a brother of General Jim Lane (Henry Lane) came in on the same coach that carried Adda's letter and stayed here at Harriman's for a few days. When I heard who he was, I immediately explained my Kansas affiliation; Eldorado and Father's association with his brother and our long connection to Lawrence. He confirmed that the Eldridge House was burned (again), as was the Whitney House, his brother's house and a good many of the more prominent houses in Lawrence, including your brother-in-law's well-stocked gun shop. They got a lot of his guns and ammunition before setting it on fire. It turns out Henry Lane knows Graton as both the local gunsmith and as captain of a Regiment of Colored troops and he knows Adda. "Though they burned other houses in your neighborhood, they didn't succeed in burning your sisters (I didn't tell him that I still own half that house.) They were certainly looking for the wife of Captain Graton to even a score for what he and Jim Lane's troops had done earlier to Osceola, Missouri, which was the home of many of Quantrill's officers and their wives and families. Quantrill has claimed that those companies under Lane and Graton were unnecessarily violent in their raid on Osceola that burned the town and killed innocent civilians, to get their hands on the lead foundry and the lead. My brother has been intent on destroying these small towns and settlements, because they have been the local means of civilian support for the Rebels. And there was another important reason for such violence from Quantrill's men. Several wives and female relatives of Quantrill's men had been captured by Lane and other Union Commanders in a round-up of four Southwest Missouri counties and incarcerated as a group in a dilapidated building in Kansas City, which collapsed, killing four and seriously wounding others." The destruction at Osceola and the unnecessary deaths of Quantrill's women were, Henry Lane says, the main cause for the retaliatory raid and such barbarism this time by Quantrill and his men in and to Lawrence.

Henry Lane said as soon as he returns, he'll send by stage more copies of the Leavenworth papers that have documented Quantrill's destruction and the lives lost, but he guesses the number will be about 200.

Shortly after Mr. Lanes' visit the stage brought in several letters including another from Adda, which went into greater detail about the terrible raid on Lawrence by Quantrill's gang in August of 1863.

Rather than paraphrase it, we will copy most of her letter.
"Dear Augusta:

I'm sure by now even in your remote Mountain camp you've heard of our terrible raid by that cutthroat Quantrill and his gang. They say there were 400 of them that may be so. I only saw two or three squads of mounted men riding all over in our neighborhood. I was home that day. The baby was upstairs.

I had rented all of our house but my own bedroom to Jefferson Conway and his small family. You probably remember his brother, Martin, from our more carefree days at Cincinnati House. He is now our Congressman.

One gang of toughs rode up and down our block on Rhode Island Street and through the yards, between the houses, from our street to the 600 block on New Hampshire Street, over to the Whitney House, trampling gardens and shrubbery, knocking over outhouses including ours, yelling for…that "bastard Captain Graton! We'll teach that S.O.B. to recruit and train them Niggers." And they were looking for Colonel Bowles, because, as you know both he and Graton had commanded Colored troops.

Well, they rode up and down our street and between the houses, over to the Whitney House, setting it on fire. They killed boarders and shot old Mr. Stone who died shortly after. Luckily Mrs. Stone and her children had returned to Michigan a few weeks ago.

Then they came back here yelling, "Remember Osceola" and "Remember our girls!" shooting at anyone who moved. Now and then they would dismount and using burning torches, set fire to random houses in our neighborhood. Then, when people ran out of their burning houses, they'd get shot.

A small squad came again and pounded on my door. When I answered it, they asked if this wasn't where Captain Graton lived. Well, of course, I said "Nobody by that names lives in this neighborhood, because (I lied) I know everybody on this block and all the houses on nearby streets and there are no Gratons around here.

Since I had been entertaining that morning, I was wearing my full hooped-skirts. While one wretch was questioning me, others were trying to set the house on fire and indeed succeeded in getting one side of our front porch burning pretty well.

Apparently I was successful in convincing them that this was the wrong house and I the wrong woman, because as swiftly as that squad came, they left thinking the fire that they started would consume the house, as it had consumed many others that day and most of "down town." They rode off towards the river, where others of them were trying to burn the new bridge.

Mr. Conway, the Congressman's brother, came out from the anteroom, where he was waiting. I didn't know what to do first, put out the fire or help Mr. Conway escape, since he'd heard his name called out, although the riders were actually looking for his brother, Congressman Martin Conway. They'd have shot him anyway. The Congressman is or has been somehow involved in recruiting ex slaves, so Quantrill's men were looking for "Mr." Conway.

Just as both of us got the fire out, we saw a different squad riding towards our house again, so I told Mr. Conway to crawl under my skirts and we quickly shuffled towards the side of the front porch that wasn't on fire. He scampered under the porch. When his side started to burn, he crawled under the west side of the house.

Two members of the second squad dismounted and while one of them questioned me again they were rather rough with me this time. This group didn't believe my story. They said someone had told them that this is where Captain Graton lived. I had my little four-shot pistol in my pocket and I considered brandishing it or actually shooting the one badgering me, but I knew if I killed either one of them, I'd soon be dead.

"The other one barged into the house and brought out newspapers and similar stuff to help set the house on fire again.

This time they got the restarted fire going pretty well, when one of their mounts, scared by the fire, ran off. What saved me that time was that horse, which they went after. All this time Mrs. Conway was hiding upstairs with her children, scared to death.

During that awful day, they killed George Burt, robbing him at gunpoint. They killed George Sangor and threw his body into his house, which they had torched. Mr. Fitch was killed in his bookstore, which the fiends also burned. His wife tried to save him but they forced her away. Dr. Griswold is dead, as is Jimmie Perune, Lem Filmore, Jimmy Eldridge, Mr. Fritch, who boarded with you at Killam's and many others including old Mr. Stone, who they shot inside the Whitney House and set it on fire. Our neighbor, Mrs. Bowles, the Colonel's wife, somehow made her escape with her children with the help of a Colored man that she was feeding at the time. Their buggy was parked in our backyard. They drove down among the cottonwoods by the river out towards the Gates' place. Luckily Mrs. Gates was not in town but they killed her husband and burned the Cincinnati House.

Graton and I had quite a bit of money in the Riggs Bank. Some of it was gun shop receipts and would be needed to buy inventory, pay rent, etc. I was worried that Quantrill might have gotten it. I learned by noon (of that day) that our gun shop had been badly burned and that they had robbed the bank, and burned it as well. By noon all of downtown was ablaze. They just wouldn't leave. They must have been here shooting and yelling awful obscenities for three or four hours. They then rode out east and south towards the Missouri Line. That afternoon I learned that the bank's safe containing our money, had been spirited out of the back door earlier by Mr. Burt and some locals (before they caught him and killed him.) Mr. Riggs (of the bank), who somehow escaped has been appointed administrator of Burt's "estate". They've since recovered the safe, opened it and found our money.

Thank god it was there! I trusted Mr. Riggs to take it to Leavenworth, where he deposited it. I would have done that chore

myself but they also stole Old Kate. I had been boarding her at the
livery stable all this time. Someone later said they saw Kate shot,
out on the prairie. They were real butchers but I hear they yelled
around town that they were evening up the score for Lane and my
husband when they burned Osceola and imprisoned some of their
wives from Bates and Cass counties. I hadn't known about that.*

*Another (ruthless) officer was Cole Younger. Two of his female
relatives were likewise arrested: they were Susan Van Diver and
Armenia Gilvey.*

*Bill Anderson, a Quantrill officer, who led forty riders the day
of the Lawrence raid had two sisters in with the other women listed
here incarcerated in the make-shift jail in Kansas City that collapsed,
killing several and crippled others.*

*It is noteworthy that the building collapsed on August 13th and
the Lawrence raid took place only ten days later.*

I learned later that three or four of their wives or female relatives
died in captivity. Others were injured. As to Osceola, I don't think
Graton had anything to do with that or I'd have heard about it
from him.

Before Graton was captured, he had sent me some money
with Mr. Hutchinson, the fellow who freighted Mary Rackliffe
and little Ermee to Colorado. I've buried that money in the
backyard. If I leave the state, I intend to take Haskey Wight,
who married Graton's older sister, Ruth. (They came out here
in 1858) into my confidence, as to where that money is. If I go
to Michigan, I certainly won't carry with me all that's buried in
the box, and if the war drags on and Alice and I need money
back East; I suspect that it will be Haskey who I must trust to
send what I need.

---

* *Added on and off months later, as more information about Quantrill, his officers,
etc. became available from various sources. One of Quantrill's officers, John McCorkle,
had a sister, Nannie, and a sister-in-law, Charity Kerr. Both women were caught
or rounded up in the execution of "Order No. 10" issued that summer by General
Ewing. This order authorized the arrest of men and women in those Missouri counties,
particularly in Bates and Cass counties, who could...or did...give aid and comfort to
Quantrill's men.*

We are all afraid that they'll come again but I don't now what good that would do them. Most of the important buildings and shops are all ruined, including my husband's. Oh yes, they also burned down the Cincinnati House and killed poor Mr. Gates.

Quantrill's gang was so unopposed that entire morning, that after burning the Cincinnati House, some of them had time to dismount and raid the main department store, stole clothing, which they quickly put on, while another group visited a local saloon, where Larkin Skaggs got so drunk that at noon as most of them rode off, he remained, riding around rather aimlessly like he was inspecting their now smoldering handy work.

When it was apparent that the main gang had rode off, some of the remaining citizens, ventured out. Most of them were armed. They spotted Skaggs, mounted, drunk, but all alone and took shots at him but missed. The youngest of the Coombs boys, whose mother worked at the Cincinnati House and whose two brothers had died that day, had a loaded musket. As Skaggs, now being shot at, rode furiously towards the boy, he fired and knocked Skaggs off his horse. Some mounted army scouts appeared in the confusion and if Skaggs wasn't already mortally wounded, they finished the task. Little boys ran out and urinated on him. They hung his body upside down and continued to take their revenge. Within a few days there wasn't enough of him left fit to bury.

I am so sick and disgusted with all this that as soon as I can, I think I'll take little Alice and go back to Michigan and stay with the Stewarts until Graton is released or the war is over.

Your loving sister,
Adda*

'In Adda's long letter is a note about two old friends, we've both known since Plymouth days. Preston Plumb was commissioned last summer as Captain in Company C of the 11th Kansas Infantry,

---

* A letter similar to this among the "Memoirs of Addie Stewart Graton is in the Archives at the University of Kansas Library, donated by Alice Graton Kincaid (KHMS 84:5, 13) It was written by Adda in commemoration of the 50th anniversary of Quantrill's raid. It appears in this book as Chapter 63.

which soon became a Cavalry Company. He quickly recruited his old friend, Alfred Pierce. The two of them and their troops were supposed to be guarding roads into Lawrence, August 20th and 21st Adda doesn't explain why Lawrence wasn't protected as it was in 1857 by Frank Swift, Captain Cracklin and the Mount Oread Rifles.

November 2, 1863
Harriman Ranch
Eastern Slope of the Rocky Mountains of Kansas Territory

Dear Adda,

Thank you for your detailed letter describing that awful day of August 21st: Quantrill's raid on Lawrence. I'm so relieved that you "out-foxed" them…and I'm not the least bit surprised. I'm also relieved that our house is still intact.

I know you won't believe this strange coincidence… but it's true. The same stage that brought your welcome letter about the Quantrill atrocities also carried Henry Lane, a brother of Jim Lane (this is a stage-coach stop.) They arrived late in the day of September 7th and he stayed with us for several days and confirmed your story and indeed added more details.

It's hard to get it into my head that so many Lawrence citizens died that morning, many of them, like poor Mr. Gates and Mr. Stone at the Whitney House. I can't believe that Mr. Burt is dead and although I knew he had been successful, I didn't know he had accumulated such wealth. I was so sorry to hear (from Henry Lane and you) that both bookstores are gone and that Mr. Fitch is dead. Did Mr. Wilmarth and his store survive?

Well, it's starting to get cold. It's a dryer cold here in Colorado than in Kansas and like Kansas the snow can drift something awful. Aside from the few coach passengers that spend a day or two here at the ranch, all the ranch hands (mostly nice young cowboys) are all gone and there is just one wintertime boarder here, George Blackman, a young miner…about my age. Mr. Harriman and he are partners.

I've become quite the gold miner since getting into the Rocky Mountains and in one of my letters this winter I'll tell you about it and a nice old Georgian, who's taught me "the ropes"

Well, that's the news from Colorado.

Your loving sister,
Augusta

P.S.:You know what I really should do for you and little Alice? I should copy all my journal entries from the time I left Lawrence with Tom Cordis. I think you would find them interesting.

Remember how we used to read each other's journals in Eldorado?

Adda, you should write-up the Quantrill Raid and send it to that newspaper in Flint.

The name of the young man at the ranch who had helped Charlie Thatcher carry my trunks and boxes in the afternoon I got here is George Blackman.

George and I are the same age, both born in 1839. Although his folks live in Iowa, he was born in Illinois. We both had the Kansas experience, although I suspect that my abolitionist zeal including our political affiliations was a little more involved than his. Two years later he came to Colorado. In recent months he became a mining partner with George Harriman. He mined sometimes up on Terryall Creek but when the mountain snow got too deep to work, he came down to the ranch, which was late October.

When he wasn't mining in the Tarryall area, he was at the ranch, which from October on was most of the time. So we became better acquainted on and off over the seven or eight months that we were both at the ranch, which stretched from late summer through a long bleak cold winter and slow to arrive spring. I had agreed to stay until April. With the war raging in the Kansas-Missouri area and Colorado mining slowing down, I was giving serious thought to returning to Michigan. In November Mr. Harriman had dropped my wages to $25 per month, which was fair because there wasn't much kitchen work to do as winter wore on. But during the day I kept busy. I mended sheets and pillowcases. I washed every blanket at the ranch and mended half of those. Afternoons and evenings I caught up on my reading.

One of the ex boarders had left a nice coal oil lamp. I claimed it and could read two hours every night. I've been able to read some of the books I've carried all the way from Eldorado that have been dormant for most of that time. Before I left Lawrence, a package of books that I had ordered arrived, but I had been so busy I didn't even bother to unpack them. In that package was a two-volume edition of Gibbons "Fall of Rome", which I had ordered after reading a fascinating book report in an Eastern magazine. The reviewer showed a revived interest in Rome and the Caesars and the decline of their empire as the concept of Christianity took root. I ordered the Gibbons but put off starting them because they looked so formidable with five or six hundred pages per book. That report by a historian at one of our Eastern colleges compares the Decline of Rome to the Decline of England, citing the inability of King George to put down the Revolt of the Colonies in North America, as a sign of England's decline.

I started Gibbons in November and didn't quit until Valentine's Day. What a writer. The problem is, he makes so many references to other times and places, like the Decline of the Ptolemy's (Cleopatra) and I have an unread biography of her as well.

After Gibbon's I began a Dumas book, the Count of Monte Cristo.

One of the stagecoach overnighters at Kenosha House this summer was an Eastern editor assigned by his newspaper to write about Colorado miners rather in the style of Horace Greeley. He had some sort of minor health problem aggravated, he said, by the elevation. (He was a big user of tobacco.) He also translated for a magazine that had serialized the French writer A. Dumas' book, the Count of Monte Cristo. He had a huge leather valise full of books and manuscripts.

When the morning stage to Denver came through, he wasn't ready to leave. Mr. Harriman wasn't here. The editor asked me if he could stay two more days until he felt better. I responded by saying, "This is a boarding house. Stay as long as you can afford. He laughed and said his paper competes with Greeley's New York Tribune and they can afford it."

After breakfast, he interviewed Charlie Thatcher. What little I caught of it, it sounded to me like Charlie (as usual) was testing the editor's gullibility. But when Charlie offered to take him up on Tarryall Creek with his rocker to show him what a miner really does for a living, illness or no, they left together. It was a glorious fall day in the Rockies. I had packed them a lunch, which included sandwiches of cold, boiled buffalo tongue. I noticed the editor had failed to throw a pair of boots into the wagon. Old Charlie was up to his usual "educational" tricks. That night, out of earshot from others Charlie lied to the young editor and said they had taken "mebbey" 5 ounces. Even the editor knew that was equivalent to 100 dollars for two hours work. By supper, after the editor had dried out, he had already begun a feature article for his newspaper on Charlie, "the famous miner from Georgia."

When the morning stage for Denver was preparing to leave after his third night here, the editor paid me and gave me his "editors" copy of the Dumas book…and that's my March assignment. This edition credits him as the translator. It took Charlie and the stage driver to carry his steamer truck out. Two days later Charlie Thatcher drove me down to the ranch. That was mid August.

NOVEMBER 29, 1863

Davey Jones was here at the ranch for supper and said Tarryall was pretty much deserted. All the people I cooked for at the Kenosha House are gone. The last time I was there was two months ago, when Charley and I had our last "dig". Davey gave me a little nugget of Tarryall gold. He thinks there is still plenty of gold in the streams and in the gravel banks and Charlie Thatcher has certainly convinced me accordingly, but conditions are just too insecure and unpredictable. He's thinking of moving on.

Mary Rackliffe visited me for four days over Christmas. She left here on the stage with eight passengers late in the day in an awful snowstorm. At the foot of Big Hill, three miles from here, at 9 o'clock or so, the stage got lost or the team gave out. They stayed there all night in the storm rather than roam around in the foothills, looking for their trail to the Michigan ranch.

Mary Rackliffe visited again in February. This time she brought little Ermee, who's about six years old now and a very nice little girl. What a shame her Daddy is dead.

For companionship, when he's here, I've allowed George Blackman to read my journal. I had, in early March written something to the effect that this is the most lonesome, God forsaken spot, it has ever been my lot to be placed in. To which George added in his writing: "*If it was not for the estimable, handsome and fine young lady, Mrs. Chase, this would be the most lonesome, God forsaken, etc.* to which Augusta wrote: he should have signed his name to this declaration: so Augusta did.

George W. Blackman of Marion, Lynn County, Iowa

JANUARY 1864

Why would a woman who's been "seeing" my sister's husband, before and after their marriage, have the unmitigated gall to write to me, more than once, seeking my "understanding"? Bereft of all morality, why would she insult my intelligence by thinking that I'm so manipulatable by her and her twisted, adolescent logic that I would somehow be persuaded to intervene with my sister on her behalf?

This is the stuff of the Old Testament! Indeed, as I made earlier entries, I promised myself that when I had time, I'd search the adulterous Old Testament to find a parallel.

Things are so slow now, I can indulge myself in this luxury, and I've always appreciated reading.

After several hours of examining the Bible, particularly the Old Testament, looking for stories that would be similar to the adulterous situation that my sister finds herself in with her husband, here are some of my findings.

Bathsheba, a young wife of Uriah, one of King David's generals, consents to an affair with the king after he watches her bathe...*or* she exposes herself to the King by taking a bath where she supposes she can be seen by him late in the day when he's finished with work and as she has hoped, he sends for her...all depending on how you see the available ambiguities, as you read the Old Testament books: Samuel and the Chronicles.

To cover the likely consequences of his dalliance, David arranges for Uriah to return to Jerusalem from the battlefield, assuming he would go home and spend some time with his lovely wife.

But Uriah, the story goes, feels he's not entitled to such marital pleasure while his men are fighting and dying, so he avoids his home. Frustrated, King David orders Uriah back to the front lines where he is killed.

After a respectable mourning period for her husband, Bathsheba now finds herself to be a young, attractive, pregnant widow. She sends a simple message to the palace, "I am with child".

What's David to do? He married the girl and she has three more children by him, of which one was Solomon.

Or, there is Jezebel, the Phoenician queen. Yes she is evil but I don't see in her resume that she's interfering adulterously with another woman's husband.

After these studies and reviewing my own experiences I do see some other comparisons to the women of the Old Testament and American women of the pre Civil War...what we have in common with Old Testament women is, we have little social or civil status and limited rights...very limited.

A long delayed letter, posted in Michigan from Adda arrived. She writes that things became so dangerous and uncertain in Lawrence that on October 17th she left, first going to Leavenworth, crossing the river there and taking the rails entirely across Missouri and on up to Chicago. She said the first news she had in Detroit was the presence of Rebel gunboats on Lake Erie, intending to burn Sandusky (Ohio) and Detroit.

She said she had not heard from her husband for months, but she had rented our house for $9 per month, that the new bridge across the Kaw is nearly complete and should be ready by early winter. Some of the houses and buildings destroyed by Quantrill are being rebuilt.

Why she wants me to know that Graton's account at the Riggs bank is $482.20, I can't fathom. She did say, "From the money buried in our backyard, she took $100 for traveling expenses and for living expenses in Michigan.

Early winter 1864

"Adda", a widow Adelaide Henrietta Stewart Graton at 49 years November 4, 1889 Lawrence, Kansas Husband: Captain John Riley Graton had been dead 17 years.

63.

HARRIMAN RANCH
TARRYALL, COLORADO
Early Winter 1864

It is pretty lonesome here now. Mr. and Mrs. Harriman moved sometime ago up to Denver for the winter. Before the snows started, the ranch hands drove the cattle towards Kansas some place, aiming to sell them, so I don't even have the ranch hands to cook for and visit with. Some of them are really nice fellows, not nearly as tough as they want others to think they are.

When the ranch hands left, I took off for a few days. I got the stage to drop me off at Michigan Ranch, where Elizabeth Cordis is staying. They found a place for their ranch but they didn't have time to build a cabin. The stage driver said that Tarryall is pretty near deserted...only Mrs. Rose is at the Kenosha House. I wonder how she keeps that big place warm...if she does. I wonder where Charlie Thatcher went for the winter. It's not like him to stay out here during the winter.

When I got back to Harriman's, two families were making themselves "at home." I had met them before at one of the Harriman's parities. The stage had dropped them off for an overnight stay. They were on their way to visit miner friends in Central City but might winter in Denver. The men want to stay and mine next spring but the ladies talk about going back to the

States. The stage that brought them brought some welcome mail, including one from Adda. It really made me jealous. It must have been written last fall. She talks of having a big party at one of the relatives in Michigan, where the highlight of the party was making several heaping apple pies from fresh Michigan apples. I haven't seen an apple since I left Lawrence.

Sometime in March when the ranch house was unusually quiet and George and I were talking, he asked me rather straight forwardly if I had ever considered remarrying. By then we had shared mutual experiences. I had told him about our trek out from Michigan, about Father joining Jim Lane's militia in Kansas, while it was still a territory fighting to vote over whether it would come in Free or Slave. Of course, he knew about that; and how Father spent the late winter of '56 in the P.O.W. camp run by pro-slavery hooligans, his New Year of 1857 presidential parole and his founding Eldorado. I also told him how I had met Chase in Nebraska, why we were there in the first place, that he and his friend Frank Robinson had followed us to Eldorado and in spite of his taciturn and independent nature, I had fallen in love with him and our marriage and the reason in my opinion for his untimely death.

He had read enough of volumes 1 and 2 of my journals to fill in other important episodes, like Father's murder and that Adda and I had sold the sawmill and three farming claims in Eldorado and moved back to Lawrence.

I told him that I was still mourning for Father when Chase died, suddenly...and that I was afraid I'd never get over that loss. I vividly recalled, but didn't discuss with George, old Mrs. Weibly's comment to me about mourning; that we continue our grief for about half the time we knew the loved one, except for females, where melancholia normally ended more quickly for biological reasons. I had occasionally thought about her biology reason. She had given me a poem that I had read several times without really comprehending it.

"For everything created
in the bounds of earth and sky
Has such longing to be mated,
it must couple or must die."

Chase died in September of '59, so in a few months that will be five years. I had trouble discussing with George the combined domestic social and financial changes that happened to Adda and me when both men in my life were suddenly taken from me.

On the long wagon ride out to Colorado I did some serious thinking about all this. I concluded that yes, I could mourn for another five years, but I'll soon be twenty-five. Time is not in my favor, in the sense of Mrs. Weibly's comment that nature diminishes our mourning out of biological needs.

George never asked me if I've gotten over my grief for Chase. What he asked was more objective. Had I ever considered remarriage? He asked it when circumstances were appropriate.

I had said to him, yes, I think I am over grieving...but in all honesty, I doubt that I will ever forget that Chase was my husband and I loved him devotedly. Without saying so, what I was thinking, was Mrs. Weibly's biology lesson. I don't think it's wise to mourn to the point where I'll be an old maid...a barren old maid.

A few days later, when the opportunity arose, I asked George why he hadn't married. His answer was that he had moved around so much or he was never in one place long enough nor did the occasion present itself at any of these places. He said Colorado and Kansas were bad places for single men because of the shortage of eligible ladies.

It was during this time, early spring, before the Harriman's came back and the ranch was still very quiet that George and I got to know each other better.

_____ 0 _____

No entries until Early April 1864

Early April the Harriman folks all came back and I was so glad for their company, especially Mrs. Harriman, who is also the bookkeeper for all of her husband's enterprises. After a day or so of negotiations, George severed his partnership with the mister for $550, which had been his plan all along. He will catch the first available stage to Denver. Before leaving, George spoke to me about rumors he had heard about the big new gold strike in Bannack, Idaho Territory.

Mrs. Harriman usually pays me by the month at the month's end except she's been gone since the last of September, so she's owed me for six and a half months. I had agreed to work through mid April. She owes $45 for October and five months @ $25 or $182.50. There was no dispute over my tally. She paid me in Denver-minted gold dollars...and you can't beat that; and that's over and beyond the deal I made with Mr. Harriman for my share of our claim up on No-Name Crick for $500 and she paid me in cash for that as well.

I had previously sold the mister some of my gold dust, at a discount, for coin. That has amounted to about $300, so for almost a year's effort here in Colorado, I've made almost $1,000 free and clear. I've also kept eight to ten ounces of gold dust and flake. When I asked him why he would buy dust, Mr. Harriman said with the war time expenses of both sides increasing, he thinks the value of gold will climb, maybe will see $30 an ounce. If that's his reason, that's good enough for me.

I've been in this area almost a year and although I've grown accustomed to the high elevation and the beautiful view of the mountains to our west, particularly in the early morning and at sunset, I think it's time for me to move on, though Mrs. Harriman's health is so poor that when the cowboys come back, she's afraid she'll not be able to cook for them and so tonight she asked me to stay over. She said the pay would go back to $45 per month and I'm able to save most of that if for no other reason, there is absolutely no way to spend it down here, except for mail order catalogue purchases and I have bought some books that way and some minor items of clothing.

I told Mrs. Harriman that since she's been gone, I have done all the laundry, made my own soap until the Lye ran out, but I said I thought I'd be moving on… maybe going back to the States. She suddenly increased her offer to $125 per month, if I'd do the laundry and cook. (The stage has begun to stop here regularly again and it's house policy to wash the bed sheets and pillowcases and guest towels after they leave. That contract would oblige me to stay through November when the cowboys go away again and the place goes into its winter hibernation. So if I accept this fine… but demanding offer…I would certainly leave in November and as politely as I could, I told the Missus that.

Maybe if I stayed through the summer and I could get Charlie Thatcher to go with me, we could prospect up on no-name creek a couple days a week. When I started to send a note to him in care of the Kenosha House, asking if we could be partners again this coming summer, if I stayed over. The stage driver said Charlie had gone to Georgia last October. I wondered why that old coot didn't drop me a note.

In the meantime, in the light of a letter from George in Denver, I may not stay here through summer and fall. George thinks we should consider marriage and that is certainly a flattering notion, though he didn't formally propose. In any event I intend to leave for Denver mid April and see what it is that George has in-mind. I'll either go through Kenosha Pass or I'll go around it, but I'm going.

I thanked Mr. Harriman for our association and during the good-byes he said he'd heard from Charlie Thatcher. He was coming back via the overland route. He'd gotten a note from Charlie posted in Leavenworth, so he should be here any day. Mr. Harriman said he believed the mining corporation was going to continue with the Kenosha tunnel-shaft this spring.

Before George left, we had an understanding that included the possibility of marriage, but didn't exclude the possibility that

I might go back to Michigan. Adda and little Alice were there and many of our Stewart relatives as well.

Sometime during the second week or so of April in another letter from George in Denver he sweetly proposed that we marry.

The northbound stage only stops at the ranch three days a week and I know most of the drivers. They often take a meal with us and it's house policy not to charge them.

I had so much "stuff" to take with me that I had to prevail upon the coach driver's good nature to accommodate me. I had my old traveling trunk with clothing and bedding but another trunk that I bought from a miner at the Kenosha House for my dishes, cups, soup bowls, kitchenware knives: the tools of my trade; included were three big cast iron skillets, (they were my mother's)...they've been in the family forever. And I needed a whole (wooden) box for my journals, books and a few magazines (with serialized books.)

Mary Rackliffe came down and took my place at the ranch but before I left, I sold my interest in a claim I told you about to Mr. Harriman for $500. The old-timer at Kenosha House, Charlie Thatcher and I had filed a claim on "no-name" Creek in the Tarryall District and took several ounces of gold out of it, using a simple rocker-placer owned by Charlie. He came down here to the ranch to visit several times before it got too cold and snowy for safe travel. Mr. Harriman and he are old friends and they always had business to discuss. Mr. Harriman knew we had "hit color", because I sold him most of my share of our dust @ $19.00 per ounce. So, over the weeks, when the weather was clement and Charlie and I mined, I had sold him over $300 worth of gold. And I suspect that a few times Charlie found someone else to dig for him but I don't think that was often because Charlie was so lazy. So Mr. Harriman believed Charlie when he said, "We'd hit color." Now Charlie has a new partner and I have $500 in Tarryall gold pieces, which, if he can persuade Mr. Thatcher to work our claim often enough he could recover his cost in just a few weeks. At $20 an ounce, they only need 25 ounces working only afternoons, but several of them we took out 1 ½ to 2 oz each time. Toward the end of our partnership we had a few days when we came back with 3 to 3 ½ ounces. The more I think about the arithmetic, if Charlie worked our claim five days a week the five month when mining is possible, paid a digger, he could clear $5,000...the more I think about it, the more I think I should have asked for double the $500.

I left the Harriman ranch about mid April after a final settling-up with the Missus. By post I had agreed to meet George in Denver as soon as the stagecoach could get over the Pass, through the remaining snow or I'll simply go around... but I'm going.

On the way to meet George in Denver, I made up my mind that I would marry him rather than go back to Michigan. Once I made that decision, I began planning for Idaho.

APRIL 1864

"Quantrill's Raid",
Another Version
August 1863

The authors found this article in the family archives written by "Addie Stewart Graton" who witnessed Quantrill's Raid on August 1863. This was written for its 50th Anniversary.

The evening of August 20th the town felt so secure that many of us went out looking for a breeze. It was so hot. There was a band concert that night.

At five o'clock the next morning (August 21st) the town was rudely awakened with pistol shots and men riding so close to my house, I could her them yelling and cursing.

We had no notice. Why didn't we have guards posted? General Ewing had established a string of outposts from Leavenworth all the way to Fort Scott. Quantrill obviously knew where they were and simply slipped around them

It was a frightfully hot day even in the early morning when Quantrill and his band of rider's made their famous and notorious raid on Lawrence…. and it was a long time in the making.

From 1854…the beginnings of the Kansas/ Nebraska Act… the Kansas Territory had been one of the most lawless areas of North America. From 1854 until the summer of 1856 with Geary's arrival as territorial governor, Missouri "Bushwhackers" came into Kansas Territory at will to attack abolitionists, free state settlements, individual farms and houses.

Some of those acts and the deliberate destruction of Lawrence were retaliated by John Brown.

The resistance was almost nil. John Brown had been in the territory for two years. He knew what to do and did take limited actions but lacked resources and manpower to do anything significant. But he did go back east and lecture and beg for help and was effective. Governor Reeder was White House appointed to maintain pro slavery politics. When he got to Kansas and saw the oppression, he joined John Brown and Jim Lane in sympathy with the abolitionists. They toured the northeast together soliciting settlers and money…and got both, though they were late in the game. By the summer of 1856, when we came out, things began to change and when they did, it was only a matter of two years and we more than evened the scales. By 1858 the Free Stators could out vote the pro slavery "establishment' and with Jim Lane's ability to organize the available manpower, he greatly reduced the pro slavery oppression and violence until the commencement of the Civil War.

By the summer of '56 Jim Lane and many others, like John Brown, numerous Eastern newspaper editors, antislavery preachers, Harriet Beecher Stowe and her brother, the Reverend Beecher, had touched the hearts of enough Northern abolitionists, to migrate or to finance those that would to the territory ostensibly to out vote the pro slavery element already there. And in time they did exactly that. Of course, that's how it came to pass that our father, Sam Stewart, my sister, Augusta, and I found ourselves out here.

But that summer "General" Jim Lane had other plans besides voting. From the new arrivals he began recruiting well-armed abolitionist militia companies to take to the field and physically confront the pro slavery forces, both those who were resident and those who rode over here so easily from Missouri. And he did that with such military rigor, organization and strength that as bad as the oppression and killing mostly by Missouri "Bushwhackers" had previously been, the summer and fall of 1856 saw that violence increase by an order of magnitude. Governor Geary barely in the territory was ordered (for the first time) to use U. S. Army troops to stop the fighting.

Some of Lane's companies were captured that summer and incarcerated in a P.O.W. camp but most of them remained semi-organized but intact as a threat to pro slavery militia made up of people from the South as far from Kansas as the Northern volunteers were for Lane's militia.

Just as the Missouri "Bushwhackers" came over into the Kansas Territory to plunder and harass the "free-stators", Lane and some of his lieutenants; i.e., Montgomery, Jennison and others, calling themselves Jayhawks and Red Legs, increased their forays into the three or four Missouri counties closest to Southeastern Kansas.

During these raids, livestock was stolen, farms burned and slaves and other property brought back to cities on the west side of the Missouri, like Leavenworth, Lawrence, Topeka, etc. Over the years these liberations created a fairly stable population of Colored folk in eastern Kansas. By the time the Civil War started Leavenworth had the largest group.

In 1859, Quantrill moved to Kansas. He left the Army, and its discipline. He was a gambler, perhaps a horse thief. There is good evidence that Quantrill, going under the name of Charles Hart, was in the area of Lawrence. There is no evidence that he had any visible means of support. When war was declared, he recruited a small band of unaffiliated Bushwhackers and raided parts of eastern Kansas and western Missouri. As early as March (1862) they attacked Aubrey, a little town thirty or so miles due south of Leavenworth. They actually captured a Union fort at Liberty over on the Missouri side. His troops grew in size and in September, the same year he struck Olathe killing three, he looted the town and set fire to several houses. In October 1862 he struck Shawnee killing two and burning houses there.

Authors' note: in chapter 59 an editor from Olathe stays at the Lawrence boarding house, where Augusta works. They discuss in greater detail Quantrill's Olathe raid.

In the spring of 1863, before Augusta left for the Kansas Gold Fields, Quantrill struck again…on the Missouri side at Plattsburg. Though we believed he favored the Confederacy, he preyed on both sides. Occasionally they skirmished with the Kansas Jayhawkers. Union officers treated him as a common outlaw. When the Union Army, including Jim Lane, ceased taking prisoners, Quantrill retaliated in kind.

In the meantime Lane, Jennison and his "Red Legs"/Jayhawkers continued to raid, particularly into Missouri counties of Jackson, Cass and Johnson, to burn, pillage, ruin crops and steal or kill livestock and liberate slaves. Some of their targets were homes and farms owned by members of Quantrill's men, their relatives or their supporters.

Union General Ewing had ordered the detention of any civilians giving aid or support to Quantrill's men. Of course, some of these detainees were female (wives and relatives) of Quantrill's men…remember he had between 200 and 400 riders. General Ewing authorized the execution of captured guerillas. Over the months Lane and or Union forces in Missouri had captured up to ten women, all relatives, wives, sisters, etc. of Quantrill's officers. These women were taken to Kansas City with dozens of other "detainees" and incarcerated in an old three-story commercial building, that was in such bad repair that even while it was being inspected for safety, on August 14th it collapsed, killing four or five women. Three escaped but with serious injuries. Prior to this event

Quantrill's gang had grown. Of those detainees killed in Kansas City was Josephine, a sister of "Bloody Bill" Anderson, one of Quantrill's meanest officers. Another sister was crippled. Some of the Kansas locals wanted to kill the women...even though some were just girls, because they were known to be closely related to and continually in support of Quantrill's men.

For some weeks that summer, prior to August 14th Quantrill had been trying without success to persuade his "captains" to raid and pillage Lawrence. The incarceration of "their women" relatives, resulting in death and injury to several was all he needed to convince his officers to mount a fierce raid on Lawrence. Indeed the Kansas City episode and the previous Osceola sacking brought more riders to his side. Some authorities claim that by August 21st he had 450.

They were particularly after Jim Lane, who *was* in Lawrence that day. They failed to get him but they destroyed his house, ditto for Jennison's, Governor Robinson's, the main hotel in town and several lesser establishments, like the Cincinnati House, where they killed the proprietor, Alpheseus Gates; The Whitney House, where they killed Nathan Stone, the hotel's operator and upwards of 200 or so in four hours of mayhem.

Just as Quantrill's raid was rationalized by him as retaliation, General Ewing issued a retaliatory Order Number 11 that forced tens of thousands of Missourians out of their homes and farms. Union troops enforced this edict. Three or four counties in Western Missouri, where Quantrill and his men lived and/or were fed and hidden, when he wasn't raising general hell, were evicted.

Quantrill trained the two James Brothers, as well as the Younger brothers, Cole and Jim. Bloody Bill Anderson was known for scalping his victims and tying their scalps in an accumulating bundle on his saddle.

After the Lawrence raid, Quantrill and some of his gang went to Texas where in time he lost control. He was ultimately killed in Kentucky in the spring of 1865.

Remembering the booty and other profitable success from their previous raids, Archie Clement contacted and then organized remnants of Quantrill's gang. They returned, post war, to their old Southwest Missouri haunts and continued their mayhem until 1866 when Clement was killed.

Soon after daybreak on that fateful morning of August 21, 1863, I was awakened by the sharp reports of firearms accompanied by wild yells and curses and then I knew that Quantrill had fulfilled his previous threat of invasion and slaughter. The raiders had gained access from the east on the old Oregon Trail, one squad coming in on Hartwell Avenue, where they killed old Reverend Snyder. In no time at all some of them were thundering north in the middle of Rhode Island Street, towards us. At 10th or 11th Street they spread out storming parts of downtown. They passed near New Hampshire and 10th to shoot up a company of new enlistments, killing and wounding several. A squad rode on up Massachusetts Street to 7th Street, the location of the rebuilt-four story Eldridge House. They shot their way in and attempted to loot it and shot any body that came into the public rooms.

That's when the first squad came over to Rhode Island Street looking, I believe, for Col. Bowles and Captain Graton (our house.)

In the early dawn a number of them mounted on horses had halted on the corner of New Hampshire and Winthrop Streets. From this point of vantage they kept a sharp lookout and dashed here and there in murderous pursuit after every man or good-sized boy who appeared within their range of vision. At first, some of them raced around the houses yelling, "Remember Osceola" and "Remember our girls" and discharging their firearms. I had to dress myself and baby, while lying on the floor to avoid stray bullets.

Later, when carrying out my household goods, I saw Mr. Vanderburgh, a gray-haired old man, in overalls, with open wristbands and untied shoes, running from the 600 block on Massachusetts street into the brush down toward the river bank.

But he was also seen by the ruffians on the corner. Two of them immediately gave chase with revolvers in hand. As I could not bear to witness the horrible deed, which I expected would inevitably result, I ran into the house. I heard one shot from them followed by others from across the river and, venturing to look out, saw the two raiders returning at full speed, one of them lying upon and clinging to the neck of his horse. It was a small band of our sharpshooters encamped upon the other side of the river which had fired the shots that saved Mr. Vanderburg by wounding one of the pursuers so badly that he died later.

During my husband's absence in the army I was boarding with the family of Mr. Jefferson Conway (a brother of Mr. Martin Conway, Representative in Congress) to whom I had rented all except one room of my house at 627 Rhode Island Street (now removed to 613 Rhode Island.)

Expecting that my house would be the next to be set on fire, I thought that I must save what I could and, during lulls in the shooting, took out into the center of the garden all of my furniture that I could carry. Meanwhile, Mrs. Conway sat on the stair-steps, apparently numb or bewildered. I urged his wife to look after his safety, and see some means of hiding him before the house should be entered by the terror. Clasping her children in her arms and uttering prayers, groans and wild cries, she would not listen to me. Realizing that it was useless to try to arouse her to action, I made an opening under the east end of my front porch and enlisting the services of a neighbor, Mrs. Luther Allen, who had just run in, directed that she walk slowly in advance of me and thereby form a screen with our skirts (we were both wearing hoop skirts), allowing sufficient room between ourselves and the front of the house for Mr. Conway to crawl along upon his hands and knees. After securing his safe passage over the porch, which was facing the group of ruffians only a few rods distant, he descended at the east end, crawled through the opening which had been made and disappeared under the house. I then closed up this opening and kept him secreted there until a crowd of prisoners, gathered from the Eldridge House, was brought down under guard two hours later and halted within a few yards of my gate. I saw that these prisoners were being guarded and, although others of the marauders were galloping past in pursuit of other prey, those in this crowd were not molested. As I had been fearful that the raiders might come in at any moment to rob and then fire my house and burn Mr. Conway alive or, if he was forced out by the fire, he would be immediately shot down, I went to the place where he had gone in and stated the result of my observations and also my fears, and advised him to come out and deliver himself up as a prisoner and take his chances with the others. This he did during a favorable moment, and the crowd of prisoners were soon after moved over to the Whitney House on the west side of the 600 block on New Hampshire Street.

Mrs. Conway, having come to her senses in the meantime, had put on the children and herself extra suits of their best clothing and given to each a small hand bundle to carry. Three men then rode up and one, the notorious Skaggs, who was drunk, first questioned Mrs. Conway. In her replies she gave him a false name. I wondered at her doing so and thought if he asks me mine, I will give him my own. Fortunately, however, he omitted that question but he asked me where my husband was, and I replied that I did not know (which was the truth as I had not heard from him for over two months), he answered, "Yes, By God! He's in the Federal Army!" Then turning to his men he ordered one of them to "Go in there and fire that house." Mrs. Conway then went to join the other refugees at the Whitney House while I remained alone and pleaded in vain with the ruffian to spare my home. Fearful that some violence might be done me if I remained longer, I took my baby in my arms and also went across the street to the Whitney House. Heartsick and faint, I stopped by the south porch, sat down on the floor and leaned back against the outside wall where I could watch my home. While sitting thus, a horseman came at full speed up New

Hampshire Street from Winthrop. When within a few yards of the house there was the sharp report of a rifle from over the river. The man instantly flung himself upon the opposite side of his horse and clung to his neck. The scream of the bullet was audible as it flew past and struck the wall of the old stone house, the Leis home, still standing in the 600 block on New Hampshire. The rider rushed on at such a furious pace that I thought that he would not be able to stop before he was upon me, but checking his horse so suddenly that he sat back upon his haunches at the edge of the porch. The rider dismounted, tied the bridle to a porch post, and stalked past me into the house. The man was Quantrill. For a year we have seen posted pictures of him.

When I became relieved that the efforts of the incendiary on our house had been futile, I too, went into the hotel where many others had gone in search for food. There was a crowd in the dining room helping themselves to that, which had been prepared for the early breakfast. After looking in vain for some member of the Stone family, I found a biscuit in a baking pan in the kitchen and divided it between Allie and myself.

Midmorning, when the raiders were leaving town, another ruffian was sent to fire my home the second time. My nearest neighbor, a very poor woman from Missouri, with her aged father and several small children were then living in the house, which I now occupy. Although her husband was supposed to be away in the Confederate Army thus her house had been spared by Quantrill after speaking with her in the early morning, she kindly placed a tub of water at my gate and sent me word. With this water, I soon extinguished what little fire there remained at my house.

Hearing that some men had been wounded at the Whitney House, I went back over, and saw Peddler Brown, and Mr. Nathan Stone, who had been shot. As he was being helped to a light wagon, he nodded a good morning to me. The men pulled the wagon down to the ferry and they were all taken across the river where Mr. Stone died two hours later. Going on into the house I found it deserted as the crowd had fled in a panic to the other side of the river as soon as the ferry could be brought over after the shooting of Mr. Stone and the others. The only occupant, a dead man, the hostler who had been killed in the early morning, was stretched out on the floor of the ironing room.

As I had been told that women and children were unharmed, I had no fears for my personal safety. But later, I learned that a paper had been recovered after the band left town, containing a list of the names of those whom they were most anxious to slay and among them were included the names of Mr. Bowles, Reverend Snyder, a friend of my husband, who was actually a lieutenant of one of the Colored companies and my own.

I learned later that day that Lt. Snyder was on leave at his farm on the outskirts of town. He was one of the first of our citizens killed by the group that rode in from that direction. My name and my husband's name were on their list! Old Mr. Brown, the father of Mr. G. W. Brown, told me afterwards that the raiders inquired of him where I was to be found. He professed to misunderstand the name, telling them that he believed there was a family here by that name but they had moved across the river about two months ago." Two of the raiders took Mr. Arthur Spicer, our neighbor, a prisoner on a horse between them and with drawn revolvers compelled him to point out the places, which they sought. When they asked him about me. He told them that he did not know anyone by that name.

He said afterwards, "I told so many lies that day that I had the hardest time of my life to remember them all to make them stick together." Two or three others, strangers, told me later that they had also been questioned concerning me. The reason given for seeking Mrs. Bowles and me was that our husbands were officers in a Colored regiment and they, with others, had been instrumental in recruiting and organizing the First Kansas Colored Regiment of Volunteer Infantry. Being unable to reach the men, the guerrillas sought revenge upon them through their families; of course, they were successful in killing Lt. Snyder. Mrs. Bowles, who was living near the southern limits of town, escaped into the country about half an hour before the raiders reached her house.

December 23, 1913   Addie Stewart Graton
Rewritten for the newspapers:
The 50th Anniversary of the
First Quantrill Raid In August 1863
This was in the family Archives

Laura Augusta Stewart Chase Blackman Denver, Colorado Territory Wedding Photo April 28, 1864 (she was 24)

*George Washington Blackman Denver-Aurora, Colorado Territory
April 28, 1864 Wedding Photo.*

64.

VIRGINIA CITY: WE'VE ARRIVED
MONTANA TERRITORY
Summer 1864
Part I

I am a thousand miles from where I was when I made my last entry at the Harriman ranch south of Denver, and owe you an entry. When the placer miners began leaving the Kenosha House late last summer, Mr. Harriman asked me to cook at his ranch on the high plains a few miles down southeast from the pass. Only those digging tunnels and shafts nearby remained, and it was likely they would leave that fall. The local east-west stage also stops at the Harriman ranch.

Although most of my time in Colorado was spent at the Harriman ranch, the three months I spent at Kenosha House were the most interesting, because I learned about gold mining by doing it, and I made more from mining than I did cooking. Of course, during the eight or so months I spent at the Harriman ranch I met and got to know the man I would marry.

George made an agreement with Mr. Harriman to buy-out his interest in their several mining claims, which they did before he left. He led me to believe that the five or six seasons he's mined out here, he has done well enough to want to stay "in the game".

George had picked up some surveying skills and after he left the Harriman ranch for Denver in March, he did some surveying in the new township there. It was in Denver that George heard more about a gold strike in Bannack (Idaho Territory.)

I had agreed to stay until April. With the war raging in the Kansas-Missouri area and Colorado mining slowing down, I was giving serious thought to returning to Michigan. In November Mr. Harriman had dropped my wages to $25 per month, which was fair because there wasn't much kitchen work to do when the ranch hands and cowboys drove the cattle to some place in Kansas to sell them. But I kept busy. I mended sheets and pillowcases. I washed every blanket at the ranch and mended half of those and I caught up on my reading.

One of the ex boarders had left a nice coal oil lamp. I claimed it and could read two hours every night. I've been able to read some of the unread books I've carried all the way from Eldorado. Before I left Lawrence, a package of books that I had ordered arrived, but I had been so busy I didn't even bother to unpack them.

On the way to meet George in Denver, I made up mind that I would marry him rather than go back to Michigan. Once I made that decision, I began planning for Idaho. We needed more blankets and I'll try to buy or make a nice thick "tick" that we can comfortably sleep on in the wagon. And I need to plan for provisions we'll need on the trip, which might be well over six weeks.

George and I married in Aurora on April 28, 1864 by a Reverend A. R. Day, a Presbyterian. Although he had a church on Ferry Street, we were married in the home of Mr. Silverthorne, a mutual friend. Afterwards we walked over to the Rocky Mountain News and wrote up our announcement, which appeared in their newspaper. We purchased a fancy wedding license/document printed by the Rocky Mountain Newspaper, which I proudly have in my trunk.

In Aurora the day after we were married, I bought two excellent off-yellow, all wool blankets, very thick and clearly marked U. S. ARMY from, I suppose, a soldier, right on the street… both for a dollar each. I should buy five or six at that price. I also bought a bolt of khaki cloth and a bolt of blue Denim from him. Miners are hard on their clothing.

From that same gentleman I bought two Army Issue coal-oil lamps and five gallons of very smelly coal oil in a heavy metal pail impressed in raised letters, U. S. Army with a screw-capped, non-leak spigot, very fancy.

From people coming into Denver with supplies and others going home or joining one Army or the other, used hardware items are available at bargain prices.

While George was looking for a suitable wagon and team, I began buying supplies. I estimate we might be on the trail as long as six weeks, maybe fifty days, so planning for that was easy. Since I knew how to run a boarding house, I thought it would be prudent to lay in supplies that I might need, should I decide to go into that trade, while George attends to his mining. If I don't go to boarding we can use these supplies 'til they give out or I'll sell them up there at a profit.

A supply wagon train had just come in from Utah with some very nice white barley and I bought one hundred pounds of that in four canvas bags. With beef stock it makes excellent soup. They also had some lean bacon at $1.00 per eight to ten pound slab and small, but fat hams @$1.00 each. I bought twenty of each and with a little friendly bargaining paid $35 for the lot. The Salt Lake City boys had some of the whitest salt I've ever seen and cheap. I asked if they were Mormons. One of them said, "Died in the wool". The Mormons also had some white flour at $10 a one hundred c.w.t. I thought that was a little dear compared to what I knew Kansas flour was selling for before we left Lawrence, so I told them I'd think about it.

A supplier from Pueblo had dried red beans at 5¢ a pound or $4 a hundred weight. I bought 200 pounds, put up in twenty-five pound cloth bags. He also had plenty of brown sugar. He had a variety of flour, the usual coarse brown grouts as well as well-milled white flour…both at $5 per c.w.t. I bought fifty pounds of grouts and 100 pounds of white grade A flour. As I passed the Mormon wagon, I told them about their Pueblo competitor with white flour at $5 c.w.t. They laughed and said they had bought their flour from him, figuring that when he sells out, they'd be all right.

The fellow from Pueblo was obviously a Mexican…a very pleasant one. His wife or female relative had a little wood fire going and she was cooking little, very thin, coarse corn pancakes, which were the diameter of a small saucer. She gave me one while we bargained. It was delicious and plain. I asked her what she called them but she smiled acknowledging she didn't understand me. While I was complimenting her, the bean salesman said they were tortillas, little tarts, whereupon she gave me another one on which she spread a thin layer of what tasted like a bean-spread-flavored with mild chili. This one, she rolled-up. I thought I would like to have these two people as neighbors. He agreed to cart all that stuff to our boarding house.

A day later I found the fellow that sold me the two U. S. Army blankets and bought three more. He also had all the coffee beans I wanted at 25¢ per pound. They obviously had come from an Army Supply Depot and had been roasted. I asked him if he could locate 100 pounds of little white Navy beans. He said he would look around.

One supplier had nothing but Missouri onions and potatoes: big ones each individually-wrapped in newspaper, a common practice to prevent spoilage…at $3.00 per barrel and each barrel guaranteed fifty pounds. I bought a barrel of each.

I went back to the Pueblo wagon and asked if he had any corn meal…he had plenty, but what did I want? White or yellow… either was at $3.00 per c.w.t. I bought fifty pounds of each for $ 5 total and said hello to his nice wife.

While I was "laying in my larder", all of it for less than $75, George bought a wagon from a miner who was doing so well he decided to stay. George had all four wheels removed for inspection and had them heavily greased. From the same miner he also bought his team of horses. That night when I asked what this rig cost, he smiled and said he'd paid with "Tarryall Flake". When I asked him how much more he had. He grinned and said, "If I tell you, others will think you married me for my money." George is a good-humored tease, but it's nice to have a close relationship with a man again. We spent two weeks in the Denver area leisurely buying supplies and enjoying ourselves. At a bank run by Southerners George traded this season's gold dust for gold coins. He actually got $22 and ounce. When I asked why they were paying over $20, he said they were speculating that gold would double before the war was over. I thought about selling my own Tarryall dust to them.

Our stay in Denver was a very pleasant honeymoon. I bought a nice dress for our wedding and had my picture taken in it. (I notice that we've had a change in our vocabulary. In Lawrence we called it a "likeness". Now they are calling it a "picture.")

As soon as we arrived in Denver, we heard troubling talk about Indian problems only twenty or so miles north of here at Bijou Creek near Fremont's Orchards; that's frightening because it's on our route north. An army lieutenant had been dispatched with adequate troops to recover some stolen mules. When they located the Indians and the mules, the Indians claimed they "found" the mules out on the plains and wanted a reward for their return.

A fight broke out when the soldiers attempted to recover the mules. Some Cheyenne were killed. During that same period a Lt. Eayers raided and burned four Cheyenne camps. In fact, he came back to Denver the third week of April while George and I were looking for agents or organizers of the first northbound wagon train headed for Bannack. By the time we hit the South Platte River, Major Downing had engaged some Northern Cheyenne along the river, killing twenty-five of them.

We were getting serious threats from Indians fighting sporadically all over the area. Indians have attacked settlements south and east of Denver along the headwaters of the Arkansas River. Before we left, all of these reports had been covered in the Rocky Mountain News. These were sobering circumstances under which we commenced this trek to Idaho.

There was, that spring, great excitement about the new big gold strike in Bannack, Idaho Territory and another one north of that in Kootenay, British Columbia, Canada. After talking it over, we decided we would go for Bannack.

During the two weeks in Denver, we located those people who were organizing outfits for Idaho and scheduling departure dates for the trains. We told them we were ready to be in the first or second outfit. I was really surprised to learn from the organizers that they already had pledges from enough locals to make up five trains. They speculated that they could double that. The first train they said was scheduled to go out the first week of May. We believe the leaders of this train are L. B. Statler, a minister traveling with his wife, O. B. Whitford, a physician and surgeon (he was later mayor of Butte), B. F. Bissell was listed as a farmer, but for two or three years I bumped into him here in Alder Gulch mining, just like Abraham Morgan, who was one of Jim Bridger's guides that didn't return with the major but came on into Nevada City and Virginia City. I served him on a few occasions when I had the boarding house in Nevada City. He moved to Wickes. One of the guides is a French speaking Mr. Amede Bessets. He too was one of Jim Bridger's guides (born in Quebec) and stayed with our party all the way into Alder Gulch. He had business of some sort in Bannack.

By the time we got rolling, it was the 1st or 2nd of May and we arrived in Alder Gulch (Virginia City) the 14th of June, so we were on the road forty-seven or forty-eight days.

By the time we got on the northbound trail, someone said that we were a separate party of about 280 men, women, children and about sixty wagons plus some cattle, milk cows, extra horses and mules. In a later published biography of George Blackman he wrote that in their party were Major Boyce (U. S. Army?) and Charles Curtis, an Irishman from County Cork. They were with us all the way to Virginia City. Mr. Curtis became a famous auctioneer and merchant...mostly in Helena, where he also became sheriff and postmaster.

George had some reason to believe that Major Boyce was on some military (Army) assignment. But he too stayed with us all the way to Virginia City. By 1870 he had become Speaker of the House (Montana Legislature.)

On the trail we continually hear about Indian fighting as close to us as along the South Platte.

For protection we were immediately organized into a military arrangement with mounted armed guides in the lead and in the rear. There are literally dozens of others, presumably armed riders on both our flanks.

Our first major destination was Fort Laramie, where our train was to meet the famous guide "Major" Jim Bridger, who will lead us on almost to Bannack.

The first leg of this trip is on the Bozeman Trail, which is also used by some Oregon-bound travelers. But at or near Fort Reno it's Mr. Bridger's plan to divert west, off the Bozeman Trail taking what's sometimes called the Yellowstone Cutoff. The purpose of the detour is to avoid Indian problems from the Lakota Sioux allied with Northern Cheyenne and Northern Arapahoes. Those Indians consider the land east of the Big Horn Mountains, in the area of the Powder River, Tongue and Big Horn River to be theirs. The Bozeman trail crosses those rivers and the River valleys.

Bridger's new Route is supposed to take us west of a generally north-south mountain range called the Big Horns, through the Wind River Country. We will cross the Big Horn River by ferry.

But the first week of May our first point on the trail out of Denver was Latham, a little east of Fort Collins. Latham is on the South Platte and I remember it as a south turning point a year ago with Tom Cordis on our way down to Denver.

Denver to Latham is about forty-five miles and due to slow starts in the morning and noontime dallying, it took all of three days.

As I recall, it was at the Latham stop or the next one that at about half-past four in the afternoon the train was stopped and the guides and guards rode by each wagon and guided us in a way that we formed a large circle, which the guides call a corral, maybe

150 to 200 feet in diameter…and that's after the teams were out of harness. The sixty wagons in our train make two corrals with the wagons as close as they can be from front to back.

The stock and team animals were allowed to graze outside the circle until sundown, then an opening was made in the circle and all the stock was driven inside for the night. And the circle was closed. Sometimes the wheels of one wagon were chained to the wheels of the next.

Guards were posted and bonfires were lighted. It wasn't cold. The fires provided some visibility.

It was quite exciting. We continued this nighttime defensive arrangement until we hit the Yellowstone River.

From Latham to Fort Sedgwick (near Julesburg on the South Platte) is about 150 miles and about ten days. Julesburg is currently the western terminus of the telegraph line. though we saw them extending it northward. We spent one night at American Ranch and another at Lillian Springs before turning northwest at Julesburg. The purpose of the east leg was to regroup with another train coming from Kansas or Iowa. At Fort Sedgwick we turned northwest and headed for Camp Mitchell, that leg was about 100 miles and is called the Bozeman Trail, named after John M. Bozeman from Georgia, who had prospected in the Bannack area as early as 1860. Beyond Fort Reno his trail goes northeast of the Big Horn Range and, we learned later, is very much an irritant to the Indians.

Midway, before we were joined by Jim Bridger, we got more reports of Indian attacks in that general area. The Army is afraid that several tribes of the western plains: the Sioux, Arapahoe, Apache, and Kiowa are uniting to fight the White Man.

After several days on the trail, we've begun to socialize during the evening meal by taking potluck. During one such meal one of this train's organizers joined us. He had a list of the people in our wagon outfit, which he allowed me to see. I cared more about what the people "did" than who they were. That was a mistake. I should have paid more attention to names. It didn't take me long to figure out this group had the nucleus of a town site.

Only four people in this train list themselves as miners and George is one of them. Well, that was a surprise. I would have guessed that half the males in this party were from the Colorado mines. Two of the miners, a partnership, have a disassembled steam-driven stamp mill in one of the wagons. It's pulled by four mules. Others listed were twenty-one farmers, eight stockmen. The other miner, another Irishman is Hugh Daly, a friend of Mr. Curtis. Later, I often saw Mr. Daly here in the Gulch. He was a carpenter but also built sluices. Now and then he mined. Later he moved to Helena with his Irish friend, Charles Curtis. They are both from County Cork. There were two lawyers, one surgeon/ physician, two preachers...one of them says he's also a freighter. It took him only three days of our communal suppers before he had us all intimidated and disciplined to wait before eating, for him to offer a long-winded prayer. Even his wife complained that the food was cold by the "Amen" time. I don't think he really cared about the blessing. I think he was simply intent on being in control of something. In a mild way he reminds me of my brother-in-law.

There were three merchants, two with extra wagons loaded with dry goods, and they reminded me of Mr. and Mrs. Strong from Indiana whom we teamed up with in Western Iowa in '56, who only stayed in Kansas a few weeks then moved to Archer, Nebraska. He too was a grocer and he had three extra wagons loaded with supplies for his new store in the Nebraska Territory. There were only two teachers; one of them lists himself also as a merchant banker. I wonder if he's carrying his capital with him. Before we get to the Yellowstone, I want to ask him just what it is he does...Does he loan money? Does he invest? I wonder if he's ever grubstaked a miner? Since he's also a teacher, maybe I'll tell him about my teaching experience in Eldorado. I wonder how long it will be before we open a school in Bannack? Another is a miller and another a brewer. There are fourteen females including yours truly. Two of the women are married to the two preachers. Minister Huge Duncan, a Scotchman has a family of five with him. He's a little nicer than the old "Bible Banger." I talked to his wife as often as I could when I discovered that she was from Scotland and had a brogue exactly like our old boilermaker friend, Mr. Eastwood. Her name was Christine, a really charming woman Their daughter is seventeen and reminds me of Adda. From what I can tell, all but an infant of their five children were born in Scotland. Yes, he's a Presbyterian. I hope he stays in Virginia City.

Fort Sedgwick is the beginning of the Bozeman Trail. In two days traveling northwest we picked-up the North Platte River at Chimney Rock, heading toward Fort Laramie, which was about one hundred miles, spending one-day en route at Camp Mitchell, another ten days were chewed up before we got to Fort Laramie. Between Fort Laramie and Fort Fetterman is Bridger's Ferry.

About 100 miles from Fort Fetterman we could see the foothills of the Big Horn Mountains some distance straight ahead of us. We began a slow, gradual wheel or turn off the ruts of the Bozeman Trail to a new unmarked trail to the West. One of the guides said this was Richards Bridge.

About a year later people began calling this spot, Fort Reno. Whether they built a fort and trading post there, I don't know.

We were now on the new Bridger cut-off. It was May 20th. It was rumored that Jim Bridger had joined our train, where we left the "Bozeman". He wanted the Big Horn Mountains to be on our east all the way to Fort Smith. This will be a long stretch, something between 110 and 125 miles.

After we departed the Bozeman Trail we stayed on the high plains heading north with the Big Horn Mountains always to our east; i.e., our right side, and the Wind River Mountains to our left or generally west of us. We saw large herds of swift antelope usually at a distance of 300 to 400 yards. They are particularly elegant in their posture when we see them in the late afternoon sunlight. The men took shots at them, hoping for fresh meat, but in this segment of our long train, I never saw an antelope fall. Some of the men did go into the low mountains to bring back deer. We crossed the Big Horn River on a ferry made mainly of logs lashed together. The ferry was big enough to handle two wagons. Each wagon paid the ferryman $2.50.That was slow going. One of Bridger's armed guides said, "If there are any Indians around, now would be the time for them to "go after us."

The first afternoon stop after crossing the Big Horn River, the guide who previously let me see the roster of our party, joined our small group for supper. One of the teachers asked him if he had worked or guided with Jim Bridger before. He said no, but on this trip he's had occasion to be in group discussions where Major Bridger dominated.

The teacher asked, "What can you tell us about him? How old is he? We had heard such incredible tales that it was hard to really believe Mr. Bridger could have done all these things."

"He's about sixty years old, had been all over this country years earlier as a successful trapper and Indian trader. He not only discovered the Great Salt Lake but also has guided Mormons to it over several westbound trails. He has been both a friend and foe of Brigham Young. He had a trading post on one of the Mormon trails. His fort was about 100 miles east of Salt Lake City, but west of the Green River.

When the Mormons threatened a general uprising and the U. S. Government sent Colonel Albert Sidney Johnston out there in 1857 to settle the matter, Jim Bridger, who was fifty-seven years old at the time, was commissioned to guide him there from the Colorado Rockies. In fact, it was Colonel Johnston who gave Mr. Bridger the commission of Major in the U. S. Army. And by the way, he's on leave from the Army this summer to guide all these trains going to Idaho Territory.

I remember one morning in early September when we were still living in Eldorado and had both the sawmill and the sugar mill working, when several east-bound companies of mounted soldiers made camp so close to us that after breakfast Adda and I walked over and asked who they were. Some of the soldiers jokingly said that they were "Utah veterans" and they explained their rather strange mission to Salt Lake City.

When I asked who was in charge, they said Colonel Phillip St. George Cooke headed their companies. Well, Adda and I had met him when he had his temporary camp across Pony Creek, just inside the Kansas Territory at Plymouth. The soldier went on to say Colonel Albert Sydney Johnston headed this Army mission to Utah but he was not among this group stopping in Eldorado.

The visiting guide continued. "One of Bridger's lieutenants on this train...also an Army soldier...was with Major Bridger in 1857 when the Army decided to explore the headwaters of the Missouri River and had hired Major Bridger as the best guide available. Bridger had told others that except for a few rapids, water navigation from St. Louis to the Pacific Ocean was possible.

They left St. Louis (1859) with about forty Army soldiers, some scientists and proceeded up the Missouri River toward the Black Hills, expecting to make peace with the Crow and Sioux Indians on the way. One officer had Indian annuity authority and Bridger could speak to both tribes to obtain a safe passage.

By August they were in the Yellowstone area... area also familiar to Mr. Bridger. He said some of the waters here are hot and the deeper into the water you go, the hotter the water. Those Army personnel thought Bridger was telling another one of his tall tales when he said there was a hot water spout in Yellowstone that shot up into the air sixty feet.

This Army group still guided by Bridger, explored all over the Yellowstone, Jackson Hole, Grand Teton area. They had meetings with local Indians, the Flatheads. Bridger had been there before and could act as an interpreter.

It was in this area where Bridger pointed out there were two possible trails generally north to the Yellowstone River, one on the east side of the Big Horn Mountain Range. The other, the one we are on now puts the Big Horns to our east. That was about three or four years ago. But Bridger had been here maybe twenty years earlier.

This party ultimately returned to Council Bluffs. The Army paid-off Bridger and he returned to his farm near Independence, Missouri.

After thirty-six days we reconnected with the Bozeman Trail and other west bound wagons at Rock Creek near Fort Smith, where we rested a day. George and I ate our meals with a family at Fort Smith.

I understand that in our party is a well-known preacher/Indian missionary but I have never gotten his name.

During our supper meal after leaving Fort Smith and after we crossed the Big Horn River, well into June, one of the leaders who I hadn't seen before, asked to join us. As he gave us a general report on our progress, he said that the party had just learned that, as of May 26th, where we're going is no longer the Idaho territory. Congress has authorized a new territory to be called Montana. It was cut out of the Idaho Territory.

I told George if I had a pistol, I could file three notches on it: one for Kansas territory, one for Colorado territory and now Montana territory. I later thought if I could find my Latin book in among all the boxes and crates, it's my recollection that Montana has a Latin root. When we settle down, if we ever do, I'll have to look it up.

After we crossed the Big Horn River, it was about 150 miles drive before we picked up Yellowstone River after crossing several streams and small rivers. Soon we were going generally west along the Yellowstone River or in its valley to Fort Ellis and Bozeman.

Someplace on the 150 mile stretch between Fort Smith and the Yellowstone River, Jim Bridger and his small party left us to return to someplace on the trail well south of us...maybe Fort Fetterman to pick-up the next north-bound train headed for Bannack. Our wagon train boss certainly knew when we lost Mr. Bridger, and his party of guides, but we didn't hear about it. We only knew the general plan, which meant that Jim Bridger and guides would pilot to this area about ten outfits along major segments of this trail this summer. From Bozeman it's a three-day hard drive to Nevada City (fifty miles.) When we stopped the 14th of June, we heard that a much bigger strike was underway in Alder Gulch, which includes Nevada City and Virginia City and that most of the Bannack miners and merchants had already moved up here. That was apparent just by looking at the activity in Alder Creek and on its banks. By my approximation, we've traveled about 900 miles.

Some of our group went on to Virginia City including the miners with the stamp mill. They told someone that there's no quartz to speak of down here among all this streambed gravel. George figured they were going on up the creek until they got into the mountains...some of our party went down to Bannack. Freighters said there was a large warehouse in Bannack as well as a slaughterhouse.

I later learned that all the wagon trains coming in that summer, ten to twelve of them from Denver increased the population of this area by 25%.

We haven't reached Bannack and probably won't even go there. It is generally west of us about seventy miles in the same valley about as far from Virginia City as it was from Fort Ellis (Bozeman), which we went through to get here. There seems to be all kinds of gold right here in Alder Gulch, which stretches from below Nevada City to beyond Virginia City and up into the mountains. Earlier, this area was called "Fourteen Mile City." There are about 10,000 miners, some with families up and down this valley already. This is a wide gravely flood plain between two low mountain ranges. Alder Creek comes down out of the mountains east of Virginia City. Over the centuries it has meandered back and forth, forming a flat, gold containing gravely flood plain several miles wide. We are in the Lower Rockies between the Ruby Mountain Range and the Madison Range. The valley swings generally from west to south.

George and almost every other miner thinks there is a Mother Lode up on the mountain some place, which is also the source of the streams and cricks that have carried down all this gold they are finding in the Alder Gulch streambed in among the sand and gravel of a large east-west running stream. Some mining is being done on the dry gravelly flood plain which is a mile and a half wide, between Nevada City and Virginia City (a distance of about two miles). Wagonloads of water in barrels are being carried to those fellows. The men panning for gold in the stream are doing very well, but they must work in the water, which even in the summer is cold up here. Of course, I know something about that first hand from my association with Charlie Thatcher down in Tarryall. Some of the younger men, boys really, work for $10 a day, digging in water two to three feet deep down into the streambed gravel, which is manually carried to rockers or sluice boxes close to the stream. The real experienced miners operate their rockers and collect the gold dust and occasional nugget. The stream diggers are inexperienced employees.

Years later pumps and heavy-duty equipment was brought in, to float on small ponds created by a dam behind the float. A high pressure jet of water is aimed at the nearby gravel bank to loosen the gravel, which is carried by water by a long boom back to the barge, where the gold is separated from the gravel in the usual placer fashion, relying on gold being so much heavier than sand and gravel, which is spewed out and piled up behind the barge as it slowly moves in stages up the steam. That stream has created Alder Gulch over the centuries.

I don't know why I'm surprised, but I am. About half the men, who we knew down in Tarryall and Harriman's are up here. So every day, as we walk around deciding just what we intend to do, we run into these fellows. It's my opinion that there are already too many people here. That's why jobs are scarce for the new comers. There's another scarcity and that's food, so I'm glad I laid in all the provisions I did down in Aurora and Denver, but George and I will keep our temporary abundance to ourselves. We left Denver on April 28th and arrived at Virginia City on the 14th of June 1864.

Although we have plenty of food in the wagon, we thought we'd celebrate our arrival with a warm supper and chose a small boarding house on the main street in Nevada City. I met the lady running the place. Since she too was up from Colorado, I told her about my Kenosha House experience. She offered me a cooking job on the spot at $40 per month. I said I'd think about it during supper.

When I mentioned it to George, his response was, "Let's not be hasty, let's look around. There are so many people already here, we might not even stay." During the meal (which was so-so), the proprietor came out, sat down and asked what I had decided to do. As I hesitated to tell her (knowing if we stay, we might be neighbors), she raised the offer to $80.

Although it was still daylight, the room, because it had no windows, was almost dark. She had a candle on each table and some candles on reflective wall tins. When my eyes adjusted to the light I realized the floor of this cabin was simply sand and pebbles.

George asked her if she had any rooms available.

"No, every boarding house in the Gulch is full up" so we knew where we're going to spend the night.

During supper George made a sobering calculation. He said, "If this entire Gulch is eight miles long (and it isn't) and if each miner can stake a 100-foot claim and there are claims on both sides of the stream and miners here are allowed to stake two claims each, there's only room for 800 individual claims. At an average of two miners per claim, that's 1,600 miners and we've both heard that there are already 10,000 in the valley. If half of the claims use rockers and employ two diggers, that's another 800 jobs, so there's going to be a lot more men than there are jobs in this camp."

The next day to explore the area we slowly drove our rig on up through Virginia City toward the summit (another six or seven miles). Between the stretches from Nevada City to Virginia City we actually got down and walked over to the claims along side the stream and struck up short conversations. About half had rockers. Many hired youngsters to dig and haul sand and gravel to the rocker, like Charlie Thatcher and I did on Terryall Creek.

One of the fellows we met from Colorado thought the elevation here was about the same as Aurora/Denver.

But the big disappointment is, every linear foot along about seven miles of this stream in the wide gravelly flood plan has been claimed, which means we've arrived too late to stake a claim right on Alder Creek. However the creek seems to be very productive. About half the people we talked to said they were doing well enough to stay. Not a soul offered to sell his claim.

Other miners have set up their rockers some distance from the stream out in the dry, flat gravel bed. Those fellows have to buy water by the barrel, so what they save in not paying streambed diggers, they more than spend on carted water.

That night we returned to the same boarding house for supper. George said, "We have three options as I see it:

One: if I placer mine in this gulch, I'll need to stake a claim out on the dry gravel bed and either buy my water or build a sluice. Remember, we saw a few short sluices, today and not too many feeder streams but there were a few streams available, which is a possible option.

Two: All this gold flake and nuggets have a source. It's got to be from up on mountain faces we saw today beyond Virginia City, which is also the source of the water for the ten to twelve mile long stream. I'll bet there are plenty of available claims up there. Chiseling's hard work...but it's dry work and will cost money for blasting powder.

Three: We can move on. He asked me what I wanted to do?

I said, "Let's eat supper".

Summer 1864

Jim Bridger

Jim Bridger

Long before the Western pioneer period of 1850 to 1875 was the period of the western explorer. Though not the first, certainly Lewis and Clark's explorations to the Pacific Ocean are among the best known

Among those who explored the best and safest trails, learning the ways and languages of the various Indian tribes, few have made more or deeper marks than Jim Bridger. Though he had been exploring the Big Horn Mountains and Yellowstone River area forty years before Augusta's party used that trail, led by him, when he was sixty years old. Major Andrew Henry had been there eleven (or so) years earlier. Jim Bridger became Henry's protégé.

Each of our early explorers stood on the shoulders of "giants" before them.

Private enterprise (the fur trade) fueled the earliest of these trailblazers. On and off Bridger acted as a guide for various U. S. Army explorations into the West. Indeed it was the Army that commissioned him a major.

Long before the Mormons arrived in Utah Bridger knew that lake was salty. During their migration Bridger was a friend of Brigham Young and the Mormons. They had a falling-out when Major Bridger guided the U. S. Army to Salt Lake City in the summer of 1858.

65.

GOLD
VIRGINIA CITY: MONTANA TERRITORY
Summer 1864
Part II

George hasn't made up his mind. There is this very successful strike here in the Gulch and in Bannack and another reported north of here in Canada or British Columbia at Kootenai or some such name.

George asked my opinion. It took so long to get here; I'm reluctant to move all the way to the Canadian strike. That might be another fifty days. We're still living in the wagon, which beats sleeping in any boarding house I've seen here. And the rent is so high. George found work, if he wants it at $8.50 a day stream—digging.

The offer of $80 a month to cook in a nearby boarding house is still available but I sense that George doesn't favor that. I've stayed in touch with the lady anyway and have visited her "kitchen". Well, her working conditions are terrible. I told her that if I did accept, I had no intention of bringing in my own wood, because 10,000 others needing wood has created a shortage of it. That place, a recently thrown-up log cabin, was just filthy: gravel floor, slippery from spilled grease, big gaps between the logs, which will be all right while it's warm but come fall and winter? And there is a pesky little knat or fly, very small, buzzing in swarms with a very irritating bite. She must serve a dozen of these little pests in every bowl of soup. Half her cooking is done outside. When I asked her what she does in the winter, she laughed and said, "Close down. All the miners leave anyway".

A few days ago two Georgia miners came into Virginia City to buy supplies. They said they were down from "Last Chance Gulch" and hinted that there was a good strike up there. We gave some thought to going up there with them. Dozens of others, who hadn't made it here or couldn't find a claim, will.

Then a few days after we decided not to go to "Last Chance", we heard of another "find" a few miles east of there…a place called "Confederate Gulch". Needless to say we considered that prospect as well.

Compared to Tarryall, I really don't like this place.

Until we decide what to do, the weather is so nice we thought we'd take a few days off, explore the countryside and go fishing on the Madison River, which is in a really beautiful little valley back towards Bozeman about three hours.

Davey Jones, the nice young man who gave me a Tarryall nugget last November, is here in this valley working for $10 a day plus his board. His employer provides his work clothes, because the work he does is so hard on them. He says he works in water all the time bringing up that sand and gravel. The deeper they dig the higher the yield. Sometimes the gravel bed is two to three feet deep over bedrock or flat ledge, all that in water one to two feet deep.

Dave takes breakfast at the same small boarding house where we ate our first supper. When I told him we were going fishing, he asked if he could come along. He said he needed to dry out for a day or two.

We all met the next morning and headed for the Madison. After two or three hours we spotted up ahead what we assumed was the Madison River. We drove up to a clean sandy bank area and the three of us began fishing up and down the river for an hour or two but " no bites". We led the horses north a little, working our way up the clear but "no-fish" Madison until we discovered the problem. Some Indians had fish traps in a stream that fed the river, and a party of white men had a trap net across it. Well we weren't going to get any fish down stream from this operation and George was told in no uncertain terms, that if he had plans to go up-river, he had better "think again". But the man said, "We'll sell you live, fresh trout...big ones for $1.50 a pound." They cleverly kept their trout alive in a dammed-up stream fed pond by the river. I've never seen such big beautiful trout. We had trout in Colorado but they were minnows compared to these Idaho fish. So we bought fifteen pounds, cleaned them, found some snow in a north facing bank, packed our fish in that, came back to Alder Gulch mid afternoon and sold all but one of our fish for $3.00 a pound at local boarding houses. I told George that I thought we might have gotten $4 or $5 a pound if we'd asked."

Mail is very scarce here. I've had none since I got here...'til I realized that no one knows where I am. I laughed about that one all day.

Joe Farley, Bill Carroll, Sam Gregory and others from Colorado are all here. They want me to start a boarding house and I may. We are still living in the wagon like Gypsies. Bill and Sam said they were averaging five to six ounces of high-grade flake a day from their claims right on Alder Creek, that's ($100 to $120), but like all miners, they have good days and bad days.

With the work that George is doing, he is very hard on clothes. I've been making his work pants out of that heavy denim I bought in Denver. Yesterday I visited a local dry goods merchant, who had moved his store up here from Bannack. I was looking for some needles that are heavier or stronger than those I have and some heavier thread. He asked me if I was in the July group. When I said, "Yes", he said, "I understand you and others are l coming in using the new Bridger Cut Off instead of continuing on the Bozeman Trail."

"Yes"

"What was it like? I had used the Bozeman Trail, what was the Wind River Valley like?"

"I'm afraid I can't give you much information, since we were only on the Bozeman Trail up to Fort Reno or it might have been Fort Casper. Where we turned west there was no fort. I can't compare the Bridger Trail to the Bozeman, except to say that the men driving the teams complained about the steep grade and rough road all along the western foothills of the Big Horn Mountains.

"Well, I guess I'm more impressed with what your outfit did, than you are. You don't seem to appreciate that your outfit and the few that followed, broke a new, probably better, safer trail laid out by Old Jim Bridger.

I told him I needed needles to sew canvas and heavy Denim …and he had exactly what I had in mind. I walked out feeling a little bit special…at least in his mind, by being some of the first settlers up here to have initiated the Bridger Trail. I guess I hadn't realized in what high regard Mr. Bridger and his accomplishments are held.

Two or three months after I sent a letter to the Harrimans at their ranch and a duplicate to Mary Rackliff telling them where I am, I received a small accumulation of mail, some issues of magazines that I had missed that carried a Dickens story serialized; even some mail from Lawrence that had been forwarded to Colorado and finally on to me up here. I had to go to the Post Office in Virginia City to claim all of it.

There were three letters from Adda dated variously in 1863. A short one dated November 1, 1863 from of all places, Gibraltar, Michigan. Adda notes that she left Lawrence shortly after Quantrill's August raid and her close call. She said she and Allie crossed the river on the Leavenworth ferry, took a boat to St. Joseph, Missouri, where she boarded the train and traveled first class with a sleeping berth all the way to Chicago. She transferred to the Michigan Central Railroad for Detroit, where, she says,

7

she spent the night. She took a Lake Steamer, the *Olive Branch* to Gibraltar and was amazed at how many in town remembered her, and she recites several familiar names. She writes that she visited our old residence, which has been improved upon with our old gardens well tended. She said hello to the owner of our sawmill who seemed to be prospering. He has a huge inventory of softwood from the "Upper Peninsula"...His biggest customer, U.S. Government for camp construction.

The disappointing War news at Gibraltar was that several Rebel gunboats had somehow steamed down to Lake Erie. When apprehended, it was discovered that they had planned to fire on Sandusky (Ohio) and Detroit. (Can you imagine?)

Another letter was posted on Christmas Eve from Genesee County (Michigan), the place of "her birth and the place of Mother's death".

In a long P.S. she says before leaving Lawrence she sold Martha (one of our cows) for $18.00 and will post my share after New Years. Why she wants me to know she sold our double-barreled shotgun that Graton had given us for protection before he left for the service is beyond me. She got $5.00 for it.

A second letter in that pack posted from (near) Flint is self-explanatory.

Flint, Michigan

Dear Augusta,

After renewing acquaintances with old friends in and near in Gibraltar, Allie and I have been having a fine time visiting relatives on both sides of our family north of Detroit.

For some months now I've been staying with Aunt Julia (Taylor) and Uncle Dan (Seeley) on their farm outside of Flint. Aunt Julia, a very strong woman, is an older sister of Mother. She is the one years ago who complimented you on the obituary you wrote when Mother died. She mentioned that the first night that Allie and I were here. She loves to talk and is determined to tell me the history of the family on Mother's side. Uncle Dan is a farmer and breeder of cattle, selling young calves to others. I wouldn't bore you with all this except their lives, like ours, has touched so much history including the Erie Canal, the westward movement, two serious Depressions: one in 1837 and another in 1857 that in each case, followed prosperous times.

I hadn't realized what a prominent family they are in this area. They moved to Flint in 1836 when there were only seven houses here. Uncle Dan built a small tailor shop in town and as Genesee County grew, he expanded it to a small "Ready-to-Wear" shop. He had been a apprentice when he was eighteen to a "Journeyman" tailor at Lockport ten or so miles east of Niagara Falls right on the Erie Canal which was being constructed then and little New York towns and villages were springing up along its route. Uncle Dan set up shop and married Aunt Julia there in 1829.

According to Uncle Dan, who like Father has always been sensitive to economic conditions, said that three years after they married the banks had such a surplus of money that farm mortgages were available for little or no down payment. So, they bought a ninety-six acre farm near Albion in Orleans County…But in the winter he always went back to "the needle trade" in town.

This turned out to be a very poor farm: too much salty marshland.

Since they had so little invested, after the "Crash" of 1833, they moved to Pontiac (Oakland County,) Michigan getting here by going north (around the Great Niagara Falls) into Canada, then crossing the river at Detroit. Uncle Dan went back to tailoring.

Eight years later they bought this 360-acre farm (Section 3) in Genesee Township near Flint. They've been on the farm over twenty years.

Their friends here in Genesee County included Josiah Begole (Begoole) who later became a Congressman, then Governor of Michigan. You know he courted our mother, Jane Taylor.

They've had four surviving children. Every winter they move into town next door to our old house, which I remember before

Mama died. Uncle Dan's father, Lewis Seeley, was born Trumbull, Connecticut.

They have a small fruit orchard on this place, so we are enjoying apples, cooked and raw, and fat tart cherries…and looking forward to their peaches. Before I got here, I visited Aunt Lucy (Stewart.) She had married Father's older brother, Addison. Well, he has died and Aunt Lucy has raised their children on her own. She has lost two sons to the war. Cousin Damon was the first child born in Flint.

Augusta, I would like to say a few words about my personal life. Although our relatives couldn't be more generous or hospitable, I'm not anxious to discuss our unusual married life with them. I'm not looking for advice, but I need someone to talk to about what's going on between Graton and me.

He's had no furloughs since November ("62), while you and I were both in Lawrence. Since then I've received about a dozen long, well-crafted letters from him, all posted at one army camp or another. Except for the first one or two, I've answered each one. Augusta, since his first battle in November '62 in western Missouri, from a careful reading of his letters, the poor man has been involved in at least eight battles. He's had officers under him killed in action. I can account for almost twenty of his (Colored) enlisted men dead…about half that number killed in action.

After one of his battles under the influence of both fatigue and gratitude that he was still alive, he asked if I could ever forgive him, admitting that, should I consider his plea, he conceded that I had much to forgive. In some of his letters he reminds me of the sinner that promises God that if God will "get him out of this", he will mend his ways. In other letters he talks enthusiastically about his post war plans in Lawrence.

He writes of promoting over a dozen of his men to squad leaders, corporals and sergeants, etc…which speaks well of his leadership, all of this over a period of about twenty months. Of course the battles only last a day or two. So there is a great deal of moving to and fro but mostly I address his letters to Fort Gibson.

Using his description of his Spartan but dangerous army life as a means of communicating, I get the sense that he truly regrets the trouble he's caused both of us, though he's too proud to come out and say so. I think by explaining some of his battles in such detail he is trying to redeem himself in my eyes that he really is or wants to be a loving husband and father. During some of those battles, I think he has confronted his own mortality and has decided or promised God that if he gets out of this alive, he could redeem himself, if we could start all over, which appeals to the maternal and domestic side of me. But living with him has taught me the difference between the hope of marital compatibility, and the reality of three horrible years with him before he joined the army.

Nevertheless my response has been to be gracious and considerate. I keep him posted on Alice's development and our activities. I don't have the experience or judgment to put my self "in his shoes", so in my letters to him, I'm careful not to be self-righteous about our past relationship.

Should I show mercy for what he's been through by a willingness to try again? And there's family unity now. Allie needs a father. He does ask about her in his letters. I suppose I should put-up with his hardness and indifference as a price for Allie to have a father. But I don't think I'll ever be able to totally surrender, to subordinate myself to him, only to earn his disrespect.

After one of his letters last year I wrote rather formally that I might try to visit him as I did when we married,. (He was somewhere in Eastern Arkansas.) He wrote back that he was very grateful for my letter and my interest in a visit but some of his troops are not healthy (one has measles) and says as happy as he would be to see me, he advises against the long trip and speculates with battles all around them, he doubts that we could even get through the lines south of Fort Scott, where most of the fighting is going on.

The long and the short of it is I think the best thing I can do is to forgive...who was it in the Bible that said, "I will forgive...but I can't forget'. I think that sums up my current situation.

Aunt Julia has told me so much about the family that I didn't know, I think, before I return to Lawrence, I will go over to New York State and visit them.

Your loving Sister Adda
C/o D. H. Seeley
Box 120
Flint, Genesee County, Mich

_____ 0 _____

With rent so high, George and another fellow are busy building a log cabin. I don't think it will be big enough to take in "roomers", but we could board five or so. Except for fresh meat, lord knows we have plenty of food supplies. We've been living in the wagon and a little along-side tent for two months. I'm almost accustomed to it. But we both know in a month or so it will get very cold and the snow will come.

Out of the blue, I received a letter from Mary Rackliffe. She said she confirmed our whereabouts from one of the Tarryall boys who had just come back from Alder Gulch with a sizeable poke. I wonder if that was Bill Carroll.

She reports increased lawlessness in their area. The east-west coach was robbed of several thousand dollars. She calls them "guerillas". They even took the six horses from the stage. Some men from the ranch went after them, killed one, but didn't recover the mine company's money. She says lots of mail has accumulated for George and me, including back issues of Leslie Magazine. She'll send it all on when she's sure that a northbound stage can get through. She writes that she doesn't know which is worse, the highwaymen or the Indians.

In a separate letter she writes that white guerillas had come into the Harrimans in late August and asked for dinner, which they got. After dinner they (guerillas) turned on Harriman's and cleaned them out of $1,500 from their mining receipts, but no one was hurt. I wonder how much of that came from the old claim Charlie and I had.

_____ 0 _____

A large group of men had been accumulating around here. There must be 600 or 700 of them. They all went "out" heavily armed, obviously carrying gold they've mined in recent months. But as fast as they go out, others come in. Claims sold by those leaving with their earnings are selling for between $1,000 and $2,000 each, depending on the month; i.e. June claims are worth more than August claims. George figures that about half the claims on Alder Creek have "turned over".

With the notorious Sheriff Henry Plummer and two-dozen of his compatriots all recently hung and those lucky ones found to be "without sufficient evidence" (to be hung!) banned from the territory, the miners and merchants feel safer. Among individual miners going home with their savings and groups in stage and wagon trains bound for Colorado or the States, there is a feeling that they are safer now than they were only last winter. But I need to explain my comment about Sheriff Plummer.

No sooner did we arrive this summer and all we heard about was how lawless the Valley was prior to the Vigilantes taking over the chore of Law and Order, about last Christmas time. Everyone knew a miner who after leaving here with his hard earned gold was never heard from again. All those who were here before last Christmas could cite cases of an outbound stage or outfit going to Denver or Salt Lake City, carrying gold that was robbed and passengers or escorts killed. Then after Christmas and New Years things gradually changed for the better. It all dealt with identifying one outlaw at a time...or a small group of them. When the Vigilantes rounded-up a nest of the outlaws, they would usually turn on each other to "save their own hides." The main trap was sprung when it was realized that the master planner and organizer was none other than the elected sheriff and a handful of his deputies.

And it all really began when the chief justice of the territory, Sidney Edgerton, appointed by President Lincoln, arrived with a prosecuting attorney and decided to make Bannack his territorial headquarters but he was gone most of 1863 trying to persuade Congress to create a new territory, Montana, out of Idaho. By the time he returned (successfully) President Lincoln had appointed him Governor of Montana Territory.

During the winter of his absence the Vigilantes captured one suspect, brought him to trial and evidence from that trial began to unwind the whole ball of string that tied one outlaw to another.

AUTHORS NOTE

Although Augusta talks of Indian scares and a state of lawlessness in Montana, she really didn't go into the details that she could have, if she'd had enough time to talk to those who had moved up from Bannack and lived through the period, and wrote about it, much like she wrote of people she knew in Eldorado or Lawrence or the Colorado mines. We think she had problems of her own: about George finding a profitable claim, the terrible living conditions, George was frequently gone prospecting and by fall she was pregnant and they finally got the log cabin finished. So we gathered up from plenty of references what we believe to be the facts on Sheriff Plummer and the events that caused his downfall.

The six months or so before Augusta and George arrived, certainly before Christmas it was assumed by the citizenry that the sheriff and all of his deputies, who occasionally formed ineffective posses, were themselves honest, law-abiding officers of the law, when in fact they were any thing but. Indeed sheriff Plumber and most of his cohorts were hardened criminals, having learned their craft elsewhere in the lawless west before coming to Alder Gulch. But none of the citizens, except Plummer's "friends" were any the wiser.

Due to their political positions they had available to them information that allowed them to know when a miner, with his hard-earned gold, was going home and on what route and what conveyance or which out-bound stage carried gold to Salt Lake City or Denver, and when it was scheduled to leave. Usually the stage driver was "in" on the planning and would be cooperative with the "road agents" when they appeared.

From mid 1863 until the first few weeks of the new year a series of unexplained out-bound coach robberies that often involved murder of both passengers and robbers and other acts of lawlessness fueled pent-up frustration among the hardworking miners and merchants of Bannack and Alder Gulch.

In the summer of 1863 a Lloyd Magruder brought a mule train laden with food and merchandise to Alder Gulch. He soon sold out, realized $14,000 and planned to return to his home in Lewiston, Idaho. Sheriff Plummer and four others knew of the sale and learned of Magruder's plans. Plummer assigned four or five of his rough necks to follow him, rob him and kill him, which they did. They made the mistake of keeping Magruder's mule and going on to Lewiston.. They were ultimately captured in Idaho and hung there.

On July 13, 1863 an overland coach with passengers was headed for Salt Lake City from Virginia City was ambushed by highwaymen. The passengers were ready for them. When called to stop, the passengers opened fire, as did the robbers. When the dust settled, most of the passengers were dead, the driver was untouched and the road agents made off unidentified with $65,000 in Alder Gulch gold.

In this case, a quickly organized posse pursued but got nothing. The driver was later convicted of conspiracy and executed in Cherry Creek, Colorado.

These attacks weren't all relegated to Alder Gulch. Helena had their road agents, as did Lewiston and Deer Lodge. But the real money was then in Alder Gulch.

During the first week of December 1863 three wagons left Virginia City/Alder Gulch headed for Salt Lake City. The caravan *contained between $75,000 and $80,000 of Alder Gulch gold and was conducted by six citizens, including John M. Bozeman.*

Needless to say Sheriff Plummer knew of their plans and he dispatched two of his gang to rob them en route. The robbers turned out to be inept and the attempt was foiled. Both robbers were wounded and brought to justice…but Sheriff Plummer remained unsuspected. Dozens of successful miners that fall headed for home with their hard-earned gold. They were never head of again.

Few, if any of the lawless acts were apprehended until the winter murder of an employee of two local merchants. From investigations of that murder enough evidence was uncovered that began to shed light on all of this lawlessness.

Nicolas Thiebalt, a young Dutchman, had sold a pair of mules that he kept at a nearby ranch to his employers, Burtchey and Clark. They paid him his price and asked him to bring the mules to town. With the money in his pocket, he went out to fetch the mules but on the way was robbed, his mules stolen and Nick Thiebalt just disappeared.

All his employers knew was that he had been gone ten days. They assumed that they had been taken in by a thief.

Ten days after the boy left town William Palmer, an owner of a Nevada City saloon, was hunting grouse when he came upon a frozen corpse with a bullet hole in his head. When he tried to get it up into his wagon, he realized that he needed help. He located a nearby camp and asked two men there for help. To his surprise they refused him with the callous comment that people are killed, like that, everyday around here and we don't intend to go out in the cold just because you found a frozen corpse nearby.

Palmer managed to get the body back to Nevada City and put on public display in front of his saloon. The spectacle of this young victim, who many of the town's people knew, caused such pubic indignation, that a twenty-five-man posse was organized. This time the posse included miners and merchants. Mr. Palmer offered to lead them out to the scene of the crime. The sheriff, who should have been attending this matter, declined to go with the posse.

They surrounded the camp where Palmer's request had been rejected and waited throughout the freezing night 'til dawn, when they questioned the camp's occupants about Nick Thiebalt's murder. One of them told the posse he didn't do it but that George Ives had. It didn't help the outlaws that one of Thiebalt's stolen mules was tied up nearby. One of the Vigilantes, a miner knew George Ives to have been an honest, hardworking miner when they both mined in California.

The posse arrested Ives anyway and one or two other suspects who the posse assumed (correctly) were "in on" the murder. Ives, who had a fast horse and lots of self-confidence, attempted an escape, but failed when his horse tired and he was recaptured. That fact didn't help him when it came up during the trial.

The posse returned to Nevada City on December 18 with George Ives.

But justice was a long way off. Confident that he could get Ives "off", Sheriff Plummer agreed to provide a jury and "friends" of the accused arranged four lawyers for his defense.

The posse of hardworking miners declined the Sheriff's offer of his handpicked jurymen and chose instead twenty-four of their own.

It could be that by the time of the trial Mr. Edgerton was also the territorial governor. He had gone to Washington to try to persuade the President and the Congress to make this area a separate territory out of the Idaho territory. Both Congress and the President had enough to worry about with the Civil War still ranging. But Congress had enough time to argue over an appropriate name. Some one suggested Douglas (after he famous senator and inventor of Popular Sovereignty.) Jefferson was also proposed and a mischievous Representative from Wisconsin, a Democrat suggested Abyssinia, teasing the Republicans for their fondness for the Negro: a side issue at that time was, should the freed Negro have the vote? Wilbur Fisk Sanders, a lawyer, had arrived in Bannack late that fall with an uncle, Sydney Edgerton, an ex Ohio Congressman, who President Lincoln had appointed as chief Justice for the territory. The honorable Charles S. Boggs (a miner) was appointed to help lawyer Sanders for the prosecution…Judge Wilson presided. He was also a miner.

Sanders, the new-comer, was asked by the posse to verify the evidence they provided, in the light of a gang of outlaws that had terrorized the Gulch for months. Wilbur Sanders summoned the courage to present a case against Ives, charging him with robbery and murder, knowing whether he got a conviction or not he would be a marked man.

The jury of miners found Ives guilty, and a few days before Christmas he was hanged. After hearing all the evidence during Ives trial, "citizens" suddenly realized that they needed more protection than Sheriff Plummer had been providing.

The tradition of posses and vigilantes were well established on the frontier, as it moved relentlessly west…and that was the case in Alder Gulch. Only after the trial of Ives were the Alder Gulch Vigilantes formed up. Prior to the trial, the apprehending group was an ad hoc posse. The miners and merchants knew they were paying Sheriff Plummer and his deputies to maintain law and order, but as robberies and killings continued, unabated while Plummer was in office, they decided to take matters into their own hands.

Masons among the local miners were quick to volunteer for Vigilante duty in the absence of that work getting done by their elected Sheriff. They realized that hanging George Ives didn't solve the problem and wouldn't bring justice to the Valley. The robberies had been too frequent and too well organized and carried out for so long for the Vigilantes to think that hanging George Ives would end it. But the apprehension and trial of George Ives produced the first tangible evidence that the Vigilantes could use to begin to round up the balance of the gang. During the questioning of George Ives, he admitted that he had had accomplices in the Nick Thiebalt murder. Aleck Carter was one of them.

First they questioned Erastus "Red" Yeager, if he knew where Aleck Carter was. Yeager was then not a suspect. He said most of the crooks, having been warned by the hanging of Ives, had moved northwest about 100 miles to Deer Lodge. That proved to be a self-

serving lie because it was soon discovered that Yeager too was a "road agent."

A twenty-four-man posse was mustered and they rode in the freezing cold toward Rattlesnake Creek northeast of Bannack to a ranch, where they had been told was a hideout. They apprehended Buck Stinson and Ned Ray, who volunteered that Red Yeager was one of their party. In no time he too was captured. Those acts quickly led to the capture of Aleck Carter. The confession of each of those just rounded-up established the guilt of the others. It was Red Yeager who spilled the beans on the king pin, Sheriff Henry Plummer. His second in command, claimed Yeager, was Bill Benton. Other outlaws named were Stephen Marshland, Cyrus Skinner, Frank Parish, Boone Helm, Club Foot George, Ned Ray, "Mexican" Frank and Bob Zacchary and that was only a third of the gang.

With their confessions it was decided to dispatch, on the spot, those in custody, and appropriate arrangements were hastily made. Red Yeager and Brown were hung where they were caught on that cold January night.

As soon as the Vigilantes returned, they apprehended the three main ringleaders, Plummer, Ned Ray and Buck Stinson. Before they hung Plummer, he still had the poise of a "Con" man to make his captives this offer: "Give me a horse and two hours and I'll bring back my weight in gold (Let's say he weighed 160 pounds x 16 oz per pound x $20/oz…about $50,000.) The irony of Plummer's fate was that he was hung on the very gallows that he had ordered built but had never used. The others too were summarily hanged…all without a trial.

We would like to report that with the hanging of the crooked sheriff, the reign of terror was over, but it wasn't. The record shows that there was little decrease in stage robberies. Of course, most of the outlaws were still "at large."

We are sure that some of the suspects, when they learned that so many of their party had been caught and hanged, escaped.

In spite of threats of vengeance and promises to rob and burn the stores owned by some of the Vigilantes made by the remaining outlaws, who were accustomed to having things their way, the Vigilantes pressed on and in short order rounded up and hung Boone Helin, Jack Gallaher, Frank Parish and two others. Six of these troublemakers were all dispatched by mid January. Of them, George Lane had also been a Virginia City sheriff!

Due to the persistent threats, the Vigilantes knew they still had work to do. Many of the names on their list were yet to be rounded up, so they pressed on through that cold January to find and execute another eight.

Bill Hunter was the last of twenty-two. He was apprehended on the Gallatin River: and hung there.

A SHORT HISTORY OF HENRY PLUMMER

When in June of '63 more gold had been (accidently) discovered in Alder Gulch than in Bannack, about fifty of its citizens moved from Bannack to the Gulch. The criminal situation was reaching such proportions that an election for sheriff was held and although Plummer didn't win the first round he managed to scare the winner out of town, and ended up with the sheriff's badge, first in Bannack, then when the bigger strike was found in Alder Gulch, he moved up there. All that was the spring and summer of 1863. Plummer immediately rounded up four or five of his fraternity of murderers and appointed them deputies. The chief deputy was _____ Dillingham, who knew each of the desperados and had another half dozen in reserve for assignments as "road agents" armed with information provided by the "honest" sheriff.

From that summer until he was hanged a few days after New Year the inhabitants of either Bannack or Alder Gulch were unaware that Plummer, though a mild-mannered, polite politician, when he was twenty-six years old, had killed John Vedder in California. He drew a ten-year sentence of which he served six months. In 1859 he killed James Ryder also in California, bribed the jailer and escaped. He killed two more before he ended up at Fort Benton on the upper Missouri River where he become engaged to the local Indian agent's beautiful sister-in-law, Electra Bryan. At that time Plummer had an arms-length partner, Jack Cleveland. When gold was discovered in Bannack, they moved there. Cleveland also had his eye on Electra. In time, Cleveland lost this competition. Henry Plummer simply shot him. How many is that so far? Five! By the time Henry Plummer was sheriff first in Bannack, then Alder Gulch, he was already a hardened killer and was organizing a gang of thieves and cutthroats to prosper from all that gold coming out of Alder Gulch.

Although Plummer had married Electra, he was "carrying on" with her married sister, Martha Vail. Indeed, when the Vigilantes finally came for Henry Plummer, it was in Martha Vail's bed that they found him. He was hung here in the Valley on January 14, this year.

By the discoveries of victims' bodies, from "on the gallows" confessions the four-month robbing and killing spree beginning with the Great Alder Gulch Placer Mining Strike, it was determined that Plummer's Gang had killed more than 120 miners or merchants. Plummer got a commission on every deal.

I received a short, rather formal for-my-sister letter dated March 10, 1864 and posted in Genesee County, Michigan.

In it she says that she's been told by her husband, who's in some Army camp in Eastern Arkansas to offer me $200 in exchange for my deeded ownership to our house on Rhode Island Street and to kindly make the deed over to her. She will instruct one Mr. McCurdy in Lawrence to draw $200 from their account in Riggs Bank and to send a certified draft for that amount to me in Montana. She adds that Mr. McCurdy has power-of-attorney to deposit or draw on Graton's money in Riggs Bank.

Graton plans, she says, to renovate the house after the War and after he is furloughed. but only if we own it.

Adda doesn't say whether she expects to return to Lawrence or, if she does, whether she will "live" with Graton in our old house or not.

It's interesting to me that Adda would use that "tone" of language…that she's been *told* to ask me. Humph!

Of course, I could use the money but I sure don't *need* it…and even if I were asked in a civil and polite way to transfer my half for a paltry $200, I would need to be in more desperate straights than I've ever been in to agree to their offer.

I think silence is the best response to this offer.

Sunday - September 1865

A beautiful fall day. George has been speculating that if all this gold, flake and nuggets that have been washing down and accumulating in this streambed all these years, there must be a source from which it comes…the Mother Lode in the nearby mountains. He's been complaining all summer about stream digging and he wants a change.

We got up early, packed a lunch and took the team up stream, through Virginia "City" (which is nothing but another sprawling camp similar to Nevada City) and continued up the valley trail along side the stream as far as we could navigate. That took three or four hours. Eventually the canyon got so narrow and treacherous to where it became even more hazardous but George thought it was passable. The stream was several feet below us. shallow and fast running. It was mid afternoon,

I stayed with the wagon. George went walking on up stream, which I could see got very steep rather quickly. Yes, I had a side arm.

George believes all that gold must be coming down from the sides of two or three mountains that form this valley that we are in, which stretches out ahead of us with almost vertical rock cliffs closing in on both sides. I think he intends to stake out a claim up here. As I watched him, he would stop now and then and peck at the side of the mountain with his little miners hammer, looking for quartz veins. It was almost dark when he finally got back.

In the meantime I had tied the horses on a long tether to some saplings along side the stream, where they could graze on the nice green grass.

I carried a few boulders that I could lift from the streambed, made a pit and had a fire going so long before George returned, the bottom of the pit was full of glowing coals. I had warmed up a small pot of beans with generous chunks of bacon, made some coffee and as the full moon peeped over the east valley mountain edge, we began a very peaceful supper.

George said he wasn't surprised to find three or four other well-staked claims up this mountain valley. One of them, he said, had several tons of rock and quartz tailings accumulated nearby, a good sign. When he asked how long it took them to accumulate that pile of tailings, one of the miners called it "mullock". George said he'd never heard that word before and the miner said, "Well, mate, that's because you've never mined in Australia." Another claim and cabin nearby was owned by three brothers up from Colorado. They had been there over a year.

George reported that about two miles up the valley the trail and the stream end at a small shallow lake. Little snowmelt streams feed it but that's the end of the trail. He said the valley narrows down to where it's only about a half mile wide at the end, where the whole mountain wraps itself halfway around the little lake.

We pulled our bedroll off the wagon and decided to sleep by the fire. In the morning George took a little fat Utah ham and a small bag of white cornmeal from our larder, which we've quietly kept in the wagon since Denver, up to the Colorado boys and was back before noon. On our leisurely drive back, George said he was going to inquire at Virginia City what the requirements were for filing a claim up there.

While George was learning about claim laws here, I thought I'd visit one of Virginia City's dry goods store. One thing about this store of which I heartily approve: he has several shelves of books, more used than new, almanacs and various magazines.

I splurged and bought five used books for ten cent each. Did I say used? Some of these are really used. The back cover is missing on two. A set of three was published in England. Can you just wonder who owned them originally? How they got to the

States? But stranger yet, how did they get all the way to a remote place like Montana Territory? One of the books has been or was obviously stolen from the Library at Princeton University, a school somewhere in New Jersey. It was checked out in May 1857. The new owner probably brought it west with him, escaping the big depression of that year that provided so many miners in Colorado and others bound for California and Oregon.

The set of three were written by English women, sisters, using pseudo-names. They were published as a set and it's the third edition of two of them. The editor explains that *Jane Eyre* was first published in 1847 written by Currer Bell, whose real name the publisher discloses in the back of this edition, is Charlotte Bronte (where he lists other books published by them in Paternoster Row, London. One other in this set *Wuthering Heights* was written by Ellis Bell with the same publisher. Indeed this book is introduced by her "sister" Currer Bell! I have never heard of any of these titles or their authors.

Well, shades of Sara Robinson...at least by the third edition she was able to publish under her own name and as I browsed through those used beauties I recalled Adda getting an article (or two) rejected by a stuffy editor of a Flint (Michigan) newspaper, because she was a female But when she resubmitted the article under the name of Addamont Stewart, it was accepted and published.

The other two book were: Hawthorne's *Scarlet Letter* and the book from the Princeton Library is a translation of Honore Balzac's *Cousin Bette*. I had read a report some time ago about this story of Greed and Revenge. Greed and revenge seems to be popular motifs of French writers. (Remember the *Count of Monte Christo* is a thesis on Revenge.)

While I was on such a literary buying spree, I picked up three "old" Leslie and two Grahams magazines in about the same shape as my five books for a nickel a piece. Heavens, they only cost five cents when they were "new".

I was careful to note that I hadn't previously read those editions. Glory-be, two of them carry missing chapters of serialized Dickens stories that I was reading in Colorado, *Dombey and Son*.

I must remember to suggest this Dickens's book to Adda. Mr. Dombey, an exceedingly successful merchant resembles in many respects her husband. Mr. Dombey seems to be totally without affection or consideration for others, including his first wife and lovely daughter. He grows so remote from his (teenaged) daughter that in one encounter with her (they live in the same house.) He asks, "Florence, do you know who I am?" And poor Florence, who has never known a kind word, an affectionate pat or even a smile from him... says, "Yes, Papa,"

Dombey becomes even more prosperous and embittered, when his only son and heir dies.

Virginia City now boasts a small newspaper, as does Bannack. Although editions are irregular, I am now a subscriber of both. One of the recent ('66) editions of the *Montana Post* carried a rather long article...a military report, really...on Indian troubles up and down what we know as the Bozeman Trail, extending from the town of Bozeman all the way down to Julesburg in Nebraska Territory. It was written by its editor, Mr. Dimsdale, an Englishman.

According to this article the Army is in the process of reorganizing and strengthening forts up and down the trail. A Commission from back east employing Jim Bridger as an advisor on Indian affairs, is trying to make a treaty or a series of treaties with the Sioux, Cheyenne, Crows and others. Red Cloud, the chief of the Sioux has attended at least one peace conference and accepted gifts, but has been frank to say that if the White Man persists on using their land along the Bozeman Trail and on land east of it, killing animals that the Indians need for their survival, the Sioux and others will kill all those that continue to use this trail.

Jim Bridger has warned this Committee from Washington that they should believe Chief Red Cloud, when he says he has at least

1,500 Sioux warriors near Fort Kearney and more further north. His attitude will not be influenced at all by a pound of tobacco and a few blankets brought out here by well meaning but naïve peacekeepers from "Back East". This Committee has scoffed at Bridger's advice, the article claims.

One of the interesting items in this news article is that our old friend from Pony Creek in Northeast Kansas, Philip St. George Cooke, heads this entire area or Army Department, he is now a Brigadier General, so he must have survived the war. This report says his headquarters are in Omaha (why not Fort Leavenworth?) and a Colonel Carrington is in charge of the troops up and down the Bozeman Trail. He reports to General Cooke and is headquartered at Fort Phil Kearney several miles north of Fort Reno. Apparently our friend, Preston Plumb, has been discharged. He was in-charge of that Army area.

I have half a notion to write General Cooke a note reminding him of his friendliness to two young girls that had "marched" into his camp eleven years ago from their little settlement south of the camp across Pony Creek to demand the return of our horses and wagon, which we saw parade into his Camp that morning. Our property had come into their possession when the U.S. Army captured Lane's Plymouth and Lexington Companies after the Battle of Hickory Point about a month before and put our father and one hundred other abolitionist in a P.O.W. camp. Adda and I were all puffed-up with indignance to have our property returned. To our great relief the Colonel cordially said, "Ladies, I'll be glad to return your horses. I'll even give you a bushel of Oats in exchange for our use of them. I'm glad to be rid of any animal I don't need or own. Our animals eat more than my men."

Adda and I proudly drove our two horses and our wagon back over to Plymouth. That was on October 10, 1856. I had just turned seventeen and Adda was sixteen.

October 1864

Typical Western Pioneer Scene Illustrator: Allan Reingold

66.

GOLD
ALDER GULCH MINING CAMP

Montana Territory
1865

Since we've been here a territorial legislature has been created. They have decided to move the capital from Bannack to Virginia City, which is flattering, 'cause we live here and the activity reminds me of the same activity after we had arrived in Kansas Territory, except here, thank goodness, the slavery issue seems well behind us.

Work here is very scarce. The food prices are "out of sight" again. Grocers are charging $100 for a sack of flour. Potatoes and not very good ones are 60¢ a pound (four to five times the price of Missouri potatoes that we were getting in Kansas). Some potatoes weigh almost a pound. Can you imagine paying 60¢ for one potato? Dried fruit…and how I hate it, is $1.00 a pound. Sugar is $1.00 a pound and eggs are $1.50 a dozen. But what really galls me and all the rest of us, is that we all know that Iowa, Nebraska or Kansas wheat is so abundant down there, available for about $3 per 100 weight (c.w.t.) If you double or triple that for the freighting risk and costs and you still have flour at ten dollars a c.w.t. But these crooks, by claiming scarcity have the gall to charge a dollar a pound…or $100 c.w.t.

A large group of miners, many who we know, have held a meeting to consider confiscating a supply of flour from two stores and to sell it at reasonable prices. George doesn't think it will work because the grocers have already hidden most of their supplies or freighted them to a guarded warehouse in Bannack or Helena. George and I are in pretty good shape from all the supplies I bought last April in Denver. We've kept quiet about it, as we gradually consume them.

All that experience I had with Mrs. Gates and her boarding house, learning to cook for large groups from Aggie Rourke and the experience with Mrs. Killam in Lawrence plus running the Kenosha House in Tarryall, all taught me how to plan for our needs, how to order the supplies, how not to pay for shoddy quality, how to hire and boss the help. Even Mr. Harriman said "I was a good manager." That's why now, with most everybody in the Gulch worried about being able to simply buy enough flour to bake bread, and complaining about the lack of beef or chicken and how tired they all are of salt pork, George and I sympathize with them, as we secretly eat out of our own larder. I have another concern: the same one I had in Kansas and that is the people here eat too much meat. Most of it is shot wild game, so it isn't too fat, but vegetables, even potatoes, are in short supply.

In using inventory of our larder after about 200 days (including the forty-seven or so days we were on the trail and ignoring the few meals we bought at Army forts or boarding houses on the way.) We've gone through about fifty pounds each of ham and bacon, twenty-five pounds of dry red beans, and little white "Navy" beans, ten pounds of molasses, though we bought ten pounds of honey from an enterprising Army wife at one of the forts on the way up here. We often eat corn meal mush or Utah oatmeal for breakfast.

We bought venison and wild turkey from hunters along the way at an average of 25¢ per pound and we ate most of that fresh or as leftovers in stew or hash. At Fort Reno we bought some nice, but small, fresh shot rabbit, tender enough to fry. Nevertheless I reckon that of the 600 to 700 pounds of larder that I bought in

Denver, we've consumed only between 200 and 250 pounds. None of it has spoiled. Those Mormons really know how to smoke bacon and ham. I've been waiting to see if the Pueblo corn meal will turn rancid. So far, so good.

At this rate and with minimal purchases, except fresh meat, we should be all right through winter and into spring. There is a slaughterhouse in Bannack that sends a meat wagon up here every two weeks or so, but they too have trouble getting beef. In August I bought a small leg of Utah lamb. Roasted, it was delicious. They pack their meat in ice. Before they go back to Bannack, they even sell that!

A letter arrived from Adda, who is visiting among our relatives in Michigan. She included a picture of little Alice, but omitted any news of her husband. I rather envy her back there among all that available farm produce. What I'd give for a few Michigan or Indiana apples right now.

News from Colorado is not good. The Indians are very bad there. There is no stage travel on the plains now due to the Indians. The ranches have closed down. Indians are stealing the stock. Business houses in Denver are closed. Everyone is out fighting Indians. Looks like we got out at a good time. Mary Rackliffe writes that there are letters and packages for George and me at the ranch. (I would really like to get my hands on all the back issue of the two magazines, Graham's and Leslie's that serializes some of Dickens' books.

A letter from Mary Rackliffe in Terryall this week dated August 1st came through in thirteen days. She writes that nine Guerillas robbed the coach of several thousand dollars, took six horses from the ranch plus $1,500. Our men chased the robbers; killed one and wounded the others, she said.

It takes weeks to get newspapers, but we do receive them and in my case, friends and relatives have always sent me clippings. This week's mail contained clippings with some good news. The best news is that on April 14th, the "dreaded and long" Civil War is finally over. General Robert E. Lee has surrendered at some courthouse in Pennsylvania and…bad news. Five days after the Armistice, a half mad actor named Booth, killed poor President Lincoln in some theatre in the capital. It appears that there was a general plan for Booth and others to kill all the cabinet members.

By 1865, a year after we arrived, Virginia City had become the territory's largest city…and in Madison county it was the area's principal seat of government. Houses are awfully high to rent or buy. A common log cabin with dirt floors rents for $100 a month. An owner with a paid helper and a team to go after and haul logs can build one for $100.

Late August George received an undated letter from his father in Iowa telling us that he was planning to bring a load of honey and maple syrup to this area and was seeking advice about the best trails, once they crossed the Missouri at Council Bluffs. If he waits until mid September, it will take two months from where he is, he won't get in, because of snows from Julesburg all 800 miles to get here.

Nevertheless we have been telling people at the west end of Nevada City if a Mr. Blackman Senior is asking for his son and daughter-in-law to tell them where we are and several times a day I look out on the road for any wagon (or wagons) coming in that might be him…although I can't imagine that he would come alone.

In recent weeks several Iowa families have arrived and are trying to figure out what they are going to do. Mr. Blackman was not among them.

This will be an awkward time to entertain relatives. I am fairly far along in a family way and am sick, irregularly

EARLY SPRING 1865

After a five-week sickness, I delivered a little girl. Thank goodness George was here most of the time and Mrs. White, my neighbor was the midwife and she too was here all of the time. I've been so unwell I didn't give much thought to a name. In time Mrs. White suggested we name her Eunice Robertie.

Directly after the birth George had to leave and he was gone… on and off…the balance of the spring. He had staked out a claim up on the mountain, where he has maintained all along that some place or several places up there is the source, the "Mother Lode" of all this placer gold down here in the valley. It would be nice for him to come home, at least on Sunday, but other miners are so ambitious, maybe voracious, such that, if you or a partner are not at your claim, if you are gone from it, when you come back, your markers might be gone and a claim jumper is there and that occasionally leads to fatal disagreements.

For the most of the winter it's been a very cold one with winds that equal Kansas. I've been alone now with a sick baby. I am so sorry to have to say that after suffering so for three months little Bertie died. She was never well from the day she was born and the last few days of her life she cried and cried. She must have been suffering so. It was so hard for me to give her up. I don't think she ever weighed over five pounds. She died at half past five in the morning and with help from the neighbors, we buried her the same day. George is still gone. I blame her sickness and death on poor nutrition, the lack of fresh fruit, fresh vegetables and not enough milk. Adda and I always had a cow or two. I suppose we should have brought one with us from Denver. We had the money.. We thought it would slow the train's travel. Then, when we joined the group, we discovered several families had cows. But we didn't. Those families who have cows, use the milk themselves.

SPRING 1865

Now that I'm feeling better I had promised myself that I'd make an entry dealing with my troubled delivery and little Bertie's suffering and death, but these recollections are more than I can bear just now. I'll continue this later.

AUTHORS' NOTE

Although Augusta says in her undated entry that she can't bring herself to describe her ordeals with the birth of their first child, Lin Fredericksen discovered in the Kansas State Historical Society Archives, 28 wartime letters that were exchanged between Adda and her husband.

Letter marked #20, April 9 1865 sent by Adda while she was in Michigan, addressed to Captain Graton, 79ᵗʰ U.S.C.I., Little Rock, Arkansas was obviously condensed from a letter she had received from her sister in Montana.

(Letter 20)

(Envelope addressed to Capt John R. Graton, 79ᵗʰ U.S.C.I., Little Rock, Arkansas postmarked Jonesville, Mich; 3 cent stamp: Notes on envelope: Important Augusta's serious illness when Eunice was born and her death; High prices in Colorado)

Jonesville Michigan April 9ᵗʰ 1865
Dear John,
Yours of March 19ᵗʰ 1865 was rec'd a number of days since, but this is the first opportunity I have had for answering it. I was disappointed in not receiving another from you this last week, hope to get one soon. We are having quite a snowstorm just now and most of the people have begun making gardens too. I have rec'd a letter from Augusta at last, She had recovered a short time before writing, from a very severe fit of sickness, which well nigh proved to be her last. She was "confined" with a daughter, which was born after two days and one-night sufferings. She then, being so completely exhausted, sunk into a state of unconsciousness, and her attendants had to work over her, employing every means in their power for hours before succeeding in restoring her to sensibility.

Three or four days passed, when she was taken with the chills and mountain fever combined, which dried up her milk in one night, but the doctor succeeded in breaking it up; three or four more days passed and "Inflammation of the womb" set in; the doctor said there would be no hopes for her unless he could check it, which he at last succeeded in doing and in addition to the (XXXX) she had the jaundice. She was left in a very low condition, from which she did not recover sufficient to sit up any for nearly six weeks. Her baby had to be fed on cows milk; it was a puny weakly little thing, had fits when only six weeks old, but they left and they begun to have some hopes of raising her, when she was taken so much worse, and at last, Death put an end to her sufferings, on the very day she turned three months old. She did not weigh quite five pounds, clothes and all, the day she died. Poor Augusta! She is almost heart broken She sent me a photograph of herself and baby (the baby in her lap) Poor girl, she is but a miserable shadow of what she once was and the baby looks so pitiful. It makes my heart ache when I look at them. The baby was eight weeks and one day old, when the photograph was taken.

Augusta wants to sell her share in the Home property, but did not know who to send her Power of Attorney to, as she heard from Sarah Lewis last fall that Mr. McCurdy had gone east. I told her of his return in my reply. She says, "of course she would like to have all that it is worth. She says her sickness and all the expenses attending it, cost at least $500.00 in gold dust or $1,000.00 in greenbacks, they being worth only $00.50 on the dollar, in coin or dust. It takes a long time for letters to go and come (she write that they all have to go round by way of California) and whatever instruction you have to give in regard to that business, perhaps you had best give them to Mr. McCurdy at once, so that should she happen to send the Power of Attorney the matter can be attended to without any unnecessary delay. They have a great scarcity of fruit there and provisions enormously high. Flour (now very low) $16.00 & $18.00 per sack has been as high as $30. Fresh pork, $1.00 pr lb. Brown sugar the same. Potatoes at the rate of $21.60 per bushel, eggs $1.50 per doz. Butter #1.75 per lb, calico $.90 per yard. Common cooking stoves as high as $100 to $200.00 etc.

The balance of this letter deals with family matters between Adda and Capt Graton.

Spring 1865: mail in and out has been irregular due to both the weather and the Indians. In fact, many of our boys here in the Valley are out this week fighting Indians. The (new) Sheriff, who is leading them, said it's better to be fighting them away from our settlements than to wait for them to surprise us here, when we would have to fight them defensively…maybe not even have time to mount an organized response. George is still out on his claim.

A small well-escorted train came in… from Denver. They carried several bags of mail with them.

Mary Rackliffe writes that she has left the Harrimans and moved to Laurette (Buckskin). I wondered if she ended up with Mr. And Mrs. Ferren who offended me with their offer. She says one of the reasons she went "over the Mountain " to Buckskin was that there are more men over there to defend the miners and their families against the Indians. All of the men remaining around Tarryall had to stop and fight Indians. Mining there has almost stopped. Even the Harrimans didn't start ranching this spring, because of the Indians. They moved to Clear Creek, bought a defunct boarding house and are running it. I'm not sure I know where Clear Creek is. Wonder if it's over by Central City?

A letter from Sarah Goss Lewis arrived. She and the doctor are living in a rebuilt boarding house. After Quantrill, they never rebuilt their old house nor did Sarah's folks rebuild theirs way out on the southwest part of town on 21st Street.

A rather "quiet" letter came from Adda. Graton is not well, but his partner seems to be managing the gun shop adequately. At the close of the war Graton had purchased a small commercial lot in town with an undamaged two-story brick building on it, which they rent.

Adda writes she's back, living in Lawrence and has begun a small private school along the lines of the private school we attended in Gibraltar, Michigan. She writes that she will use a classical curriculum: reading, Latin, penmanship, English, arithmetic, etc. "I will try attracting youngsters from the better families here: ages eleven and twelve…and work with them for a minimum of four years in very small classes, which I will teach right here at 627 Rhode Island street, but I note that she doesn't say what her relationship is to Graton.

NEVADA CITY — 1865

Even though it's late spring, we had an awful snowfall. We must have gotten 2 ½ feet. The men had started mining again and had to stop abruptly from the snow.

Prices have come down a little. Flour is $50 per 100 wt. (I paid $5.00 per c.w.t in Denver, and that price reflected being freighted in) so even $50 per c.w.t. is just ridiculous. Adda and I knew the Hayworths up in Chelsea, north of Eldorado. They milled wheat for farmers and sold it profitably at $1 per 100 wt. The retailers sold it in smaller quantities…ten to twenty-five pounds for 2¢ to 3¢ a pound.

I certainly believe the freighters have a right to a hauler's profit, as do the wholesalers, who speculate, but to be able to buy Kansas wheat (flour at $2 to $3 a hundred weight, freight it up here and have the gall to charge from fifty dollars to 100 dollars for that same hundred weight is outright criminal.

Believe it or not I still have some of our Denver rations left and compared to others financially we aren't "bad off" but we don't talk about it. George had purchased any extra mining tools he thought he'd need before we left Denver, so we didn't have those expenses here. We paid the fellow $100 who helped George build the cabin. So George has hung on to most his savings fairly well and I'm only down $200 so far. If we did decide to leave, we could land some place else in fair shape. But, though mining has its ups and downs, I don't see George willing to "call it quits."

One problem now is a labor surplus. Men who were earning $8 to $10 a day as paid laborers last summer, are lucky to get half that today and they can't live on that. Some of the (better) diggers are Chinese and some of them, I understand, are quite good at placer mining. There are several here in the Valley. I suppose they are up here from California. On the other hand, from some of the miners up here, who we knew from Colorado, those who operate sluices and rockers, the more experienced miners, can average six to ten ounces per day per rocker, but they have to give up 10% to 15% of that to stream-diggers. Some rockers are big enough to employ two diggers but those poor fellows are not only wet all the time but these rocker men work from dawn to dusk, so some of the diggers work six-hour shifts. That water, even at the peak of summer is snow run-off and we can't be more than eight to ten miles from its source. The miners who own claims right on the stream…actually both sides of the stream…tell me that all those claims are taken; must be 700 to 800 of them. About half of them are sold during the year, because either the miners have done very well and are going home with their gold or they've done poorly and want to move on.

Last week there was a large assembly of people, some of them we had met before at a noisy meeting expressing serious complaints again about excessively high food prices. Nothing but complaints came from the first meeting. This time a much bigger crowd is agitating to take action. Before the week was out they had confiscated several 100-pound sacks of flour from a shipment that had just come up from Salt Lake City.

We knew some of the freighters, so we knew what they were selling flour for at wholesale to the merchants, that wasn't anywhere close to the retail prices the local merchants were asking. Anyway the "confiscators" sold the flour they took for $27 to $30 per 100 wt or 30¢ per pound (and that's high) to those in real need. The confiscators knew that the freighter paid between $5 and $8 per c.w.t. in either Denver or Salt Lake City. The freight from the next train in was transacted and secreted fifteen miles from here up toward Bozeman. The merchants brought down only what they wanted to sell over three or four days at a time and quickly jacked their prices back up to $60 to $70... some as high as $85. They told us down here that flour was scarce. George and I have been using flour out of our own larder and we've used almost all the corn meal I bought from the Pueblo Mexican, so in these shortages we haven't been directly affected.

I was talking to one of the families just yesterday about the food riots. The situation seems to be much more serious than I had thought. This couple thought there were 4,000 people in the most recent riot. Although they appointed a posse of twenty-five or so men, some with wagons to be the confiscators, I wasn't there...had no need to be...I just heard about it from others but 4,000 people from our total population in the Valley is a very big number.

Sheriff Neil Howie has his hands full. He sympathizes with the confiscators and their cause but he has continually warned them not to loot the actual stores here in the Valley that have been manipulating flour prices. In recent weeks the posse "nabbed" twenty-three wagons loaded with food including flour for storeowners Tootle and Leach. And they confiscated eight to ten wagons contracted for by Cyrenus Biers and his partner's store in Virginia City.

The leader of this posse, James Williams, lives up in Virginia City (a miner). He has promised Sheriff Howie that he will control the passion of his people. Many of the boarding house operators and their boarders have threatened to "beat-up" the grocers. So far that hasn't happened and Sheriff Howie sees to it that the grocers get paid fairly for the flour (and some vegetables) that have been confiscated and sold off the wagons to the populace.

A committee has been asking in all the boarding houses and door to door either for new volunteers to form another posse to ride back down the trail or for donations of cash to defray their expenses. They plan to go as far as Bozeman to intercept these supply trains, make them the same offer that the merchants would offer. If they refuse, the posse would pay them a fair profit but confiscate the entire train. The merchants have been creating scarcity by regulating the supply, then they agree among themselves what the retail price (for flour) will be after they buy up the contents of a freight hauler coming in. This posse is the citizen's response to that behavior.

Well, a week has passed since I wrote the entry about the posse of miners going out from the Gulch and meeting the trains. After two confiscations several freighters have been allowed in and now we have about balanced the supply with daily demand. Potatoes are sixty cents a pound, dried fruit and sugar a dollar, eggs $1.50 per dozen and lo and behold flour is down to $16 to $18 per c.w.t. That's still a mark-up of over fifteen times their cost! (At those prices I might buy 100 pounds myself.) There are several folks in the Valley who didn't have flour for up to four weeks. That means no bread for them. George and I have quietly given away about twenty pounds of Red Beans and maybe ten pounds of both white and yellow corn meal to people we know who are down on their luck.

George and I both like corn bread about as much as bread from wheat flour. When George goes back to his claim, I send with him a big bucket of cooked Red or White Beans with ham or bacon rind, which he loves and I give him ten pounds of corn dodgers (little hard cakes of corn meal with a little sugar and molasses added and I grind some cooked bacon or ham rind into the dodger dough before I bake it. He has a small caliber rifle, which he uses to shoot game, which although it isn't plentiful, it is adequate. Now and then George shoots a rabbit that's too tough to fry or roast. I've taught him how to make Rabbit Stew.

Sarah Lewis writes that now that the war is over, Lawrence is rebuilding very fast. They've rebuilt the bridge over the Kaw River, so solidly that the railroad from Leavenworth can run daily through Lawrence to Wyandotte. Well, that means that they've extended the railroad from Iowa City all the way to the Missouri River. How could they have done that during the war?

In good times the railroads seem able to raise prodigious amounts of capital and the Federal Government grants them large tracts of land for their rails because they know that when the rails come in, commerce increases sharply. When commerce increases, tax revenue for the Government increases.

She writes that Mrs. Gates, my old employer and friend, who was such a comfort for me right after Chase died, whose husband was killed during one of Quantrill's raids, has remarried a Mr. W. Y. Roberts. I don't believe I know the gentleman, but I must write her and send my best wishes. In hindsight she was really very nice to Adda and me. Her little Fanny must be seventeen or eighteen years of age by now. With Mr. Gates having died during one of the Quantrill raids, I suppose Mrs. Gates rebuilt the Cincinnati House and is running it.

_____ 0 _____

George is trying to hang on to his claim in Big Canyon on the Mountain, which has yielded a little, but less than his expenses. He is still gambling on finding gold-rich quartz veins, and then digging and blasting into the mountainside to loosen the rock, so he can follow the quartz into the mountain. There is one Irishman in the Valley, who will chisel holes and provide blasting powder and "know how". George pays him by the day for chiseling but the powder work and the powder is extra. We've spent over $250 for powder, caps, fuse cord etc., yet so far, to recover that cost.

The fellows with the stamp mill are within a quarter mile of him and they have it running. They charge by the 100 wt or $20 by the ton. George said he'd like to see the day when he can take a wagonload of quartz rock up to them.

He took on a limited partner, a Mr. Shoup, both as a helper and as someone who can be on the claim when George is elsewhere. No sooner did George take him on and they were ready to blast into the lower face of a deep vee-shaped notch that ran half way up the Mountain. George and the Irishman had already blasted and tunneled in ten to twelve feet, and had put in some overhead support across the open "vee." Anyway, following the blast, the whole contraption collapsed. Rock chips, dust, loose gravel, everything came down some of it from 200 to 300 feet up that notch, and buried Mr. Shoup right up to his neck. The blast knocked him down, then the rubble covered him-up, George and the "powder monkey" got him out alive, but he is still having trouble getting around.

I asked George how this could happen. He said Shoup wouldn't listen to the powder fellow. He clearly told us after he had put the sticks of powder deep into the holes and was getting ready to set the long fuse that we had a count of ten to get out and away from the opening, and he added every fuse is a little different. It might be an eight count or a twelve count. Well, he lit the fuse, George said, and they all had plenty of time to get out and down to one side of the rock face of their claim. Even at twelve count the charge hadn't gone off, so Shoup decided to go up and see what went wrong. He said he thought maybe the fuse cords had pulled out of the holes. Just as Shoup got within eight to ten feet of the face where the powder had been placed. The charge went off. Luckily for Shoup that he didn't get closer or the blast would have killed him, the Irishman said. As it is, he was almost buried alive, and Mrs. Shoup will be picking little pieces of sand and quartz out of his head and neck for a while.

George said he and the Irishman had worked out an arrangement called by him, "double jacking." "He uses a rather short stone chisel to get a blast hole started, then we shift to a longer chisel (owned by him and made of Swedish steel.) He pounds while I hold the chisel and give it a one-fourth turn between hammer blows. Sometimes I use a spanner for that. I tried this process with Shoup but he doesn't have the upper body strength to pound and when he holds the chisel, he allows it to wobble and I'm afraid I'll hit his arm, and he lacks stamina, which really comes from lack of ambition.

"John has several hammers of various weights. We start out with a four-pound maul (hammer) and gradually get up to the eight-pounder. The hole goes faster with heavier hammers.

"In these mountains John likes a hole eighteen to twenty-four inches deep. We place eight to nine holes in the drift. Each hole takes us about one hour plus or minus, depending on the hardness of the rock, so we spend a week or a week and a half just drilling holes. After we get say, eight holes drilled, he puts powder in all but one or two. He wants the blast to force the rock towards the hole or holes with no powder. He buys powder packed in cylindrical sticks about eight to ten inches long and a fuse cap goes in after the powder stick.

"When we drill eight holes, he lights off two sets of powder sticks, one slightly before the other, which is regulated by one fuse cord being cut two inches shorter than the other...or he lights one fuse cord, counts one, then lights the other.

"Each blast yields about three to four tons of rock, most of which comes down onto a large sheet of metal or a wooden floor that makes shoveling easier.

"When I'm drilling into quartz, I take one to two tons per wagon loads up to the stamp mill; pay then $20/ton to stamp it and I stay there until it's done. So I need to get more than two ounces of gold 'to make it pay'. Some days I beat that...but most days I get so little quartz I don't even load-up the wagon."

Before George abandoned the Big Canyon claim, he had a tunnel with little short diversions, which totaled over fifteen feet.

The Whites, (that's Mrs. White, who was with me with Bertie) had a party and it was very nice...nicely attended...even though it rained cats and dogs. The night of the party, there was a big mudslide in our area that pushed some of our neighbors' cabins off their foundation or mud and rocks broke in a back door or a sidewall and flooded some of the houses near us with mud. We escaped through pure luck.

Oh, big news! The roof of the most popular saloon in town, the "Sonny Boy," collapsed yesterday and broke one man's jaw and another's leg. I heard about all this from George's partner, Mr. Shoup, who with little sores all over his forehead and face "hobbled" in for cup of tea. He thinks he's sprained his leg. I asked him how he knew all these details about the saloon's roof and he said, "Augusta, I was at the Sonny Boy, when it all happened. I teased him and said he should be very careful. Bad news seems to follow him around. I was glad when he left. George is a little impatient with him. He thinks Shoup is perfectly able to be guarding our claim, even if he can't work. George has been offered a job by a three-man partnership of Georgian miners that we both knew in Tarryall, to build a sluice that would bring water to their rockers. They call the sluice a "Tom" or "Long Tom". These Georgians are digging in dry gravel several feet from the main stream, and they need large quantities of water. Their claim is on the north side of Alder Creek about half way between Nevada and Virginia City. They found encouraging color but can't afford to continue to buy water by the barrel for their rockers. If Shoup could guard our claim on the mountain, then George could accept the sluice job. They've offered to take George in as a partner in exchange for his surveying and carpentry. He needs to bring the water in from several feet higher than their location, so it need not be a long sluice. They will provide the lumber and some of the labor. They need George's surveying skills and his surveyor's level to determine the correct grade down from the source of water. They found a little crick that feeds into Alder Creek about 200 feet distance and a little uphill from their rocker site. George says they get about a five-foot head or drop in elevation. They blasted enough rubble to make a low dam or penstock at their stream source. The sluice starts there. Water for this kind of mining is in such short supply that at a similar operation one team of miners work nights, because that's when their share of water is available.

In late summer a pack of mail arrived in a train up from Salt Lake City. In it was this letter from my sister.

June 20, 1865

Dear Augusta,

Late this spring Allie and I left Michigan to visit relatives, particularly Grandma, Mama's mother in New York State near Rochester and the old Erie Canal. Grandpa Taylor is dead. I'm staying with Uncle John McLarens and Aunt Aurelia, who is one of mother's sisters. They have a farm almost on the edge of Lake Ontario. The nearest town is West Webster, right on the Erie Canal a little east of Rochester.

Once I got across the river at Detroit we caught a train at Windsor, Canada for Rochester and Webster. (We traveled part way on that little peninsula of Canada's that runs south west of Niagara Falls/Buffalo) about 300 miles changing trains at Buffalo. In fact in Windsor we had to change our money to pound sterling and pences for Canadian train tickets. Canada accepts no "Greenbacks".

While I was visiting the McLarens, we learned that Grandma Taylor was "under-the-weather". So I took little Alice to visit her, where we were joined by other relatives. She was clear-headed and understood, who I was and said, "Oh, yes, it was your father who married Jane, wasn't it, over in Michigan? Why in the world she chose, a sawmill operator, when she could have married that nice Begoole boy, who was later a congressman, then Governor of Michigan, was more than we could fathom".

As politely and gently as I could, I explained how Father had gone to Kansas in 1856 and fought the Missouri proslavers, spent time in a U. S. Army P.O.W. camp. Then he established a new voting district of Free Soilers farther west and was elected to the territorial legislature.

She was lucid enough to ask if Kansas had ever become a state and I explained all that. Then she asked how our sawmill business was going and I explained to her Father's unusual murder. She asked, if we were so far west, why he didn't form a posse of vigilantes to go after the horse thieves!

She asked about Sam's "other daughter" (meaning you, Augusta) and how life in Kansas is now without slavery and I began by explaining how Graton and five other Army captains had trained an entire regiment of ex slaves and had fought the Rebels all through the war.

As I was talking, she closed her eyes. I thought she had dropped off to sleep, so Allie, I and others quietly stepped out of the room. An hour or so later, when someone went to inquire if she was going to eat some supper…she was dead. She was eighty-five years old.

I helped in the funeral arrangements, including organizing the mourners, the funeral and the graveyard service.

Little Alice has had her first encounters with death and the ceremonies. By the time you get this, Augusta, Allie will be four years old. She's about average in height and weight and has known her ABCs since she was three. Can count to one hundred, talks a "blue streak" and is very active physically. She's over most of her childhood diseases…with scarlet fever and mumps to go. All the relatives love her and she gets along with everybody.

The McLarens remind me of the Seeleys in Flint. They have a very well built snug farmhouse, which is not too far from Lake Ontario. They say the winter weather is fierce up here.

I asked them why they, Uncle Dan and Aunt Julia had moved to this area, when they did. They said, "Jobs", thousands of jobs were available when they were building the Erie Canal and as all these towns from Albany to Buffalo sprang up along the Canal and grew, the area became very prosperous. Wages were up, commercial property values were very high as well as farmland along the canal on both sides. Then the railroads came in almost parallel to the Canal and they brought in more jobs. Although the Canal lost business, farm produce still moved on it but most passengers switched to the railroad. Prices continued to go up, but they could afford it.

Then…BANG! Everything collapsed in 1857! Too much expansion, too much speculation!

All the Irish that came over here to build the Canal stayed and worked on the railroads. Until the war there was a serious depression up here, several banks in major cities, like Buffalo, Rochester and Syracuse closed. Then the war created a shortage of help and farm crop prices have risen to where the area is prosperous again.

In your last letter you asked why I was boarding with the Birbecks in Flint and that you didn't believe they were relatives… they aren't. He's a local shoemaker with room to board Allie and me. I wanted to visit Aunt Lucy (Stewart), Uncle Addison's wife, but as she is a working widow raising a family, I didn't want to impose, so Allie and I stayed a week or so with the Birbecks (at $3.00) and I helped with the housework. Of course, they knew as many of Father's relatives as Mother's.

While Allie and I were boarding in Flint, we had occasion to visit Uncle Isaac (Taylor), a brother of Mother. They are (or would be) about Father's age. They have a beautiful daughter, Clara, who really took to Allie. Uncle Isaac works in a "department store".

I realize now both sides of the family were members of a very strong church in the Flint area with much antislavery sentiment and a willingness by those who didn't want to go to Kansas to support financially those who did.

With Graton's future still uncertain my own plans to return to Lawrence are uncertain.

Your loving sister;
Adda
c/o John McLaren
West Webster P.O.
Monroe County, NY

Late summer 1865

Augusta Stewart Chase Blackman Taken during a visit to Lawrence, Kansaa in 1882 Augusta was 43.

George Washington Blackman circa 1882 age 43
Butte, Montana

67.

ALDER GULCH MINING CAMP
MONTANA TERRITORY

Fall 1865

Mrs. White, intending to open a boarding house paid over $200 for several little cabins for "roomers" added to their main cabin, which is really just a mess hall, big enough to feed thirty-six at one setting. She has offered me a job. The first day it was apparent to both of us that I knew more about this business than she does. If she'll increase my pay, I'll bring some of my kitchenware over, do the buying, which includes wild game, assign work to the girls and make sure they do it. Dumping slop jars from thirty-six miners every morning is a task nobody wants to do. I told her, we already have more business than we can handle, so we don't have to extend credit, which she had done to sign-up her first boarders. I advised her to begin requiring one week, paid in advance. There are too many shiftless miners in this camp to give them even one week's credit. Lawrence was a much more stable community than this place, yet in Lawrence we had people skipping out after owing Mrs. Killam for two weeks.

JULY 11, 1865

Ten years ago today Adda, Father and I left Michigan and here I am, sitting all alone, in the kitchen of my employer's boarding house, making a note of it in my journal, volume three.

This spring Mrs. White took terribly sick with something that caused her breasts to swell to double normal. She thinks it came from a bad tin of sweet corn. We have one doctor here in Nevada City and nothing he has tried worked. He did say that she also has dysentery and that has nothing to do with her body swelling. We called Dr. Zwissler down from Virginia City. He seems to have helped a little, but Mrs. White is of little help to me now and she's honest enough to apologize for the situation she's put me in. I told her for all the help and comfort she gave me when I was sick and almost died with little Bertie, this is the least I can do. Anyway I have no trouble getting good help. I told her to just stay in bed and get well. I'll run the boarding house.

As busy as I am, I'm lonely for my husband. I thought he could find time to send me a note once in a while. I don't even know if he's still working on the long-haul sluice or if that's finished, knowing him, he's back up on that blamed Mountain, looking for quartz veins.

George got home in the middle of the night. It was so good simply to have someone to share my bed, though it's a little warm up here for July, but not as hot as Kansas Julys.

George seemed disappointed. They continue to sink the same shaft that had previously collapsed, six to eight feet deeper into hard rock, following a thin quartz vein, hoping to see it get wider and be gold-bearing…but not enough color yet to pay for the powder and drilling.

The one thing that encourages George is that at least two other miners out of maybe six on the same face he's on are doing well enough to send their quartz rock to the stamp mill.

I asked him how the sluice job was going and he said that was finished. They paid him half cash and he has one-tenth ownership in the operation. They have so much sluice water they can operate two rockers: day and night. The night shift fellows don't own their own rocker. They rent it for a split of 50/50 of what they get with these Georgia owners, collected at dawn every day, when the night shift pans out their dust. George gets 10% of the take from both shifts. The daylight rockers have been getting between ten and twenty ounces per day. Now that the sluice is working, the water is free and they don't have to pay diggers, George says he's been getting $30 to $40 of gold dust a day for his share. There have been some months where George spends $250 just for drilling and blasting. Well, halleluiah, he's getting ahead now, three or four hundred dollars a month. George thinks this will last until about November 1st…when the Georgians will go home. The week that their sluice began operating, the two Georgians, who own the two rockers began taking board and room with us.

In July and August a petition was posted on the saloon's outside wall, looking for prospects to join a train to go out in late August or early September and I saw the White's name on it. I bided my time to make them an offer for this place. It would be a shame just to close it down. We've got thirty-five or so full time boarders. About two dozen sleep here as well. We can put six to eight "sleepers" in one cabin. Most of them have their own bedrolls. We charge 25¢ more, if we provide a tick and two blankets…no extra charge for the bed bugs.

We've had no trouble getting female help. One of the problems in a place like this is infidelity. I don't mean the men cheat on their wives. I mean frontier and mining towns are hard on family life and marriage. When some of these miners get down on their luck and can't find work here, they leave their wives in search of work elsewhere, or vice versa. There must be a dozen young women who have arrived in various trains in the last twelve months, many of them with husbands, but the husbands are gone now, so they are willing to work for board and room, plus a little spending money: $25 per month. I have four of them working for me now, one with a little boy. Of course, some of them will come back for their wives if they find a paying job or claim elsewhere. Others are gone for good.

Mrs. White hasn't worked a day during her recovery from that food poisoning and she's not very good with the books either, so I have helped her in that department as well. It was a surprise to her that she owed money to two stores in Bannack and our wood supplier. All that, she said, reduced what she thought she had made this summer.

Mrs. White put off making a decision about selling her place until just a few days before the train was scheduled to go, which is now September 1st. Maybe they've tried to sell it to others, I don't know. Though I am running the place, they live here and they are all packed. Finally today she said, "Augusta, this place is better than a gold mine and you know it. At $6.00 per day per boarder, you'll gross almost $900 a month. I'll sell you the business, the buildings, furniture, bedding everything, even the pantry, lock, stock and barrel for $1,000."

I said, "Between George and I together we couldn't scrape up $1,000, but I will give you $500 in gold; no "Green backs",… mostly for the stuff inside. She interrupted to say, "Augusta, there's $200 to $250 worth of food in the pantry."

"I haven't looked carefully at your larder, but I will.

"I don't think all these flimsy little cabins are worth $150 and when winter sets in and the miners who room here now, leave, the cabins won't be worth that. Little by little the miners will dismantle these cabins for the logs, which they will chop up for firewood." And I let her think about my offer for a few more days.

The next day she said she'd take my $500 offer, I said, I've been thinking it over and I've looked more closely at your larder. Wild pigs wouldn't eat that a barrel of salt pork. Most of your cereal has weevils and your bedding is in terrible shape. We've only got September and maybe October to make any money and I'm not sure I want the load of thirty-five boarders. Five of them owe you for two weeks already and that's a $500 deduction from your asking price that neither one of us will ever see, never mind what you've spent to feed them, but I tell what, if I collect a nickel from any of those five, I'll mail it to you. Foodstuff is going to go up come October, because of the weather. The best I can do," I said, "is $400 and you take your pots and pans. I've got my own."

She laughed and said, "I guess I'd better take it. If I wait another three or four days, you'll be down to $200. So, George and I own "the White" house, the biggest boarding house in the Gulch. I immediately told any boarder, who owed two weeks or more, to pay up before supper or leave hungry. Five left but that didn't bother me one whit. That was her loss not mine. I had estimated that if five or six of these fellows, on credit left, she'd be short between $400 and $500, so I had already deducted what they owed from her $1,000 asking price and she knew it. I suspected I wouldn't collect from that gang…all from the South. If you carry some of these fellows for two weeks the next thing you know, they will owe you for three. When the word got out that I had five vacancies, five new ones lined up and begrudgingly paid one week in advance. If they didn't have coin, I took a minimum of two ounces of dust. What I'd really like to get is a cow but none of those prospectors or families who are leaving owned one.

When these fellows leave, I try to launder some of their bedclothes. I can't seem to get water hot enough or lye soap strong enough to kill those damn bed bugs. St. Mathew said the meek will inherit the earth. He'd never met a Montana bed bug. They will inherit the earth. Heavens, they've got it already. One of the girls brought up a Chinese fellow, who offered to do the laundry on the premises. He has his own soap and big bleached white wooden buckets. We heat the water for him, if he brings in the wood. Although he's rather quiet, I've tried to strike up a conversation with him. Yesterday I asked him to come in for a cup of tea, which he liked. From what I can tell his name is Ah Boon Haw.

He has a tight little pigtail of hair and wears an oily leather skullcap. By drawing pictures, I've learned he lives on a big river in China called Whang Poo, with a wife and two children. He carries a two-edged knife on a belt. Its scabbard is visible above his waist hanging in the middle of his chest, which when the weather is hot and he's doing the laundry, is bare. He's really a rather big fellow.

After a while, as we got to know each other, he brought me a present. It was a little hollow baked terracotta Buddha with a round open mouth sitting on a little saucer. By lighting a little brown biscuit he showed me that it was an incense burner with rather pleasant aroma, which comes out of the Buddha's mouth.

After working for me for two weeks, and over protests from some of my "regulars", who dislike eating next to a "Chink", he's become a boarder. He likes to stream-dig three or four days a week for anybody that needs a digger.

I told George I thought we could do all right if we stayed open until November 1st...maybe November 10th for the stragglers. What I'm afraid of is, when miners know you're going to close on a certain date, some of them will skip out on you the last day you told them you'd be open, owing two weeks or whatever they can get away with. They'll even steal the blankets if you don't watch them. Five of the boys have given me their poke of ten to twenty ounces as a safety deposit.

I'm bound and determined that the day I close down, no miner will leave owing me money, if for no other reason than, after he pays me on Friday night, he'll expect me to be "open" the next week, and I have a week's deposit in coin or dust from all those remaining.

I asked on October 1st how many intend to stay through the month. Almost all of them raised their hand. So, again, I spoke in private to those who were in arrears two weeks and gave them my ultimatum of pay up or skedaddle. This time I lost five but only replaced them with three. From those three I demanded a week in advance. I said I'd take coin or dust. More laundry for Mr. Ah Boon Haw.

I'm worried about the three girls who work for me. What will happen to them this winter?

In mid October I took another poll to determine how many of my boarders thought they'd stay through the winter: eight of them. How many through October? All. I've finally got every boarder current as of Friday. Then the last week of October, we had a big snowstorm. A notice had been posted at the saloon that the last train out, headed for Salt Lake City would be October 30th. All but eight of the boarders had signed up.

I always collect what's owed every Friday before supper. I go out of my way to let them know I record their payment or lack of it. In that way they will think I'm staying open for another two or three weeks. If I don't do something like this and if they know Friday is their last meal here, enough of them will leave that day and then there is no way to collect what's owed. On November 1st, give or take a day or two, I'm closing down, but I won't announce that. I'll simply announce at breakfast that I'm closing that day. The Friday before November 1st, I will have collected all I'm ever going to collect.

Those fellows who are staying all winter are staying to protect their claims, and to prevent them from preemption in the spring by early new comers. Four of them run rockers and hire younger men to stream dig for them. They will need a place to stay this winter. They will also need one hell of a pile of wood laid in before the snows come to keep this drafty place warm. We have no stoves in the three little add-on cabins. But we have a very big stove in the kitchen and two pot-bellied "Ben Franklins" in the Mess Hall. The fellows who do stay over can bunk in those two rooms.

On November 2nd or 3rd when it's obvious that I have closed, I'll offer to sell the place cheap to the eight miners who are going to stay through the winter.

NOVEMBER 5TH — HERE IS MY REPORT

I wish George were here to go over my numbers. I ran the place for two months and stopped operating it on November 3rd. When I bought the place, I knew what the food and labor costs were and I knew the board and room rates. From that I budgeted that I could make between $700 and $800 per month for the next two months free and clear. Well, you know about the best laid plans...the Friday before November 1st four miners skipped out owing me for two weeks, but I was holding a $40 to $50 poke deposit for each miner, so I wasn't too concerned...until I took my little tobacco bags of dust to the Assay Office on Saturday. Mr. Worsig said, "Mrs. Blackman, these eight to ten ounces don't pan out well at all, you've got more sand than flake. Until I do my next test, I'd guess you're got between $25 and $50 here. How did you come by this stuff?" I was ashamed to admit my folly. "But let me be much more accurate," he said. Showing me a little cylindrical brass weight (with a little knob on top), he said, "Mrs. Blackman, this is a one-ounce weight certified by a government agency in Washington, D.C. How much gold do you think you have in each bag?"

"Two ounces. I charge $6.00 a day for board and room. I ask cash or gold one week in advance, so I expect there is at least two ounces of gold in each bag and I'm putting a value of $20 per ounce."

"All right, I'm going to put two, one-ounce weights in this left pan." Watch what happens when I empty your bag onto my pan on the right. Do you see what happened?"

"Yes. The beam didn't balance."

"Not by a long shot. Now you see this little arrow that points to a calibrated scale in the middle of my balance?"

"Yes."

"Well, it reads a little over one ounce and you're expecting two. So, let's test it more accurately. I'll leave the contents where it is, but I'll remove one of the one-ounce weights and replace it with smaller weights and see what happens. Now it's balanced, isn't it?"

"Yes"

"So this bag weighs slightly over one ounce, so obviously that's part gold and part sand with more sand than gold, I'm afraid,"

"Your sand will weigh between a quarter and a third what the gold weighs by volume. It will take a little more work on my part to determine how much actual gold your boarders paid you."

It took him a few more minutes to weigh the other bags and calculate the proportion of sand to gold.

I walked out of his office with fifty-five dollars…and I was expecting at least $160 to $200.

But this story doesn't end here. If you've ever read the Count of Monte Cristo, within a few days I was to have my Edmond Dante's revenge, though my satisfaction wouldn't hold a candle to what Edmond Dantes was entitled for having been falsely accused, arrested and imprisoned for years before escaping, then finding a treasure, which allowed him to locate and settle his differences with those that had so seriously wronged him.

One of the Southern miners, who had cheated me by diluting his deposit of gold dust with sand, had the gall to drop in, saying he'd left a pair of wool socks drying in the cabin they had occupied. I guess he hadn't figured on my visit to the Assay Office.

Presently he came into the mess hall holding his socks to say thanks. It was noon. I asked Mr. Spoon, "Now that you are here, would you like to have dinner with us? He said, "I shore would." I told him our starter today was a big bowl of thick Navy Bean soup with pieces of ham hock and that I would serve him personally.

I keep a quart jar of alkaline salt crystals in the kitchen for miners who complain of constipation. The label on the jar proudly says, "Movement Guaranteed within 24 hours or your money back." They are from a company in Missouri, named Eno, and they claim that their little crystals are effervescent. Well, I ladled into Mr. Spoon's soup a double dose of Mr. Eno's little persuasive crystals, stirred them until they fizzed and dissolved; grabbed a chunk of warm corn bread and served it with the soup.

"How soon are you leaving us, Mr. Spoon?"

"Tomorrow morning at sun-up."

"How are you traveling?"

"I'll be on horseback. We're a party of twenty-five or thirty, some with wagons…some are your old boarders."

"Well, good luck. I hope you don't run into any irregularities between here and…where you are going?"

"Julesburg on the Platte to Council Bluffs… down to Missouri and on to Georgia."

I interrupted, "Bye-bye. I must get back to the kitchen."

It's episodes like this when I miss my little sister. In her prime Adda would have ridden down the trail with this rascal, waiting for that effervescent bean soup to run down his pant leg and onto his boot. She would ride up to him and say something like, "Say Mister, yore laig is leakin."

If I had Mr. Alexander Dumas' address in France, I'd send him this journal entry. He might make a story out of it.

So I cleared $1,200 for the two months from board and room and I haven't sold the buildings and stuff inside yet. I offered to sell the place to the eight miners who were going to stay over for $250 or about $31 for each of them. Well, that reality scared out four of the eight. The remaining four made me a "take it or leave it," offer of $100. I said, "Give me $200 and a promise that the girls, if they stay, get a roof over their heads, though they will have to run the place and maybe pay something toward their board and they could keep all the bedding, except for six Army blankets that I bought in Denver as well as all the larder that's in the pantry, including that barrel of "high grade" salt pork. As bad as it is they'll be eating that by New Years. They get the big kitchen stove but I'm taking one of the "Ben Franklins".

Their spokesman asked if I'd take dust?"

"Yes, indeedy."

He smiled. Then I said, "If you intend to give me dust, I'll need ten ounces. They agreed to that. I added, " We'll complete this transaction at the Assay Office." In the end I took $50 in coin from each of the four of them.

They accepted my counter offer.

So I've come out of it with $200 for the house and cabins, which is fair and $1,200 for two months operation for a total of $1,400 over and above what I paid for it and I've made $80 per month while I worked for the Whites. I don't think George, for all his work and sacrifice has met expenses on his claims but he did right well with his share from the sluice before those two miners went back to Georgia...wealthy, I'm happy to report. Of course, if he "hits it" on his claim, he'll hit it big...not 500 feet up the trail from his claim, on the same face two miners just sold out for $20,000 and promptly hired two, full-time bodyguards.

The new owners, both experienced hard rock miners with experience in California and Colorado, immediately bought out the stamp mill operation. The original stamp mill fellows, according to George had a good claim, but never found any real gold. What money they made, they made by crushing quartz for others. I asked George if the new owners of the stamp mill would crush his quartz. He said, "If my quartz is looking good, they will, because they will be thinking about buying me out. If they won't, I think I'll hire an arrastra built. There are two Mexicans in the valley offering to build them...and they will sell me a mule to run it. How's that for enterprise"? George said the arrastra is similar to ancient horse-driven flourmills and/or olive presses. They've been around for thousands of years. I'll let the Almighty provide food for my mule, which is much cheaper than the wood that the stamp-mill operators need to buy to keep steam-up on their boiler.

George drew a picture of a large round pan or depression cut into a flat rock surface four to six feet in diameter with a stout wooden or metal axle standing vertical in the center. Connected to the center pole or mast is a horizontal pole that rotates in a horizontal plane about the axel. A mule or horse or human pulls the end of that horizontal pole round and round. Attached to the pole is a very large smooth boulder or millstone fixed to rotate. As the boulder is dragged round and round or the millstone rolls in the pan, any quartz rock dumped in its path gradually gets ground down to fine sand, releasing the gold. There are several ways to collect the dust and to separate it from the gold flake.

I immediately saw a similarity between the arrastra and our syrup mill. The crushing rollers were made to turn or roll in the large pan by the vertical axel, which in our case was rotated by a leather belt driven by a small steam engine.

When the Whit left with the big train September 1ˢᵗ, they promised to write and today we got a nice lettr from them posted at some fort over on the Yellowstone brought in by an "Express" rider.

July 15. 1865
West Webster, NY

Dear Augusta

Although the war is finally over, and I had been thinking all along come the armistice, I'd return to Lawrence, but a recent letter from Graton has caused such uncertainty that I think I'll stay here until I know what it is he is going to do.

Graton said he had been thinking about the future and had decided to ask an Army Review Board for an appearance to apply for post war Army service. He was told to report to regimental headquarters on June 23rd, and he did. The Review Board told him they would recommend him for a post-war commission. That he didn't consult me in this important matter is mildly offensive in the light of almost a dozen letters over the last two years from him talking of his intent for us in Lawrence, his plans to rebuild his gun shop, repair the house to livable conditions, etc…now this! If he is going to stay in the Army, Lord only knows where he'll be stationed and I'm not sure I want Allie living on one after another military camps as she grows up, although he recommended that Allie and I do precisely that in his June 25th letter to me from his camp in Little Rock, Arkansas.

Although he's saved $3,000, he thinks this will be insufficient to rebuild his business. And a captain's pay is now $1,500 per year, with a raise "coming up". He's not sure he can make free and clear $1,500 a year as a Lawrence gunsmith.

Your affectionate sister;
Adda
West Webster, N.Y.P.O.

When the Whites left with the big train Sept 1ˢᵗ, they promised to write and today we got a nice letter from them posted at some Fort over on the Yellowstone brought in by an "Express" rider.

A week or so later two letters arrived by coach. They posted these at Forts Halleck and Kearney in Nebraska Territory. Since then we've had a hiatus of mail and coach arrivals through October and November, due I'm sure to Indians and bad weather. I'm just amazed that the U. S. Army can't spare a Company to guard wagon trains or a Squad to guard the stagecoach carrying mail and official communications.

After their sluice began early this summer, those two Georgians started boarding with me. And because George had built it, we've had a pleasant, mutually respectable relationship. I've known for some time that they were going out with the train due to leave the first week of November and I've known they must have done very well for themselves after George built them that sluice, if for no other reason than the amount that George got all summer and fall ran $1,000 a month and that was only 10% of their take.

Thinking ahead to next year, I asked them not to abandon their legal claim but to sell or sign it over to me in exchange for their October board and room.

The other miner laughed and said with the war over, he wasn't planning on coming back anyway. So I pressed my luck and said, "Well, leave your rockers with me and I'll keep them for you. If you do return, I'll be here.. If you don't come back, I may find a partner and return to mining and I told them about my old Georgia gentleman-friend, Charlie Fletcher. It turns out they both knew the Russell Clan but they didn't know Fletcher.

A wounded lone rider straggled in here a week ago, reporting that he had been a mounted (private) guard for the northbound Denver coach with nine passengers and two drivers. One of the passengers was a hired detective. The Indians had killed all but him and took the horses. He said one of the passengers was an official from a Government agency that makes regular Indian payments, called annuity. The Indians are paid according to whatever treaty exists between the Government and the local tribe. The agent had been met by a party of Indian elders at some fort on the upper Bozeman Trail and the annuity money distributed. The next day after the coach left, braves of the tribe that had just been paid their annuity, attacked his stage. General Patrick G. Connor is the annuitant administrator for this area of the Montana territory. He seems to have adequate money but inadequate Armed Forces.

A recent letter from Adda says that she's in New York State visiting manufactories, buying supplies for their gun shop in Lawrence. But Graton is someplace in the South…with the war over, I wondered what he's doing in the South? Maybe he's buying surplus guns and ammunitions from Old Confederate armories now taken over by the U. S. Army? Both the Union Army and the Confederates had, according to Graton, a much-improved revolver design, but when Graton had his shop in Lawrence, he had trouble getting them, because the government was buying them all. She sent a very nice picture of little Alice.

And there was a letter from Mary Rackliffe. With the war over she and her children have returned to Hardin County, Iowa. I wonder if she will ever remarry?

A few days later I returned to the Assay Office and asked Mr. Worsig if he could melt down an ounce or two of gold flake into a single cube or sphere. He said no but he had some molds that yield (unofficial) coins worth ten dollars (a half ounce) and twenty dollars (one ounce.)

I told him I had a niece in Eastern Kansas and I wanted her to have a solid piece of Colorado gold containing at least one ounce.

Mr. Worsig said, "Anytime you're ready."

I still have about $300 of Colorado flake from my partnership with Charlie Fletcher. Mr. Worsig joked with me before I left by saying, "We'll see if your Colorado flake has any sand in it." A week or so later I took some of my Colorado dust to him and he smelted, then molded a fifty dollar gold piece out of it for my little niece, Alice.

A week or so after the big exodus carrying Mr. And Mrs. White, George's father and one of George's brothers plus two freight drivers and an armed guard (that they hired in Julesburg) arrived. They had joined a larger train In Nebraska City, and came out on the Overland Trail. Then part of that train, settlers and freighters, broke off at Julesburg: some for Colorado, some for Idaho). There were twenty-five or so wagons. Most of them had freight for Nevada City and Virginia City. By the way, they used the Bridger Cut Off.

Mr. Blackman, Sr. has two wagons and between the two of them they have about 4,000 pounds of freight. One is a covered wagon, like ours, with household effects: bedding, food, etc. it's their home on wheels. Most of the freight is in the large wagon with a black canvas cover.

I've never seen so much honey, sugar; cane sorghum in barrels and one-gallon terracotta crocks; with twenty 100-pound sacks of sugar…some white, some brown, and two fifty-gallon barrels of Iowa maple syrup. They brought into our place a partially used 100-pound bag of Kansas white flour and some corn meal. I baked several loaves of bread from it. We enjoyed it with some Iowa butter that I was happy to see had not turned rancid. With their honey, it was the best dessert we'd had since we've been here.

He said that on and off their train had an Army escort. For safety in Julesburg they hired an armed (U. S. Army veteran). He rode on the freight wagon. They were forty-five days from Julesburg. But they had been "on the road" over two months.

Considering their late arrival and the dangers of traveling now between here and Iowa, I asked Mr. Blackman, Senior (who is a widower) if he planned to stay over the winter. He said he had given some thought to either going to Denver or Salt Lake City. He has friends in both places.

I told him he was welcome here and if he stayed, maybe we could dismantle this cabin, that George and I moved into when I sold the "White house". This house has a decided list to it, because it simply doesn't have a foundation. He laughed and said he'd noticed that when I had served him soup in a shallow bowl. The mudsill logs were just laid on rocks. We need to build a real foundation, using very large stones (several tons each) and laying large logs, adzed flat on two sides on those stones. After getting foundation logs level, we could put in a real wood floor from a sawmill now in Bozeman. Then we could use the logs in this cabin, to reconstruct a new one. I can afford it. I don't want to spend a winter in a cabin with a gravel floor.

He said first I've got to see how much of my freight I can sell to the grocers here in Alder Gulch. If I can't sell it all here, I'll try Bannack, then Fort Ellis. That's my first job. Then we'll get to your new cabin. I promise you and George this much, I'll stay 'til we've rebuilt your cabin.

It took less than one week for Mr. Blackman to sell-out. When I asked him what he realized on a per-pound basis, expecting he'd sell sugar for at least 50¢ a pound, honey at a dollar, maybe a dollar and a half a pint, etc., he evaded my question. But that same day the gentleman that they hired in Julesburg as an armed guard, asked if he could take board and room with us. When we discussed terms, he said, "Your father-in-law has hired me as a body guard, though he did most of his transactions with local merchants, using a 'draft' payable to him only against the bank in Bozeman."

For his age Mr. Blackman, Sr. has a lot of energy but after listening to his son for two evenings and visiting George's claims up on the Mountain east of Virginia City and seeing what he does, he says he has very little interest in joining George as a miner.

While George's father was in the process of selling his freight, one of the Army Veteran's who acted as an Armed Escort came by for a discussion with him about the perils of the Bozeman Trail. He said he'd been asked to write a report for the Army about troubles on the Bozeman Trail.

I invited the gentleman to stay for supper and we all talked well into the night, In fact, we used up all the kerosene in the lamp and I'm having trouble getting coal oil or kerosene up here. What

I do get comes up from Salt Lake City. Do you suppose those Mormons have learned how to make coal oil?

I've written up a summary of our discussion and told him he's free to use this in his report.

What Bozeman did was to find a way for travelers that had come West along the Platte River system, (The Overland Trail) to get to Oregon or points west of Omaha/Council Bluffs by turning generally north at Julesburg Junction, actually at nearby Fort Sedgwick, where if they followed the South West Trail, they'd end-up in Denver, like we did in '63. By turning north and staying east of the Big Horn Mountain Range all the way to the Yellowstone River Valley...then following that generally west, the traveler could rest in one of the valleys of the Jefferson, Madison, Gallatin or Missouri River valleys and settle there or press on for Oregon. So the trail blazed by John Bozeman stretched from Fort Sedgwick to the Gallatin Valley, which ultimately included the settlement of Bozeman.

The problem was that the Bozeman Trail traversed land that had always been the Hunting Ground and generally living area of at least a half dozen Indian tribes: the Crows, Snakes, Flat Heads to the west. Along the north/south stretch of Bozeman's Trail were the Sioux, Cheyenne, and Arapahoe. Jim Bridger (and others) knew this land and had learned enough of their languages to have traded with these Indians twenty to thirty years prior to Bozeman.

When gold was discovered in Bannack and Alder Gulch in 1863, there were already thousands of White men in the general area of the Central Rockies. They too were either looking for gold or were servicing those that were. Only a fraction of the miners ever "struck it rich", but they all thought they could. So when the word got to Colorado, California, Kansas, Iowa, indeed, the world that another "Big Find" was there for the taking in the Idaho Territory, by 1864 the area stretching from Bozeman Village down to Bannack and nearby branches, like Alder Gulch, the population quickly swelled to 10,000 to 15,000.

The people getting there using mostly the north-westbound Bozeman Trail accelerated the threat to all those tribes I mentioned, and probably others I've failed to identify.

Indian attacks had already increased in ferocity and number by 1864 along the Eastern Slopes of the Rockies around Denver and became very severe in 1865. By the summer of 1866 there was so much traffic on the Bozeman that 300 wagons were lined up waiting to use the ferry at the Big Horn River. Then as immigrant trains formed up and started to roll towards Alder Gulch, this threat to the Indian homeland increased their resolve to resist…and resist they did. Attacks and killings went on almost weekly from 1863 on, peaking in "Bloody 66" and the Fetterman massacre. The Government hastily built three more forts along the Bozeman that year. But the Indian wars continued until final battles of 1876 when the ranks of Indian warriors of that vast region had been almost terminally eliminated.

As far as we were concerned, the fighting along the Bozeman and into the Yellowstone Valley threatened our survival. In 1865 twelve people were killed by Indians near Fort Benton and that's getting close to home. They kidnapped some children. Governor Edgerton called for and got 500 volunteers to serve a short enlistment. For months little mail got through and when it did, it occasionally got there via the Lander Cut-Off and up from Salt Lake City on the Virginia City road. Supply wagons from Kansas or Colorado were constantly under attack, if they were on the Bozeman. The ten or so Army Forts from Julesburg to the Yellowstone River including the three new ones built in '66 bore the worst of the Indian hostility. Not a fort went unmolested. Some of them were (temporarily) almost wiped out, particularly those at Fort Phil Kearney down to Fort Laramie.

And the fighting wasn't confined to the spring and summer months. Some of the bitterest fighting was in midwinter, occasionally in mid blizzard.

In October, Virginia City had a very nice party sponsored by two merchants and a ladies auxiliary of Masons. The Masons had built the lodge where they had the party. They had hired a small (traveling) orchestra and engaged a troupe of actors from Chicago for a whole week. The orchestra leader announced that each night they would try to play some music to please every taste. Wednesday night was an evening of instrumental solos...a German pianist from St. Louis played piano pieces that ranged from Mozart and Beethoven to pieces composed in recent years. Before the night was out the pianist and the clarinet player played a beautiful clarinet solo that I'd never heard, but reminded me of Adda's music teacher in Detroit, when Adda was playing the clarinet.

After the concert I asked the clarinet player for the name of the piece was he played. He said it was an arrangement of a clarinet concerto written by Mozart about seventy years ago. He had an accent. When I inquired as to his origins, he said he was from Austria but was now living in Chicago, teaching music in a high school, but toured like this in the summers. He was proud to say that by traveling summers he had visited cities like, Cincinnati, Memphis, Springfield (Ill.), St Louis, Omaha, etc.

George was able to get Mr. Shoup or one of the other miners up there to shoo off any claim jumpers for five nights of this wonderful party. George said he was thinking about becoming a Mason.

During the evenings of social activities, I met Mrs. Electra Plummer, the widow of the ex Sheriff and her equally attractive mother. She looks much younger than I expected. I didn't know how old Sheriff Plummer was when he was hung. She had been in St. Louis when the vigilantes hung him and she didn't even know about it. That was a year and a half ago. Sometime later, I suppose it was last summer that she and her attractive mother came back. The old Bannack crowd here seemed very cordial to her and she is also a very outgoing lady. I wouldn't be surprised if, like other citizens here in Alder Gulch, that she was totally unaware of her husband's nefarious past and his murderous behavior here. On the other hand I have heard speculation Electra Plummer is here simply to locate caches of gold hidden by her husband in the hills surrounding Alder Gulch prior to his "demise". Several remember that when Plummer was apprehended, he asked for a horse and a couple hours and he would bring back from hiding places in the hills "his weight" in gold.

George's father and Mrs. Plummer's mother are about the same age and I noticed he spent quite some time with the lady at the Masons' and Merchants' party.

A week or so after the party, Mr. Blackman Senior and the two freighters started hauling, well, actually dragging, in some very large boulders and digging out space for them, using their team of horses. One of the freighters seems to be reasonably skilled with the adze. They had to go half way to the Madison River to get the size and length logs they wanted. They are rebuilding and enlarging our cabin, reusing some of the logs that George had brought in originally. I may want to take in boarders next summer. We also want to be several hundred feet from any of the dirt banks that were formed years ago as the stream meandered back and forth. Houses east of us, close to the banks, suffered from recent mudslides, when the rain was heavy.

A week or so following the Mason's Winter Party, while George's father and two workers were hauling/dragging those heavy boulders for foundation stones, a wagon with two ladies drove as close as they could to the building site. One lady alighted and began talking with Mr. Blackman, Sr. I could see it was Electra Bryon Plummer's mother. Those two spent several evenings together during last week's party in Virginia City.

Tonight, as we all had supper together, George's father announced their intention to wed on December 23rd and they were. It turns out that Mr. Blackman, Sr. is a Mason and they elected to have the wedding in the Virginia City Mason's Hall. It was a nice quiet ceremony with some rituals unfamiliar to me.

Saturday, two days following the wedding, the honeymooners came by. I was happy that George was here and not on the mountain We discussed whether they would spend the winter with us...I would like their company...or whether they would go down to Salt Lake City.

I told George and his father about a notice on the bulletin board outside the Sonny Boy Saloon, announcing a train going south on the Virginia City Road to Salt Lake City.

George suggested to his father they walk down to the saloon to read the particulars. They were only gone about half an hour. When they returned, they were both laughing. I asked George, "What's so funny?"

"A dozen people had signed up so far, each agreeing to pay $25 for an armed escort, but Dad has decided to spend the winter here in the Gulch." But I knew there was more to the story than that.

"What's so funny about that?"

"I'll tell you the funny part later."

After his father left, George, who has a rather pleasant, earthy sense of humor, said he had suggested that they stay over the winter up here and he suggested that Electra Plummer stay with them.

George said his father asked if there was any particular reason for that suggestion.

George said he told him that Electra's husband, the notorious sheriff, told the posse that caught him and hung him that if they'd give him a horse and two hours, he'd bring back his weight in gold. People, who knew him, said that would come to near $50,000. There's plausible speculation that Electra didn't come back to the Gulch to visit old friends. It makes sense that Electra might know where that gold is hidden. George said it was that revelation that caused his father to be laughing.

The Winter of 1865

Ralph & Marjorie Crump

68.

NEVADA CITY & VIRGINIA CITY
MONTANA TERRITORY

1866

Winter has set in cold and blustering. George's father and two helpers finished the cabin a few weeks ago. We have a nice wood planked floor and our walls are substantial. We have windows on three sides and reasonably tight fitting doors.

A remnant of a squad of freighters came in a few days before Christmas '65 without freight and in bad shape. One was from the firms we knew when their outfits went through Eldorado: Russell, Majors and Waddell. The other one was Creighton from Omaha. Both had lost their freight to Indians. Majors was out of Nebraska City (their headquarters.) Creighton had foodstuffs and St. Louis hardware. Creighton lost 200 head of cattle, which is no small loss considering the high price (meaning scarcity) of beef. Two of these men have moved into our old boarding house.

I had occasion to speak with these fellows about the circumstances of the Indian troubles. It's their opinion that the Government isn't supplying enough protection from Julesburg north. They said that a Lt. Col. Preston Plumb had a squad of soldiers patrolling the area and the Colonel had a partial company in the area of Fort Laramie, where they fought and in these fellows' opinion they lost to at least 2,0000 well-armed Sioux, who attacked them at a bridge on the upper North Platte.

I told these fellows that I had known Lt. Col. Plumb since the summer of 1856 in Kansas and we've kept up our acquaintance. They both speculated that if Plumb doesn't get heavy reinforcement from the Army this winter he's a "gonner."

Between Christmas and New Years of '66 a lady knocked on my door soliciting money to support the Vigilantes. I had donated $10 before in October, when I was running the boarding house. Apparently a record of my philanthropy was made because this solicitor asked if I could repeat it. She wore sort of a uniform hat with a red, white and blue ribbon. She said she was a member of the Ladies Auxiliary of the Masons, the wife of a miner (also a Vigilante) and they lived up in Virginia City.

I asked her to come in out of the cold. It had stopped snowing and the sun was out. She had been driven by a middle-aged Negro. I suggested that she should call him in. There are a few Negros here. Many of them dig in the stream…obviously freed up from the early days of the Civil War. He did come in, smiled, had a cup of tea, but didn't say a word other than "thank you."

I offered another ten dollar gold coin and after thanking me, she said her husband had just returned from the Snake River with a few more of the robbers that had robbed the Port Neuf Canyon stage…and killed some (or all?) of the passengers. This was his second posse in pursuit of them.

She thought the fellow they brought back was the stage driver. They have been questioning him. He has named fifteen or so of the road agents involved.

"When was this coach robbed?"

"July.

"It was going from Virginia City to Salt Lake. When we received news of the robbery and that passengers had been killed, my husband went with a Vigilante posse. He left here the last of August under the command of Captain Williams." Of course I've seen him here in the Valley.

"Jim Kelly and James Brady from here tried and failed to kill a man (maybe one of their own). Kelly was quickly arrested. Brady,

I believe admitted he pulled the trigger, but there was insufficient evidence to convict Kelly. Brady was hung right here...well, in Virginia City. They gave Kelly fifty lashes and an order to leave the Gulch, which he did. Well, that was a mistake.

No sooner was Kelly released and he traveled toward Salt Lake City. He probably followed the Salt Lake City coach he was to rob. Anyway about fifty to seventy-five miles north of Salt Lake the trail goes through a canyon called Port Neuf. It was there that Kelley and several others, we believe, robbed the coach. We think he was in cahoots with the driver.

"Captain Williams, the current Vigilante leader, upon hearing about the robbery, raised a posse and rode south, which included my husband. Somehow, some northbound Californian prospectors down there had already taken Kelley into custody for some offense to them.

"They apprehended another robber on that trip by the name of Dolan. He had been a recent partner of Kelley. By the way Kelly was hung right there on the Snake River, but they brought Dolan back here. Dolan also confessed to having stolen $700. (He still had half the money with him.) Dolan was also hung at Virginia City. The Vigilante Committee will take that money to cover part of the expense of going after him. What happened to the coach driver on the Port Neuf Canyon robbery?"

"After catching him and questing him, he confessed...so he's been hung."

'You said there were fifteen besides Kelley. Have they caught them all?"

"I'm not sure. But you maybe sure they'll keep trying until they do. Until we get some law and order up here, we must take care of these matters ourselves. The public hangings are intended to let other outlaws know that we'll get 'em...and we'll hang 'em."

Before she left I asked her to explain the meaning of the numbers 3-7-77 displayed on a little button she was wearing.

She said it's meant to be a secret recognition symbol among those of us who support the Vigilantes and it's a warning to the crooks that we are united and we'll "get 'em." She said the Masons brought the symbol with them from California and Colorado mines.

She departed, making a note that I had donated another $10 for a good cause.

St Patrick's Day has come and gone. I'd never given much thought to it, but up here it's quite a holiday. I hadn't realized how many Irish or Catholics we had in the Valley until I heard about the Midnight Mass the Catholics had up in Virginia City on Christmas Night. Now we've had another big Catholic celebration in February by the Irish. Much beer was consumed.

Speaking of Irishmen, last September the territory acquired a new Secretary, Thomas Francis Meagher. Governor Edgerton left for Washington, turning the territorial operations over to Mr. Meagher. I have a newspaper clipping carrying an outline of his biography. He is an Irishman, who hasn't changed his "stripes". He got into some political trouble in Ireland (like our Eldorado Irish friend, Frances Dempsey), who escaped the English sheriff by going to the mines in Wales, Mr. Meagher was arrested and sent to Tasmania, the colony where the toughest "criminals" were incarcerated...most of them, Irish. He escaped, somehow getting to New York City, another hot bed of Irishmen. Like many of the Irish who comprised the (Democratic) Army to fight in the Mexican War, Mr. Meagher organized a Union brigade to fight in the Civil War and distinguished himself in the process. After Lincoln's assassination, President Johnson appointed Mr. Meagher, Secretary of Montana Territory this year and that's why he's a hero among the Irish here in the Valley. He's frequently drunk and frequently seen in the company of some of our ladies of dubious virtue. For reasons he can't articulate, he wants the capital to be moved from Virginia City to Helena.

After a lapse of six months I received a letter from Adda. She was in New York State visiting with relatives on both sides of the family (Onondaga County.) She and Allie are boarding with a family for $3.00 per week.

Before we left for Colorado a year or so ago, Adda had written that Graton and some of his darkie soldiers had been taken prisoner during one of the battles around Fort Scott.

In my last letter to her I asked her what she had heard from her husband.

All she says is that after the letter she received, while we were both in Lawrence (January '63) he continued to write and she responds about every three months. He's survived several battles, she says, and he's now out of the Army and is back in Lawrence but is not well. That left me wondering if he had been taken prisoner and how long did they hold him. Adda had said in one of her letters that Graton had reported to his superiors that eleven of his men were still prisoners. Maybe the two armies carry on some sort of prisoner exchange.

She also says that shortly after she went to Michigan, our renters on Rhode Island Street moved out and the house, empty, has gone into terrible disrepair. Graton doesn't think it's worth repairing, but she says, if I will sell them my half for $300, they will rebuild it. Otherwise, they'll build elsewhere.

She is thinking of staying in New York State until spring. (She wrote this in the middle of the winter.) Then she says she will return to Lawrence and resume housekeeping. Although Graton has left the Army for good, at the close of the war his record was so good he was offered a post as 2nd Lieutenant in the 81st regiment then stationed in Louisiana. I wonder if they kept him in a convalescing hospital for a while, before he returned to Lawrence and opened up his old business, with a partner. They have had to rebuild their war-ruined shop on Massachusetts Street. She writes he intends to meet her in New York, to buy more supplies, then go up to Massachusetts and visit his relatives. (He can now take the railroad from New York straight through to Boston. Isn't that amazing!)

April 1866

We almost moved to Confederate Gulch (up a little east of Helena). We heard from two Georgia miners we knew in Tarryall that they've "struck it rich" up there. They came down to Virginia City for some supplies that they can't get in Helena and boarded with us. George and I both got pretty excited about joining them when they go back but several things came up. I couldn't find a renter for this cabin. It's one of the nicest ones in Nevada City… thanks to George's father…and we sold the team two years ago when we got here…and George didn't want to pay what people were asking for horses. So, while I was looking for a renter, George went back up on the Mountain to prospect.

The fellows, who had the rocker last year that did so well running it with sluice water, didn't come back this spring. I suggested to George that we operate the sluice and rocker this year. He said winter snow and rock-fall knocked down parts of the sluice. Other miners have stolen all the planking that was in the sluice. Some of the short support posts were stolen during the winter for firewood.

George has given up his claim in Big Canyon, the one he spent so much time and effort chasing quartz veins twenty-five feet into that stingy mountain.

George took a different claim on the Mountain, this time a little closer to Virginia City, that is…six or seven miles from here. He recorded it as the "Borgia Lode". I told him if he could file an adjacent claim for me, I'd pay for the dynamite. So, he said, "Ill give you the Borgia Lode. It's a 100-foot claim and I'll file on five more. I think I'll do that while I have the opportunity. He said it was strange that there is so much open area for unclaimed sites in that area. The next day he gave me filing records on "The Blackman", the "Lucky Jim", the Hoss" and the "Mary Said" lode. We spent an hour or so planning on how much we can afford to spend on these claims before we're down to "going home money". George and the Irishman will need to chisel and blast on all these new claims to chase the quartz veins. George has been very frugal with the money he made in Colorado and he earned several hundred dollars for his share last summer in the sluice fed rocker until winter froze the water source. We've banked in Bozeman what we don't need for current expenses.

While he was still home on this visit George showed me a notebook dealing with information on gold yield from quartz rock that he had been collecting.

All of it dealt with various amounts of gold that can come out of an average cubic yard or ton of quartz bearing ore.

Starting with the poorest yield of zero gold, it costs $20 to stamp or crush one ton of ore.

One unnamed mine or mining area has yielded fifteen ounces of gold per cubic yard or $300at $20 per ounce of gold.

A mine in the Pike's Peak/Colorado Springs area, after crushing twenty-eight tons of quartz rock, each average ton yielded 400 ounce or $8,000. That was considered to be 1.3% gold.

Another Colorado mine yielded $130,000 of gold per ton or 22% gold, which was labeled very unusual.

A mine in Cripple Creek area Colorado yielded a low of $1,000 per ton of crushed quartz rock up to $20,000 until the vein "gave out".

This source said that the ten years of mining in California from 1849 yielded about $400 million total.

In terms of cost: $20 to crush one ton of mined rock compared to about $5 to wash by panning a ton of streambed sand and gravel, compared to $1 to wash with sluiced water one ton of streambed sand and gravel.

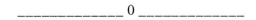

I received a terrible letter from Mary Rackliffe. She says that Elizabeth Cordis has died but had posted a letter to her, while she was sick (in Iowa) asking Mary to take care of her children. What in the world has happened to Tom? Mary's letter is silent about him. That letter has really upset me. It brought tears to my eyes. I just can't get it through my head that Elizabeth Cordis could be dead. She was so smart for her age. It seemed to me she could just do everything. Now she's gone? All these people, such dear fiends, are dead.

Out of the blue I received a letter from my brother-in-law, the gunsmith. First he reports on the sad condition of "our" house while he was away in the Army. I know what he's "up to" in telling me about the condition of the house. In the next letter the rascal will offer me half what my share of the property is worth. He writes that Adda and the baby (who's not a baby any more) are in Michigan. Well, I knew that. He thinks Quantrill did more damage to Lawrence than was done to most towns by regular armies. (What he means is that Quantrill was simply an outlaw raider. He wasn't "in" the Rebel Army.)

He said although he is still not well, he plans to go to New York this summer and he gave me his railroad itinerary…straight through from Lawrence, across Iowa, then on to New York, all on the rails: amazing that the Union could do all this construction and carry on the Civil War, simultaneously.

All of his old arrogance is gone along with his animosity for me, and there is nothing recriminatory in his letter about our previous strained relationship. I haven't heard from Jule Johnson, since my first days in Tarryall.

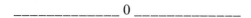

0

George came in the night before last full of optimism. He recorded two more leads yesterday next to those we already have, The "Discovery" and the "Olivia", which he put in my name as an extension of half of number 4 S. E. Dis. on the "Borgia Lode" as well as an extension of No, 4 N. W. from Discovery on the "Olivia". He said he filed those claims because of the presence of quartz veins when he scratched down to raw or base rock

We bought another house on this street and have moved into it. As good as the old one was, this one is better. Now I'll have to find a buyer for the old house.

George is still a hard rock miner, prospecting. He did find some gold containing quartz on my claim "The Olivia". To a miner who was complaining that George had no right to all these claims, George said, "Well, I have the miner's right of priority, I got here first, but I need company. I'll sell you the "Olivia" for $500, which is cheap, but when I'm not here, you guard my claim and when you need a spell, I'll watch yours."

I asked George for the $500. He laughed and said, "I bought and filed another lead for you called the "Widow Lode".

"George," I said, "I know you. You might sell a claim up there for $500, but you sure didn't buy one for $500. I still want the money."

It's so nice to have a husband to banter with.

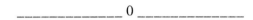

One of the girls who worked for me at the boarding house, Ellen Hoffman, remarried in a nice ceremony that George and I attended. His folks also live in the Gulch. After the wedding they all left for Elk Creek…but I don't know where that is.

MID SUMMER — 1865

A clipping from an Emporia, Kansas the town newspaper, founded by Preston B. Plumb and partially surveyed by my father) reports on Mr. Plumb as follows. He was promoted from Major to Lt Colonel Feb. 1865…while in the 11th Kansas's volunteers.

He had earlier served in Washington, D.C.. with the Kansas Militia Volunteers with General Jim Lane during the interim between the Buchanan presidency and Abraham Lincoln's inauguration on March 4th, 1861 and into April to guard the White House and the Capitol area.

After the Washington, D.C. assignment he volunteered for the 11 Kansas Voluntary Cavalry in May 1864 when most of the Regiment was ordered to Fort Riley. Then he marched out to Fort Kearney, Nebraska Territory (a miserable winter march along the Platte River.) That took twelve days...on March 7th was ordered to start for Fort Laramie and the Platte Bridge area, where he established Regimental headquarters, as a check against the Indians who were marauding the telegraph lines.

Soldiers from one of his companies were given the duty of protecting the overland stage line from Camp Collins (Colorado) to Fort Bridger just beyond the Green River in Utah, a 400 mile stretch: both ways. Prior to the availability of these soldiers, stage service had stopped operating.

Other companies of the Kansas 11th were attacked by 2,000 Sioux Indians on July 22, 1865.

What was left of his Regiment remained in the Fort Laramie area until the summer of 1865. The Regiment was mustered out in September of 1865.

The article closes by saying that Colonel Plumb was healthy in spite of the rigors of his Army life and he intended to get involved with the local newspaper, practice law and maybe get into Kansas politics.

The stage brought in a letter (at least two months old) from my loving sister. She is back in Lawrence and trying to decide what to do about "our" house, which apparently is in bad shape. A neighbor has been keeping our cows and I might add getting the milk, which is the main reason people keep a cow, isn't it? One of the cows has calved each year of the recent two, therefore she thinks they are entitled to keep the calves, because she's been taking care of all of them.

Adda writes that when she was in Flint (Michigan) visiting with relatives, she looked up many of the people, who we went to high school with. She asked me if I remembered Jim and Ed Parsons. Well, of course, I remember them. Ed was by far the dumbest boy in our class. Well, he's at Ann Arbor almost finished with law school! One of Father's brothers, Uncle Charles, is dead. There was so much in her letter about all the friends and relatives, we had in Michigan, that it has made me very homesick. I spent hours trying to figure out how I could do what Adda is doing.

4ᵀᴴ OF JULY 1866

I'm afraid I must report that I spent this 4ᵗʰ of July in exactly the same way I spent the 4ᵗʰ last year, when little Willie Lehner, whose family came in with us from Denver two years ago, died. The brokenhearted parents asked me to "lay him out' and I did. His funeral was the next day.

Yesterday was another sad 4ᵗʰ of July. Mrs. Matte McClarren died suddenly. George was in town and we sat up with the corpse all night. I see my husband so infrequently that, though it disturbed me, spending our time under such unusual circumstances, it was nice to have him home and so we caught up for lost time, while poor Mattie lay in her casket nearby. Mrs. McClarren was perhaps a year or two younger than me and she leaves a darling little girl seven weeks old. The family was very much liked and the funeral held a day later, had the largest attendance of any I've seen here since we arrived. Sickness and death is so much with us.

It's been unusually warm and we are wondering if the heat isn't contributing to the death toll. (A Mr. Stein died at home during the funeral for Mattie McClarren.)

Even my husband, whose robustness reminds me of Adda, is not feeling well. The doctor said it was Bilious Fever.

I told him about my nursing episode the second summer we were in Kansas Territory when I volunteered to nurse a little ten-year-old daughter of my employer, with a serious case of Small Pox. Three of her relatives had it as well and they too were assigned to my care. After three or four weeks, they all recovered. Then I took sick. They sent this local doctor out, who had been absolutely worthless in helping me with my Small Pox patients He asked me some questions, poked about on my body and said that I had Bilious Fever.

Later when a younger associate doctor of his came out with him. They changed his earlier diagnosis and said I was simply run-down from nursing those Small Pox cases. The new doctor prescribed an extract of Ginseng and six glasses of warm water a day. It took two weeks but I recovered. I contacted our local doctor (who couldn't help Mrs. White) and asked if he had any Extract of Ginseng. He did. I bought two bottles and I'll have my husband on his feet in one week.

Summer is almost over and I've had an awful time getting any fruit to speak of. The 1st of August I bought four apples (probably from Missouri) for $1.00. Can you imagine my paying 25¢ for an apple?

To make matters worse, every apple had a worm…but that's common. I haven't seen an orange or a lemon or a grapefruit for twelve months. Three of us wives of miners went over toward the Ruby River Valley in late July, thinking there ought to be wild grapes or wild plums. We had such nice wild plums and mulberries in Kansas. We wasted our time.

It's been some time since I've felt like making an entry. We've had rather pleasant weather so far. I might as well be a widow, George is on the Mountain all the time. Well, not totally, since he filed the new claims closer to town, he's only six or seven miles from home, so he comes home Saturday nights and goes back up on Monday morning (early!) I would like to say that we've mined so much gold; we don't know what to do with it. But that's not the case. Speaking of case, I can't tell you how many cases of powder we have used up with our Irish friend. Since George filed those new claims last April I don't think that the gold that' he's recovered has even covered his expenses. But he just won't give up…and winter is here. He and that fellow who bought the "Olivia" have built a rather substantial lean-to against the almost vertical face of the Mountain at their claim. Twice this fall I went up and cooked for them and walked around the area. It's quite nice up there, but would be nicer if that old Mountain were a little more generous with us.

Mrs. Lehner, who came into Montana with us two years ago moved to Helena shortly after the death of their son, Willie. She writes that as soon as the first available boat that goes down the river this spring, they will be on it. She hints that they have done quite well at Confederate Gulch, although when she wrote earlier, she said their claim was at "Last Chance." Maybe they are both the same place. But what surprises me is that shallow draft passenger boats can come all this way. I haven't seen a map of the area, except for the sketches in the Lewis and Clark journals, so I don't even know what river they are on. I suppose, sooner or later, they must get on the Missouri and take it to Omaha and catch the train there or stay on the boat all the way to St. Louis.

George came in a few days before Christmas. He said that John (the Irish "powder monkey" had run out of fuse caps.) When they came into town for more, they found there's not a fuse to be had here, so we've had as jolly a time as we can over Christmas, considering the circumstances. I asked him if he's going back out there and he said, "Just as soon as John can get some fuses." I suppose he's tried Virginia City. I certainly hope they don't have to go to Bannack or Helena in this weather.

I said to George, "Why don't we just build a cabin up there?" thinking that he would reject that idea. Much to my surprise and relief, he said, that was a great idea. Of course, I have another reason to spend more time with my husband...I am with child. From what I can tell, I should deliver about April 1st.

This is my Christmas Eve entry: although we've had one of the nicest winters since I've been in the mountains, it's snowing now and I'm hoping my husband will come home with a Christmas present for me, such as a ten ounce nugget that he's picked from a blasted quartz vein or I'd take one the size I saw yesterday. It was about the size of a child's marble, almost round, and weighed about one ounce. He's been up there all fall and all winter, so far. Yes, he does come home for the weekend and although there has been some claim jumping near him when the originating miners are gone temporarily, his claims have not been violated.

I read Adda's November letter again. She reports that somehow she's settled her differences with the neighbor over the ownership of our cows and had sold the two calves to a local butcher for veal, which is all the rage now in Lawrence. She says she posted my share of the money…but it has not arrived, but I appreciate her honesty in the matter. With all the snow accumulating here and on the plains over which the mail must come and go I suspect it will be some time before I'll get any more news by mail.

In the pack of mail that I did get with the last letter from Adda, was a letter from Mary Rackliffe posted from Portland, Maine.

LATE JANUARY — 1867

Augusta Stewart Chase Blackman (photo undated)
(Taken in Butte, Montana Territory)

The Blackman House built by George W. Blackman - 1867-1868
Silver Star, Montana (about 30 miles from Virginia City)

J.D. Conner Eldorado Grocer in 1858 taken during a visit October 1905 Left to Right Mrs. Conner, J.D. Conner, Augusta, Adda. Mr. Conner, an Irish immigrant, opened a store in Eldorado in 1858. He was a friend of Jacob Chase. The Hildebrand trial was held in his store.

69.

WE BEGIN OUR FAMILY AND MOVE TO SILVER STAR, MONTANA TERRITORY

1867

W*ith Chapter 69 "Augusta's Journal" comes to its end. Her entries span a period in the history of the U.S.A. that witnessed monumental events. Several new states were added (all free of slavery). The West was opened up. Our terrible Civil War ended. Augusta continued her entries up to the eve of World War I.*

There is much talk here in the Gulch about a big gold strike someplace on the Salmon River. Julia Williams, a neighbor, and her husband visited today, asking if Julia can board with me in the event that her husband goes there in the spring. I would certainly like her company, for I am alone so often and I have another reason for preferring her company. Early this spring I should deliver this package that I am carrying around and I'm sure I'll need some help. Of course, there's not much to talk about regarding that (delicate) fact: it's so obvious. Mr. Williams says there is already a large crowd signed up to go to the Salmon River, which I believe is southwest of Bannack, but I really don't know.

Oh, yes, in with the last pack of letters is a bill from the county treasurer posted in Lawrence. Can you imagine that: I'm paying county real estate taxes on a house I haven't seen or lived in for three or four years! I wonder if I failed to pay and they seize the house for my share of back taxes, would Adda and Graton pay-up? It wouldn't be nice to subject them to that prospect, but it certainly would be a relief, for me. I get absolutely no benefit from my ownership. If Graton possessed an ounce of responsibility, honesty or fairness, he would have, long ago offered a fair price for my share of that house.

Although Sheriff Plummer is long gone, we are seeing a sharp upsurge of robberies and general lawlessness in the whole territory. We've had reports that entire wagon trains, destined for Virginia City, have been attacked, the cattle and supplies stolen and sold elsewhere. Four years after the Plummer episode a new Vigilante posse was formed in mid December. Actually this posse was a revitalization of the old posse from miners and merchants still here. I haven't heard of any arrests or hangings.

One by one George has sold all but two of his claims on the mountain outside of Virginia City. He's made more money from the sale of the claims than he's made from gold taken from them. His buyers are miners, like him, who have given up on placers and are, like him, gambling on hitting the Mother Lode or they are new-comers and don't like the idea of working in the water, even if they could get a claim on Alder Creek (without buying it), which they can't. So while they still have some money, they come up on the mountain east of Virginia City and either look for a new claim or buy one with veins of quartz showing, he hasn't sold any for less than $500.

He said if he doesn't hit a vein of quartz with gold in it by spring, that he will leave this mountain and try his luck elsewhere.

March 13, 1867 our son was born...looks like a healthy little boy...weighs about ten or eleven pounds.

Thank goodness George was able to be here a few days before and after my delivery. It's April 8th and I've never seen such a snowstorm in my life. The roads had started to dry up from the winter slush...now this.

I've recovered nicely from the ordeal of bringing little George into this world.

There is considerable talk, worry and anxiety about this coming summer and the Indians. This spring they massacred every living soul at Fort Buford and even more at Fort Phil Kearney in Nebraska. All of those places are along the Bozeman Trail. I hope my old friend, Lt. Colonel Preston Plumb, has been discharged and avoided those fights. Last I heard he had been attacked by 2,000 Sioux somewhere over on the Bozeman Trail. Mr. Bozeman himself was killed over there. We seem to be isolated and surrounded by savages.

A female letter carrier from the post office in Virginia City brought several letters. One in particular was from Mrs. Lehner, our neighbor before they moved to Last Chance Gulch (Helena). They were with us on the train up from Denver three years ago. They mined close to us for two years. She had posted this letter on their river trip to the States. I will include most of it, as this day's entry. She had written last winter that it's possible to get from the Helena area back to the States entirely on the river system all the way to St. Joseph, Missouri. This accommodation has been in place about a year. She had written during the winter that they intended to be on the "first boat" out this coming spring or summer. Well, it looks like she's met her goal.

Dear Augusta,

We are in Fort Union, which is at the junction of the Yellowstone and the Missouri rivers. A stage and military escort are leaving here headed for Virginia City. I will give this letter to them with the hope it will reach you to thank you again for all your help last year when we lost our dear little Willie. I thought you'd enjoy hearing about these new traveling accommodations. We will be two nights here. They say we are 500 miles from "the Gulch", so we are about halfway into our trip.

I told you we'd leave on the first boat. Well, what really happened was, traveling by boat is so popular that there are over thirty boats employed by our group. Some hold ten. Some are called Mackinaw boats. They are pointed "fore and aft" for better steering in swift *water. Our fare to St. Jo, Missouri is $30 each. (We could have purchased our ticket in Virginia City!) But since we were up here, we bought ours here. I mention Virginia City only because, much to our surprise, about one hundred in our party (300 all tolled) came up from Virginia City via Bowsman (she means Bozeman), and are in our "Floating Outfit." Many of them know you and George.*

We floated down to Bowsman, then onto the generally east flowing Yellowstone to where it joins the Missouri. The Army has built a dock to accommodate riverboats here. They say those boats are 75 to 100 feet long and able to carry 250 tons of cargo. There are none of them here now. Some of our boats have sails but mostly we float with the current. The scenery has been magnificent. Occasionally, we see Indians watching us from the shore.

Each night we disembark, look for dry wood, and build a fire. Some men have ridden ahead of us and shot game and often supper is ready when we get off the boat. We get some form of wild game each evening meal. Yes, we sleep on the flat, some times grassy banks of the river and we knew that would be the case before we left. Armed men stand four-hour watches, fearful of Indians. So far, so good.

We recently floated through the intersection of the Yellowstone and the Big Horn. We knew where this was because the Big Horn water is muddy whereas the Yellowstone is fairly clear.

Two young men on our boat troll or drag some sort of bait on a fish line as we float, so we frequently have fried trout for dinner and occasionally cold-poached trout for breakfast. Other travelers do the same.

We will enter the United States in Sioux City, Iowa. From Sioux City we go down to Council Bluffs, where in our case, we will catch the train to Chicago.

About half our party are Southerners. They will go on to St. Jo (Missouri) and take trains to St. Louis.

From camp (or is it Fort?) Sully on the Missouri the water will be deeper, so we are scheduled to board steam-driven stem wheelers or stern-wheelers there. I'll try to post a letter to you from that place.

I will write again and try to post it either from Fort Sully or Sioux City.

I hope George and you strike it rich in Virginia City.

Your friends,
The Lehners

A guide came into Virginia City two weeks or so ago, warning the posse that there was a massing of a large body of Indians over on the Yellowstone. The largest group of Whites in this part of the country is right here in this Valley, so we must be the reason for their coming together.

You would think that now that the Civil War is behind us that the Federal Government could afford to send some real Regiments up into this area and give us some security from these Indians.

FETTERMAN MASSACRE

Since mid January ('67) rumors, reports and news articles have been filtering in about a terrible Massacre over near Fort Phil Kearney. The Indians (Sioux and Cheyenne, led by Red Cloud) a few days before Christmas in a single fierce battle appear to have wiped out all of several Army Companies under the command of Capt. Fetterman, more or less on the Bozeman Trail. With about eighty men he had marched north of the Fort, so close to it that those in the Fort could hear the shooting.

The Fort was under the command of Colonel Carrington, whose headquarters are at Fort Phil Kearney. (He had continually been asking General Cooke in Omaha for more troops, supplies and ammunition to no avail.)

Colonel Carrington's formal report after the battle accounts for ninety-four soldiers killed, the entire contingency that had been sent out. It was his opinion that Red Cloud had bettered his statement earlier, which was confirmed by Jim Bridger during the failed peace treaty with the Indians that the old Oglala warrior could bring 1,500 warriors to bear along the Bozeman Trail to drive the White Man out of and off of their hunting ground and living area, if the White Man persisted on trespassing and living on their land (in forts.)

The day after the battle Colonel Carrington sent supply wagons and a new Company of soldiers out in a blizzard to resupply those (presumed to be) still living and waiting for the next attack. They discovered to their horror that not a single soldier or officer remained alive. They returned with forty-nine badly mutilated bodies, which is all their wagons could hold.

Returning again to the battle site they recovered the balance of those killed including Captain Fetterman. Colonel Carrington insisted on this recovery, saying that the Indians would interpret as a sign of weakness if those alive in the Fort could not or would not recover all the bodies of their dead.

The situation was so desperate that Colonel Carrington left orders that while the search party was gone leaving the Fort undefended, if the Indians attacked it and were successful in breaching the walls, all the women and children should be moved into the "Magazine" where the remaining ammunition and powder was stored. Rather than let the Indians capture the women and children alive, the guards were instructed to blow-up the Magazine.

The telegraph line had not extended to Fort Kearney. Colonel Carrington dispatched a guide, "Portuguese" Phillips to ride with his message for Omaha Army headquarters to the closest telegraph station, which was thought to be at Fort Reno, about fifty miles south in very heavy snow. But at Fort Reno technical difficulties prevented telegraphing the message. So poor Portuguese Phillips had to ride on...believe it or not...all the way to Fort Laramie (see map) at least another 150 miles.

Four days later on Christmas Night, he arrived caked in snow and on an exhausted horse. The Fort was having their Annual Christmas Party, the soldiers, all in their best uniforms and the ladies in formal gowns. When Phillips got off his horse and staggered in with his message of the Massacre to General Palmer, it sent such a chill throughout the party that the Christmas festivities were discontinued. Many of those at Fort Laramie were friends or relatives of the victims.

For Phillips it had been a four-day, treacherous ride. Once inside the Fort his thoroughbred horse dropped dead,

When Colonel Cooke ordered General Palmer at Laramie to send two Calvary Companies and four Infantry Companies to relieve Fort Kearney and Colonel Carrington, the weather was so bad that this relief party couldn't get away until the 3rd of January.

Whether the telegram that Colonel Cooke received was transmitted word-for-word to Army headquarters in Washington, we don't know. But we do know that then, as now, the bureaucrats put their own self-serving interpretation on the situation. The Bureau of Indian Affairs that had been sending peace committees to appease and treat Indians turned the story upside down and blamed the Fort/Army personnel, assuring Congress that all was well with these Plains Indians…That taxpayers' money had been well spent. Their story (without a bit of proof) was that when the Indians went to the Fort asking for food and help during the blizzard some sort of fight broke out, but surely those peaceable Indians, who had signed the treaty and took our gifts couldn't have committed such atrocities. Maybe the soldiers simply froze to death.

The Army's response was to reorganize all the Fort Commands along 100 miles of the Bozeman Trail.

SUMMER 1867

Another letter from Mrs. Lehner

Dear Augusta.

Well, Hooray! We are in the good old U.S. of A. and got here on a river paddle-wheeled boat named the Abeona, which we boarded at Fort Union (as planned). There are about 150 of us plus some horses and mules. We also took on twenty-five cords of wood. This boat's

boiler will take wood or coal. We understand it goes north on coal, which it picks up at St. Jo, but goes down river on wood. Our wood was dumped on from an elevated deck or landing eight to ten feet above us, coming down with a horrendous roar and a cloud of dust.

Two days later we were out of wood and had to buy more en route. This boiler burns twenty-five cords ever twenty-four hours There are three men on this boat that do nothing but carry wood that's piled on the deck and feed it to the boiler.

A squad of twenty-four Army soldiers also joined us at Fort Union with wooden crates of ammunition. One of the corporals told Mr. Lehner that Indians enjoy shooting at the boats from the riverbank.

The third day some Indians took shots at us…some hitting the smoke stack with the ball going through one side and out the other. But the "Indian" shooting stopped as abruptly as it started just as soon as our soldiers opened up on them. Two teenaged boys (going back east to school) were given rifles and got some shots in before it all stopped. Won't they have stories to tell when they go to school with those Eastern Sissies.

The sixth day of the trip we ran up on a sand bar at a bend in the Missouri. But the officers ingeniously rigged two heavy ropes to trees on the riverbank and using a steam winch on the boat, we were off the sand bar. We saw other boats in the same fix on the Muddy Missouri.

So far on this fifty-day journey we have passed a northbound boat named Gallatin and the Taconic passed us southbound in a wide stretch of the River.

We will be in Sioux City two or three days for repairs and to take on water for the boiler.

We hope, since we wrote last, that George has found the Mother lode up on that mountain.

Your friends,
The Lehners

This summer George had talked to the owners of the Green Campbell mine at Silver Star about forty miles from here on the

Jefferson River. The owners have plans to either put up a stamp mill (steam driven) or build an arrastra. Mr. Charles Everett and Mr. Saulsbury are originally from Cleveland, Ohio.

OCTOBER 1867

I have neglected my journal in recent months. My excuse is the baby, who we haven't named yet. He has been so sickly that I was afraid we were going to lose him, but so far, so good. He has awful bowel troubles...loose, runny yellow stool. By mid June he weighed nineteen pounds...that at four months, according to Gunn's *Book of medicine*, which I've kept all these years, it says that weight is a little above average.

At three or four weeks I noticed when I was giving him a bath that his scrotum was unusually large, not inflamed, but seemed swollen. I asked the doctor to examine him and he said muscles in his lower abdomen had parted (a common male pediatric occurrence.) When he cries or strains himself a small segment of his lower intestine drops or slides down through this muscle opening into the scrotum with his testicles. That's what makes it appear swollen. The doctor showed me how to make a hernia belt or truss and said in all likelihood the muscles will grow together, holding the intestine where it should be. He remarked that this is an inherited trait and one that he will pass down to his sons and so on.

At seven months he has no teeth. I asked the doctor if that wasn't unusual. He said, "Yes" and that I had not been getting enough calcium from certain vegetables, certainly milk and cheese.

In October George came home for a few days and brought Mr. Everett and Mr. Saulsbury with him, the owners of the mine in Silver Star. We invited them for a dinner and had a nice visit. I was so grateful for their company.

They are all working on a rather large arrastra located in the outskirts of Silver Star down on the Jefferson River.

George sent a note saying that work is progressing well on the arrastra apparatus and when he has time, he's building us a house in Silver Star.

DECEMBER 1867

There was an unofficial meeting at the Masonic Hall (Virginia City) yesterday on the Indian situation but most of the time was taken to discuss the recent peace treaty between the Government and the Indians occupying the vast range over east in the Powder River Country. It's been mostly Sioux and Cheyenne in that area that has made travel on the Bozeman trail so treacherous (and induced Jim Bridger in his wisdom to lead trains like ours in 1864 west of the Powder River and the Big Horn Mountains.)

The gist of the treaty is this. All the forts from Fort Smith near the Yellowstone down to Fort Laramie, a 250 mile stretch, are being evacuated and closed, giving up the land to the Indians and giving up any future military protection to immigrant supply trains,

It is expected that the farmers and ranchers already here must provide our supplies. Well, there is a flourmill in Bozeman that's milling wheat from this area. In fact, it's owned by T. W. Cover (whose original name may have been Couvier.) He was a partner with John Bozeman. Someone reported a nice potato crop this fall. Travel between the Gallatin Valley and Salt Lake City (the Virginia City Road) will not be affected by this development.

I don't know when the Bozeman Trail was established by him but I suppose most of the traffic and subsequent bloodshed started in 1863 and Jim Bridger knew that travelers who trespassed the Wind River Territory Eastern Foothills of the Big Horn Mountains that stretched from the Yellowstone River all the way down to a little north of Fort Sedgwick, near Julesburg were always at serious risk. That's why he opened up a more westerly trail in 1864, which is the one we and most of the other trains took in 1864, and maybe 1865, I don't know.

So here we are four years later giving in to that old Chief Red Cloud.

Someone asked if the Army for our protection over here would expand the forts in the Gallatin Valley, like they expanded Fort Ellis (summer of 1867) near the settlement of Bozeman. The answer was a "Yes – maybe". Right now the problem is dismantling those Army outposts and evacuating the personnel on the Bozeman Trail.

Someone asked if this was an Omaha decision or one from Washington. The speaker (a politician unknown to me) thought the decision was made in Washington but the details would be carried out by Omaha Headquarters under General Philip St. George Cooke, who is near retirement. So he's not going to do anything to put his pension in jeopardy.

Someone asked if we knew how much land was being treatied. The speaker said he has read the legal description but it is difficult to "decipher". This much seems certain. All the land from the Missouri River west to and including the Eastern Slopes of the Big Horn Mountains. North-South is more difficult but generally it embraces the land north of the northern border of the Nebraska Territory all the way to the Canadian border, but there are some ambiguous carve-outs that have been agreed to. And this treaty forbids all but White officials to enter or pass through, trade with, etc. this land.

Some men up front, obviously Union Veterans shouted that it looked like the Army "Lost this one but the Bureau of Indian Affairs won theirs. "

Someone asked what will happen to the telegraph lines up and down that stretch over there. The speaker thought the treaty protects it.

Someone else asked, "How about mail"

"Recently, lots of mail is being carried by boat now. As for mail trains using the Bozeman trail, he said that would be discontinued."

One of the ladies piped up and said, "Well, the Indians have been able to stop mail for months every year we've been up here. Now our own Government is in cahoots with the Indians. That's the limit!"

The Ladies Auxiliary served hot coffee and cookies. But the weather outside was threatening, so I left. George was at Silver Star and I'll send him my notes.

A week later, editor Dimsdale of the *Montana Post* put out his version of the meeting in an editorial. I don't know what meeting he attended but his observations sure differ from mine.

I was always skeptical about the editorial quality of the *Montana Post* and that editor, Mr. Dimsdale. Well, I see where they've closed-up shop and moved it to Helena. I wonder if they've taken the editor with them?

All we have now is the *Democrat*, which is not any better than the *Post*.

MAY 1868

I received a nice letter from Mary Rackliff. She married on New Year's Day to Bradford Stuart. I recognized that name as a miner, who we both knew in Terryall. Then as I read on she confirmed all that. They are living on a farm two miles from Concord, Massachusetts. (It must be near where the first battle of our Revolution took place.) She doesn't say anything about Ermee and her other surviving children or those of Elizabeth Cordis. I figure she remained unmarried for fifteen years. Sumner died in 1863 and "little" Ermee is thirteen years old now.

George was with me until today (May 10, 1867) when he left again for Silver Star, down on the Jefferson River. George said before he left that if all goes well down there, we'll move as early as spring but no later than summer, next year.

JULY 1868

We were delayed in moving, because George has been working full time, which hasn't left much time for him to build our house. But with the help of an itinerant carpenter, they were far enough along that we could move in on July 23rd, almost four years to the day that we arrived in Montana. Using the wagon George bought in Denver in '63, we moved from "Nevada" (Alder Gulch, near Virginia City) about forty miles to our new house in Silver Star. Little George Chase was seventeen months old. We are within walking distance of the Jefferson River, where on a sunny day, if I don't cast any shadows, I can spot Rainbow Trout, big ones.

I had gotten pretty well adjusted to living in Nevada City. The house was adequate; the neighbors were nice but far from permanent. Those who "made their poke", always moved out in November and many of those who hadn't, moved on anyway.

Down here the Musquitoes look like immigrants from Kansas. And I do believe these Montana snakes (Rattlers) are as populous here as in Kansas. Silver Star is going to take some getting used to.

Here in Silver Star they had been running the Quartz Mill (which is a Stamp Mill) at the Green Campbell Lode for about four months before I moved here. I wonder what happened to the planned arrastra? I've visited the mill while it was running and must say it makes an awful racket and George is right in the midst of that noise. He is a "feeder". That is, he feeds the quartz rock, which contains the gold under the mauls of the stamper...and he's getting deaf as a post for all his efforts. His partner-feeder, Fred Hutchins, is already deaf.

1872

In the fall I received a letter from Adda postmarked Falmouth/ Bourne, Massachusetts, July 30th

Dear Augusta,

As you can see, I'm in Massachusetts. Quite early this spring Graton, who was, in my opinion, not fit to travel, decided to make the rounds of his suppliers for shotguns, rifles, small arms and ammunition in Connecticut and New York State. I think he enjoys talking "shop" with these manufacturers. Many of their managers now had been young apprentices with him during their armory days and they've stayed in touch with each other over the years and many of them are Veterans, which adds to their camaraderie He left his partner running the shop, which has been doing tolerably well in the seven years since he left the Army. I know because I keep the books.

In no time at all I received a telegram from Ithaca, saying that all was well, and since he was already in the East, he decided that he would visit his relatives in Massachusetts, which would delay by a few weeks his return. They all live about fifty miles west of Boston.

Then two weeks later in May, I received a telegram from the Boston area, saying that he was feeling so poorly that he thought he would go out to Falmouth on the South Coast and rest. He suggested that I might enjoy the New England seacoast in the summertime. But the way I read it was he really wasn't getting any better and it was his way of asking for help without surrendering any of his enormous self-sufficiency.

I left immediately and traveled the entire distance on the rails. There are new coaches now and rather elegant service in the dining cars. Most passenger trains now have berths. (When Graton mustered out, he had saved over $3,000, so I thought I would indulge myself a little and bought a sleeping berth the entire distance…very luxurious.)

When I got to Boston, he had not gone to the coast as planned. He was there waiting for me at the Parker House Hotel. We left immediately for Falmouth, taking the rails to Bourne and a coach to the coast., my first sight of the Atlantic Ocean. This is a Colonial seaport and fishing town, directly on the ocean facing south. We took rooms in a delightful old house almost on the shore, where, when Graton was feeling well, we could walk along the old waterfront. Sometimes we'd rent a carriage and drive into the bays and old shipping wharves. On occasion we'd visit the fishing boats coming in late afternoon with their huge hauls of fish, mostly Cod. Several times we bought fresh Cod at ten cents per pound for the lady who runs our boarding house. But the fish I like best of all is Flounder. It's much tastier than Cod.

We were there most of June. In July, even when the weather was pleasant, he complained of being tired and we stopped taking our walks. But the boarding house had a nice wide front porch where, in the afternoon, we could sit and watch the ocean and the boats coming and going.

Mid July he felt so weak he didn't want to go outside. Some days he didn't get out of bed.

Finally on July 24th Graton passed away.

It was his wish to be buried in Kansas. But railroad restrictions prohibited transporting bodies of the dead during summer. I left instructions for his remains to be placed in a local tomb until October, when it was sent to Lawrence. That year Alice was eleven years old.

Your loving sister,
Adda

Adda's letter about Graton's passing has really moved me, not over his passing; I never liked the man, but for what my sister has had to put up with from him, which started within a few months of their wedding. A sense of fairness, honesty, openness and charity as well as some earthy humor runs deep in the American character and I include the immigrants I've known in that appraisal. I saw little of those qualities in Graton.

I wonder if I dare ask Adda if she's ever forgiven his behavior… or now that he's gone, will she forgive him? I know it's none of my business, but as an observer of those I've known and loved, I'm curious. I forgave Chase, indirectly, by simply remembering the better parts of our relationship and discarding the rough patches, but his behavior towards me was almost saintly compared to the torture that Graton put Adda through.

Well, Adda has the house, which she's had all along, whether she's shared it with Graton since the War, I don't know. I should send her my deed assigned to her and be done with it, and I will. I assume she has Graton's share of the gun shop and I know they owned some rental property in Lawrence, so she gets some income from that. When Graton mustered out of the Army, he had accumulated over $3,000 and knowing how tight he was, other than what he invested in rebuilding their gun shop, he kept every nickel of his Army money in cash or as investments. So I guess Adda and little Alice will be able to weather the storm.

_____ 0 _____

Two years later Adda wrote that she had learned that she might be entitled to a Civil War widows' pension and that she had mailed in the appropriate forms to the Army. She never said whether she got the pension or not, but there is no doubt about her husband's distinguished and faithful service to the Union as a captain. It's too bad that he couldn't have been as faithful a husband and father to his loyal wife and child, as he was to the U.S. Army.

Our daughter, Adelaide Beryl Blackman was born on February 16, the following year.

Our next son, Charles Stewart Blackman, was born on April 18, 1875. I wanted him named after my grandfather, the "Minuteman", who fought in our Revolution.

In 1883 I was able to revisit Eldorado.

In preparation for its 50th year anniversary, I was contacted to write an article about the founding of Eldorado and to describe what life was like during those early days (1856 to 1860) of pioneering the territory and being in the founding family of Eldorado. I spent weeks, on and off rewriting my journal, adding things here and there that I had omitted originally, particularly about Father's political activities in the Territorial Legislature, pre statehood, which he never discussed with Adda and me. An excerpt of all that was sent to Eldorado.

The *Walnut Valley News* did me the honor of printing every word… most, if not all of it, of course came condensed from volume I and II of my journals that I had started in note form as we traveled across Iowa in our ox drawn covered wagon, when I was sixteen (almost seventeen) years of age. Shortly after we arrived I turned seventeen. I was only twenty years old when Kansas achieved statehood.

In 1905 I was fortunate to visit Eldorado and Lawrence again. We went on to Chicago and in one of the better department stores, ordered from Limoges, France a complete set of white chinaware, decorated with little light pink cyclamens, similar to the set belonging to Mrs. Weibley that she spread out for our tea that afternoon in May almost fifty years ago after Elizabeth Cordis, my sister Adda and I (with the help of the Doctor's wife) cleaned up for burial that dead Irishman, Mr. Curl. It was Mr. Curl who provided Eldorado its first funeral (chapter 20 of volume II of this four volume series.)

Several weeks after we returned to Bozeman, the chinaware arrived directly from France, carefully packed in wooden barrels, everything in perfect order, and nothing broken.

Montana gained "statehood" on November 8, 1889. Three years later George died. He was only 53 years old and was already recognized in history books as one of the new State's pioneers.

I was so happy that he lived to see Montana's statehood, for he so loved this place.

Laura Augusta Stewart Chase-Blackman

Died May 31, 1914

At the age of seventy-five

Is buried in the Silver Star Cemetery

A Pioneer of the State of Montana

A pioneer of the Colorado gold camps in 1863

A pioneer of Kansas when in 1854 it was intended to come into the Union as a Slave State.

The Abolitionists, like the Stewarts, turned that intent upside down at the territorial polls Augusta's father, Samuel Stewart, served on the Territorial Legislature to write the new Constitution, banning slavery in Kansas, known as the Wyandotte Constitution. It was ratified in October 1869 about a year after Sam Stewart's murder, Sam's major reason for uprooting his family and moving to the new territory was to prevent Kansas by the vote from becoming a state with slavery.

Kansas was admitted as a Free State just prior to the Civil War on January 21, 1861

A few months later our Civil War commenced. It's ironic that the War was fought, not specifically over Slavery, but whether Southern states had a right to secede. At the height of the War President Lincoln in effect abolished slavery by his Proclamation of Emancipation. By then many Colored had enlisted and were fighting for the Union against their old slaveholders. Augusta and Adda lived through that period and, lucky for us, wrote about it.

Augusta Age 66 taken during a visit to
Lawrence, Kansas in 1905

INDEX
Vol. IV

Bissell, B. F. , farmer and miner in Alder Gulch, 214

Blackman, George Washington, xvii. 17, 181, 184, 207, 273
"The Blackman" a mine 302
George and Augusta marry in Denver, 206, 210
Laura Augusta Stewart Chase Blackman dies, 331

Blackman, Sr, Mr. 256, 294
Brings load of honey and sugar, 289

Black Regiment, 69

Blunt Lt. Col. ,114

Boggs, Charles, S. a miner, 242

Boiled ham with boiled potatoes, 156

Border Ruffians, 64

Blackman's mine, 302, 304

Boston, 9,

Boulder, CO, 139

Bourbon County Kansas, 112

Bowles, Colonel John, 133, 175
Mrs. 133, 177

Boyce, Major, 214

Bozeman the town ,xviii

Bozeman, John M. from Georgia 241

Bozeman Trail, 214, 215, 218

Brady, James, 298

Brant Reverend, 12,

Breckinridge, John from Kentucky, 33,

Breckinridge, CO, 141

Bridger, "Major" Jim, 215, 220
Oregon-bound travelers. 215
Bridger Cut-Off, 231, 289

British Columbia, 147

Bronte, Charlotte, 249

Brown, George W., 113

Brown, John, 22, 36, 63, 77
Speeches, xiii

Bryan, Electra, (nee Mrs. Plummer), 245

Buchanan, President xiii, xxv 30, 33, 35, 38,

Buckskin, CO, 136, 154

Buckskin, Laurette, Colorado157,

Buffalo tongues, 145
boiled, 156,

Buffalo Town, Kansas Territory 30, 269

Buffalo, N.Y., 269

Bureau of Indian Affairs, 325

Burt, George, "famous mesmerizer", 3, 30, 41, 127,
is killed by Quantrill, 177

Butler and Hunter County, 27, 34,

Byers Bill, 138

C

Cabin Creek, Kansas, 106 , 162,

"cabooner", 29,

California, 1849, 22, 125

California Gold Rush, 135

Camp Mitchell, 216, 218

Cantrell, John, 27, 139,

Capt. Frank Swift, xvi

Carey, (Mr. and Mrs.) 7, 26,
Mr. joins Union Army, 103

Carroll, Bill, 231

Carrington, Colonel, 251, 319

Niagara Falls, 234
No-Name Crick, (Augusta and Thatcher's claim on), 192,
North Carolina, 143,
Northern Arapahos, 215
Northern Cheyenne, 213, 215
Northern Missouri,, 66

O

Oates, Steven, book on Jim Lane, xii
Oglala, a warrior, 319,
Old Sacramento, a brass cannon, 31,
Old Testament, 155
  Samuel II 162
  Women, 185
"*Olivia*" (G.W. Blackman mine), 304
Omaha, 152,
Onions, Missouri, 212
Onondaga County, NY, 300
"Order No. 10", General Ewing's, 178
Osages, 140
Osceola, 112, 174
Oskaloosa, 133
Overland Trail, 29, 151

P

Pacific Ocean, a water passage to, 220
Palmer, William, saloon owner, 241
Parish, Frank, hung by Vigilantes, 244

Parker House of Boston, 4, 156, 328
Perkins, Reverend, marries Sarah Goss and Dr. Lewis, 23,
Perrine, Mrs. (midwife) 45, 74, 91
Perune, Jimmie, 177
Philadelphia, 38, 140, 142
Pierce, Alfred, 31, 68, 82, 164 180
Pike's Peak, 137, 139
Pinkerton (detective), 37,
Pittsburg, 37
Platte River South Fork, 135
Platte River Trail, 134, 144,
Plumb, Preston B., (founder of Emporia, K.T.), xvi, 31, 68, 82, 164,
  (Leader of 1856 supply train) appointed aide de camp to General Lane Captain of Company C of 11th Kansas Infantry, 180
  As Lt. Col., 297
Plummer, Sherriff, xvii, 238
  Vail, Martha, married sister-in-law 246
  Wife Electra and mother return to Virginia City, 293, 295
Plymouth, Mass., 2, 49, 231,
Poe, Edgar Allen, 11,
Poison Springs Battle, 106
Pomeroy House, Topeka, 51,
  Caters to Legislators, 54
  Augusta, chief cook, 52, 58
Pomeroy, Senator, 117
Pontiac (Oakland County,